Theoretical Logic in Sociology

The task is this, to understand the discourse just as well as and even better than its creator.

Friedrich D. E. Schleiermacher,
Hermeneutics

Theoretical Logic in Sociology

Volume Three

THE CLASSICAL ATTEMPT AT THEORETICAL SYNTHESIS: MAX WEBER

Jeffrey C. Alexander

University of California Press
Berkeley • Los Angeles

University of California Press
Berkeley and Los Angeles, California
© 1983 by
The Regents of the University of California
Printed in the United States of America

1 2 3 4 5 6 7 8 9

Library of Congress Cataloging in Publication Data

Alexander, Jeffrey C.
  Theoretical logic in sociology.

  Includes bibliographical references and index.
  Contents: v. 1. Positivism, presuppositions, and current
controversies—v. 2. The antinomies of classical thought:
Marx and Durkheim—v. 3. The classical attempt at
theoretical synthesis: Max Weber
  1. Sociology—Philosophy—Collected works.
  2. Sociology—Methodology—Collected works.
HM24.A465   301   75-17305
ISBN 0-520-03062-1 (set)   AACR2
ISBN 0-520-04482-7 (vol. 3)

CONTENTS—OVERVIEW

Volume Three
THE CLASSICAL ATTEMPT AT
THEORETICAL SYNTHESIS: MAX WEBER

THE CLASSICAL
ATTEMPT AT
THEORETICAL
SYNTHESIS: MAX WEBER

Contents

VOLUME THREE
THE CLASSICAL ATTEMPT AT THEORETICAL SYNTHESIS: MAX WEBER

Preface To Volume Three

This is the third part of a four-volume work. Naturally, I hope that the work will be read in its entirety, but I recognize that this may not be possible, and so have written each volume in such a way that it can be read independently of the others.

Since the work is of one piece, it is inevitable that each successive volume will in some important ways build upon the arguments of those preceding. The present volume relies in important respects on the framework and arguments laid out in volume 1, *Positivism, Presuppositions, and Current Controversies*, and volume 2, *The Antinomies of Classical Thought: Marx and Durkheim*. In these earlier volumes I made certain statements about the nature of science and the relationship of its parts, about the status of contemporary theoretical debate in sociology, about the elements of good theorizing, and about the role of interpretive readings in social-scientific theory. Further, I applied and developed these ideas in relation to the founders of sociological materialism and idealism, Marx and Durkheim.

I cannot recapitulate these arguments here, but I will try, nonetheless, to provide the reader with enough background so that the understanding of the present volume can proceed apace. I will, of course, be returning to these issues throughout the present volume. Many of the questions that were considered abstractly in volume 1 will here be thought through in a more concrete way. Likewise, many of the points made in volume 2 about Marxism and Durkheimianism will reappear as counterpoint to my discussion of Weber. Still, many of the earlier themes and points will not be elaborated, certainly not in the depth they deserve. The very concreteness of the theoretical discussion in the present volume

makes an *abstract* that much more necessary, and my continual reference to the theories of Marx and Durkheim makes a compact summary
of my previous interpretation that much more helpful. Needless to say,
for those who have read the preceding volumes, this review is redundant
and unnecessary.

In volume 1, I conducted two simultaneous polemics. First, I argued
against the positivist persuasion in contemporary understandings of science, evident not only among philosophers and sociologists of science
but among its practitioners as well. The crucial proposition of the positivist persuasion, I argued, is the belief that factual statements can be on-
tologically separated from nonfactual statements or generalizations.
From this central tenet, the other components of the positivist persuasion inevitably follow: the notions that philosophical or metaphysical issues play no essential part in a true empirical science, that theoretical
disputes must be decided by reference to crucial empirical experiments
alone, that methodological techniques of verification or falsification are
of critical and ultimate importance. In opposition to these positivist tenets, I suggested that general as well as specific thinking is crucial to science, and I defined this "theoretical" (in contrast to "methodological" or
"empirical") logic as the concern with the effects of more general assumptions on more specific formulations. Indeed, this more general concern with "theoretical logic" permeates the analysis through the entirety
of this multivolume work.

My second polemic in volume 1 was directed against theoretical arguments that have occurred within the antipositivist framework itself. I
argued that recent debates in sociological theory have sought to reduce
theoretical argument to one or another particular set of nonempirical
commitments. Theoretical empiricism has, for example, sought to reduce sociological theory to assumptions about methodology, conflict theory to assumptions about the relative equilibrium of the empirical world
at a specific time, antifunctionalist critique to assumptions about the nature of scientific models, and ideological criticism—practicing a "strong
program" in the sociology of knowledge—to the political components of
a theorist's perspective.

I proposed, to the contrary, that science be conceived as a multi-
layered continuum, one that stretches from the most general, meta-
physically oriented presuppositions, to more specific ideological
assumptions and models, to still more empirical concepts and methodological commitments, and finally to empirically related propositions
and "facts." Each of these levels, I insisted, has relative autonomy vis-à-
vis other kinds of scientific commitments, although each is powerfully
interrelated to others at the same time. It is the task of *theoretical* logic in
sociology to explicate what each of these commitments entails and how
they are interrelated. Only with such a differentiated understanding of

science, moreover, can the dichotomy of idealist versus positivist, or materialist, understandings of science be resolved, for with this understanding it becomes clear that every scientific statement is the product of
the interaction between pressures from both the empirical and the metaphysical environments. Figure 1 is my schematic representation of the
scientific continuum, which I presented in volumes 1 and 2 and repeat
here for the reader's convenience.

Figure 1

THE SCIENTIFIC CONTINUUM AND ITS COMPONENTS

Metaphysical   Empirical
environment   environment

As part of this second polemic I also made a final point: not only have
recent theoretical arguments been reductionistic, or conflationary, but
taken together they have usually ignored the most generalized elements
of social-scientific argument. I called these elements "presuppositions"
and defined them as the assumptions any social scientist makes about the
nature of human action and how it is aggregated into patterned
arrangements.

These presuppositional assumptions address the problems of action
and order. First (and here I must unfortunately simplify complex issues
which were treated earlier at some length), action can be defined either
in an instrumental, rationalizing way or in a manner that pays more attention to nonrational, normative or affective components. The former
takes the materialist path, the latter the idealist, although there is also, of
course, the possibility for a more integrated and synthetic, or multidimensional, position. Second, theory must also adopt an orientation to
order. Are social arrangements the results of individual negotiation or do
they present themselves as collective structures that have sui generis, or
emergent, status? Individualistic approaches often reveal important as-

pects of empirical interaction, but they ignore the invisible parameters within which such action takes place, parameters which inform the substance of action itself. If one takes the collective course, on the other hand, action remains vitally important, for assumptions about the nature of action will determine how such collective order will be described. If an idealist understanding of action is pursued, collective order will be given a normative hue. This position has the advantage of allowing collective structures to be combined clearly with the voluntary agency of individuals, for normative order rests upon internal, subjective commitments. Yet, taken by itself, this approach exaggerates the responsiveness of the collectivity to subjective concerns. Yet if action is assumed, in the name of greater realism, to be instrumentalizing and rational, collective structure will be described as if it were completely external and material, for if motives are always calculating and efficient, action will be predictable on the basis of external pressure alone. Subjectivity and the concern with motive drop out: order is then viewed in a thoroughly deterministic way. These two solutions to the problem of collective order form the traditions of sociological idealism and sociological materialism, traditions that must be sharply separated from idealism and materialism in a purely epistemological sense. Of course, once again, there remains the theoretical possibility that more synthetic and multidimensional understandings of collective order may be achieved.

It is within the contexts of these various polemics that I introduced certain technical arguments which might at first glance elude those who are reading the present volume alone. These are: (1) the dangers of "conflation" in scientific argument, (2) the importance of multidimensional thought at the most general presuppositional level, (3) the dangers of "reduction" within this presuppositional level itself. Within the context of the preceding summary these technical points should now be more accessible. (1) Conflationary arguments attempt to make each of the components of the scientific continuum primarily dependent on one particular differentiated commitment. Thus, "conflict sociology" is conflationary, as are so many of the arguments for "critical sociology" and the arguments for or against "functionalist sociology." (2) Within the presuppositional level—the most general and ramifying level of scientific reasoning—I insisted on the theoretical power of multidimensional thinking over either its idealist or materialist alternatives. Critical benefits accrue to both forms of one-dimensional thought, but there are also debilitating weaknesses which make each, taken by itself, theoretically unacceptable. (3) I suggested that one-dimensional thinking was often camouflaged by a form of reductionism within the presuppositional level itself: the reduction of the problem of action to the problem of order. Sociological idealists and materialists often—in fact, almost invariably—argue that a collectivist rather than an individualistic approach can be achieved only if action is perceived in an instrumentalist or normative way. This simplification is appealing but false. The questions of action and order are themselves relatively autonomous, although they are thoroughly interdependent. Normative and instrumental understandings of action can both be collectivist, just as they can both inform individualistic thought.

I made other arguments in volume 1. Most importantly, I suggested that nonpositivistic thought need not be merely relativistic, that it can attain its own kind of objectivity. I also argued, in the introductory chapter to volume 2, for the critical importance in social-scientific argument of the interpretation and reinterpretation of classical work. In the nonconsensual world of social science, "readings" of the work of dead theorists, or of completed and past theoretical statements, is a fundamental means, though not of course the only one, of establishing the validity of general orientations.

These assertions, which for polemical purposes and for clarity's sake were put as sharply as possible—and here are being reproduced in an unforgivably foreshortened way—may have seemed tendentious to many readers. I hope that the intervening discussion in volume 2 has demonstrated that they were not. There I tried to show through a detailed examination of the writings of Durkheim and Marx that presuppositional "multidimensionality" is such a generalized and universalistic criterion that it allows a certain kind of disciplined objectivity. It does so because it provides a reference point from which every interpretive and theoretical debate can be judged and, in a truly Hegelian sense, negated and included at the same time. The evidence for this, of course, can be established only through the actual interpretations and theoretical arguments of volume 2, and I cannot hope to reproduce these arguments here. I will, however, try to provide a brief overview of that earlier discussion, summarizing my understanding of how the classical antinomies of sociological idealism and materialism were first constructed and elaborated. Since I view Weber as attempting to transcend these dichotomies, and also as unfortunately reproducing them, such an overview is essential not only for comprehending my general theoretical position; it is a necessary framework for understanding my specific interpretation of Weber as well.

This work as a whole is dedicated to the construction of a multidimensional sociological theory, and in volume 2 I examined Durkheim and Marx in order, first, to understand the different elements from which such a theory must be composed and, second, to comprehend the analytic barriers which prevent such a synthetic theory from actually being constructed. Marx and Durkheim both considered themselves as committed to collective understandings of social order, but the uncertainties of their conceptions of action made this social order difficult for them to define. Marx began with a normative and voluntaristic approach to revolution and change, an approach in which cultural critique was essential and which posited the subjective alienation of reason and the desire for its reconciliation as the central mechanisms for transforming social life. But the encounter with the radicalism of his day and especially with the science of political economy initiated far-reaching changes in Marx's work. Instrumental action now seemed the appropriate form for any analysis of the capitalist period. Alienation changed from a source of critical subjectivity to a rationalization for its theoretical elimination. Marx could now conceive collective order only in external and coercive terms. From this transition, sociological materialism was born, and with it an enduring sensitivity to the external dimension of social constraint. But so too was born an antivoluntaristic theory with all its fateful implications.

Durkheim was from the beginning committed to avoiding what he justly regarded as this utilitarian error. He sought to combine a recognition of individuality and voluntarism with the necessity for social order and control. The history of his early writings, however, is the record of his failures to make this intention into a scientific reality. Because of his difficulties in conceiving of the individual actor in an analytical rather than a concrete way, because of his tendency to conflate empirical equilibrium with collective order, and because of a continuing residue of utilitarian thinking about action itself, Durkheim's first great work adopted—ambivalently, to be sure—a theory of instrumental action and external order. When the obvious "pathology" of the capitalist division of labor abolished the deus ex machina by which Durkheim had thought voluntarism could still be maintained, and when critical reaction brought home to him the truly deterministic theoretical structure he had actually wrought, Durkheim recoiled from this quasi-Marxian adventure. He now sought persistently to subjectify order, and he rediscovered the notion of culturally interpenetrated and solidary individuals from his earliest work. His revelation about the true nature of religious life allowed him to reformulate these insights in a more systematic and elegant way, and in the last two decades of his life he developed a theory of society that in every significant respect was the mirror image of Marx's own. Durkheim understood more acutely than anyone before him the subjective and voluntaristic aspects of modern life, and his understanding allowed him to solve the riddle of the fate of religion in a secular world. It was upon a religious model that the great successes of sociological idealism were forged, but it was this same model that was also responsible for its greatest failings. Religious fervor must deal with the limitations of the human soul, but there are more external and material barriers to action that are equally obdurate, and these barriers sociological idealism finds hard to explain.

The limiting assumptions of these sociological founders confined their thought in rather narrow ways. The fact that in some sense they "knew better" created pressures that burst the formal barriers of their science altogether. Marx managed to be extraordinarily consistent in his explicitly scientific writings, although not completely so, but his more informal political work—his pamphlets, letters, and speeches—reveals an effort to achieve a more synthetic scope. The residual and peripatetic nature of these efforts leaves them theoretically confused; Marx could not "theoretize" the elements whose existence he informally recognized. Durkheim, too, was forced to recognize at least the existence of the objects he had striven so hard to overlook in his formulations of scientific theory. "Utilitarianism," he admitted, existed in the pathological interstices of modern life. Yet although in crucial ways it played havoc with moral solidarity, such utilitarianism still could not really be explained, at least not in a systematic rather than residual way. For in Durkheim's idealist view, material facts were always individual, never social and collective in their sociological status.

The limits of one-dimensional theory are even more strikingly revealed in the schools that these founders of the major sociological traditions established. Under the guise of homage and obeisance to the master's work and memory, Durkheim's most distinguished followers tried to reconcile his religious theory of society with the telling obduracy of "material" facts, with class stratification, group conflict, market pressures, and the bureaucratic state. The most important Marxists moved just as persistently in the other direction. Their commitment to the voluntarism of revolution, combined with their sensitivity to continuing academic criticism, made them search for a way to voluntarize and subjectify Marx. The history of these revisionist efforts is extraordinarily interesting and each has contributed powerfully to elements of multidimensional thought. Each, however, has ended in failure, for as long as the effort is made to squeeze these broader insights into the narrow framework of the founder's work there is no escape from profound intellectual contradictions. To avoid contradiction, new starting points would have to be firmly established.

In this volume, Max Weber is presented as the theorist who laid out these starting points. As in the earlier volumes, the historical and chronological dimension of my discussion is fundamentally qualified by more general analytical and theoretical concerns. Thus, although Weber was a contemporary of Durkheim, my presuppositional interest in the problem of multidimensionality leads me to consider his work as a response, in part, to the idealist tradition which, in the second volume, I have taken Durkheim to represent. Finally, even less than the other two founders of classical thought was Weber able to avoid fundamental irresolution and ambiguity. I will, then, also examine these weaknesses and the efforts at "paradigm revision" which they entailed for the postclassical generations.

The many acknowledgments which I owe for this and the other volumes of this work are made in the Preface to volume 1. At the beginning of this volume on Weber, however, I would like specifically to thank Colin Loader and Steven Seidman, who provided invaluable assistance in checking and translating German texts, and Guenther Roth, who graciously provided an eleventh hour reading of the galleys.

Chapter One

WEBER'S EARLY WRITINGS

Tentative Explorations beyond Idealism and Materialism

Alongside Durkheim and Marx, Max Weber stands as one of the fathers of the modern sociological tradition. Because of this seminal status he has been accorded the honor of being "read" in contradictory ways. Working on the assumption that "as Weber goes, so goes sociology," leaders of different sociological perspectives have used Weber, over the decades, to legitimate their own specific theoretical ideas. Weber's thought has been reduced to every different point on the scientific continuum, each effort an attempt to conflate his great achievement with a commitment to one particular position.

On the most specific and concrete side of the continuum, Robert K. Merton used Weber to legitimate his campaign for theories of the middle range. Merton insisted that Weber had worked with a "severely delimited problem"—that is, the delineation of propositional relationships—and that his discovery of the Protestant ethic, for example, merely revealed "the ways in which religious commitments and economic behavior are connected."[1†] Directing themselves toward broader empirical generalizations, "conflict theorists" claimed that Weber's most ramifying commitment lay in his sensitivity to disequilibrium. From this empirical insight, John Rex argued, emerged Weber's instrumental

NOTE: In addition to the citation of sources, the backnotes include numerous substantive discussions—refinements of points that occur in the main text and digressions about relevant issues and secondary literature. To enable the interested reader to turn immediately to this substantive annotation, I have distinguished these substantive notes by marking them with a dagger(†) following the note number. A ribbon bookmark is provided to facilitate such referral.

approach to action and his understanding of coercive order.[2] Ralf Dahrendorf and David Lockwood similarly equated this conflict perspective with a presuppositional commitment to power and substratum rather than to values and superstructure; Dahrendorf argued, for example, that the "true Weber" viewed legitimate authority as coercion rather than as a matter of belief.[3†] More recently, Randall Collins has reduced Weber's thought in much the same way, suggesting that it was his understanding of empirical conflict that allowed him to jettison functional models and normative action.[4†] Addressing himself to the meta-methodological assumptions that inform such empirical observations, Hans Zetterberg claimed that if Weber had been more committed to verification and had employed the logic of proposition building, the controversy over his work would have been avoided.[5] Still others have located the crucial commitment at the level of model. For Reinhard Bendix and Don Martindale, Weber was the anti-systems theorist par excellence, his focus on institutions and individuals allowing him to transcend the anti-voluntaristic status of modern functionalist theory.[6] Weber's work, finally, has been explained as the reflection of his ideological commitments and social position. Raymond Aron and Wolfgang J. Mommsen explain the instrumental cast of Weber's political theory by reference to his political beliefs, Mommsen describing the scholarly work and political creed as "two sides of the same coin."[7] Herbert Marcuse argued for a different ideology, but his theoretical logic was the same. Weber was a bourgeois apologist, he contended: "Philosophical, sociological-historical and political motives are fundamentally connected in Weber's analysis of industrial capitalism."[8]

Each of these interpretations has pointed to something of significance in Weber's sociology, yet their reduction of the general work to one of its parts makes their polemical intention not hard to find. Certainly Weber's work has offered powerful exemplars for empirical study, and there is no doubt that his emphasis on conflict is significant in itself. His opposition to "functional theories"—no matter how misunderstood by contemporary "presentist" readings of his writing—certainly was important to the formation of his particular sociology; and the force of his profound political commitment sent shock waves throughout his theoretical and empirical work. None of these levels of commitment, however, was determinate for his sociology. Indeed, if each claim is partly true, all have to be at least partly wrong. But if these critiques obscure the partial validity of competing claims, they have also resulted in what is perhaps the most serious error of all: the relative neglect of the most general and ramifying level in Weber's sociology—his presuppositions about the nature of order and action. If Weber's work has functioned as an exemplar, it has also been massively influential on the level of its most general themes. If Weber was inspired by certain empirical observations about the correlations between religion and economy, he could see this relation only because he presupposed the kind of order that gave to each an important status. If Weber appreciated conflict, how he explained this disequilibrium depended upon more generalized reference. If Weber opposed certain models, the nature of his own orientation to actors and institutions must still be explained. The same must be said, finally, for his political concerns. Other German intellectuals, though by no means many, shared his ideological focus—but how many of them produced the same kind of sociology?

Though I will not neglect the impact of Weber's more specific concerns, my principal interest in the following pages is Weber's presuppositional stance and its formative impact on his sociology. Even among those who have recognized its importance, this presuppositional level has been interpreted in various ways. In part, these contradictory interpretations have occurred because of misunderstandings about the nature of theoretical logic; they have also resulted from purely polemical intent. Some analysts have insisted that Weber must be viewed as an individualist rather than a collectivist thinker. Arguing that Weber is concerned primarily with nonrational action and meaning, Aron places him among the existentialists;[9] starting from a more instrumentalist position, Richard Ashcraft sees Weber's lack of concern for "structural" explanation in his purported depiction of an "atomised" struggle for power among individuals.[10] Within a more collective framework, Weber has consistently been seen as an idealist concerned exclusively with normative order. Seigfried Landshut wrote about Weber's idealist construction of history, Gabriel Kolko about his exclusive focus on *"geist."*[11] Though Talcott Parsons claims to see Weber as a multidimensional theorist, there is a strong tendency in his interpretation to portray Weber as supplying a normative answer to order.[12†] Yet while Parsons ties Weber to Durkheim, other influential interpreters have tied him just as strongly to Marx. Albert Salomon wrote, in fact, that Weber was simply a "bourgeois Marx," and Joseph Schumpeter that "the whole of the facts and the arguments of Max Weber fit perfectly into Marx's system."[13] George Lichtheim supported this collective instrumental reading, describing Weber simply as a "Marxist epigone."[14] Irving Zeitlin takes a similar perspective, and Hans Gerth and C. Wright Mills profess to see "a definite drift in his intellectual biography towards Marx."[15] Finally, Weber has been described as the ultimate synthesizer of the materialist and idealist traditions, the final arbiter of the conflict between Durkheim and Marx. Bendix's is the classic articulation of such a reading, following, in a less ambiguous way, the earlier claim by Parsons.[16]

The incredible range of these interpretations has often been seen as resulting from the fragmented character of Weber's final corpus. "Since the original remains incomplete," Bendix writes, "Weber's . . . work demands an interpretation."[17] The same contradictory claims, however, can be observed in the interpretations which have been made of the more "completed" writings of Marx and Durkheim. Theorists read strategically, and any great thinker will eventually be read in ways that reflect the entire range of theoretical commitment. Although I, too, am bound by theoretical commitments, I will try to read Weber in a more objective way, to do justice to the complexity and ambiguity that actually characterize his work. Bendix wrote that one purpose of his important intellectual biography was to make Weber's work "more thematically coherent."[18] Yet perhaps this is precisely what should not be done. The interpreters of Weber, even the most perceptive, have eliminated the true drama of Weber's sociology by smoothing over the radical tensions that permeate his work. While the intention clearly has been to facilitate contemporary learning, what we have learned from such readings has ultimately narrowed rather than expanded our comprehension of theoretical logic. For Weber's tension and ambivalence are no less than those of sociology itself. As he struggled to overcome the classical antinomies of social thought, so must contemporary sociology.

1. THE HISTORICAL AND IDEOLOGICAL BACKGROUND FOR WEBER'S SYNTHESIS

Germany's peculiar historical development forms the background to Weber's thought, the foil against which his early intellectual orientation emerged. Germany came to industrialization only late in the nineteenth century, and its formation as a nation-state barely preceded this period of intense economic development. In the cultural realm, too, the German path of development was distinctive: against the "rationalizing" values of the French Revolution and English democracy, it expounded a traditionalistic Romanticism. Because of these developments, the German middle class was comparatively weak. Although Germans of that class shared certain individualistic and democratic aspirations with liberals in other nations, they never were able to promote a successful revolutionary movement. Politically and culturally they remained subordinate to the aristocracy and to the state bureaucracy; in the 1860s, Bismarck had unified Germany without any significant liberal help.

The condition of the German intelligentsia was tied to the fate of the middle class. By the latter decades of the nineteenth century, the professoriate generally approved of Germany's traditionalistic and sharply unequal stratification system, tolerated the repressive elements of Bismarck's rule, and shared the ruling circles' fears about the spread of Social Democracy. They also had the same disdain for the "vulgarity" and "materialism" of the emerging industrial order.[19] This "German ideology" became formulated in the analytic terms of intellectual life. There is no better representation of this than the term *Geisteswissenschaft*. Dilthey had translated this word from Mill's "moral science," yet in the German context it came to have a particular meaning. Translated generally as "social science," its more literal meaning is "spiritual science." *Wissenschaft* itself had idealist overtones that the Anglo-Saxon word "science" never possessed. Windelband rightly compared it to the Greek "philosophia," which, he insisted, "means exactly that which we describe with the German word *Wissenschaft* and which . . . fortunately includes much more than the English and French *science*."[20] Troeltsch described the cultural background of this *Geisteswissenschaft* tradition as a "mystical-metaphysical" reaction against the social atomism of the French and English experience. According to the German conception, he wrote, "the state and the society are not created from the individual by way of contract and pragmatic [*zweckrational*] construction, but from the suprapersonal spiritual forces which emanate from . . . the volk spirit [*Volksgeist*] or the religious esthetic idea."[21]

In view of the fate of German liberalism, it is not surprising that this intellectual Romanticism was combined in the German professoriate with strong support for the military accomplishments of the German state. Ever since their decisive defeat in the Prussian constitutional conflict in the early 1860s, German liberals had manifested a profoundly ambivalent attitude toward the state. Although they continued to support individualistic goals in domestic economic and political life, they cooperated with Bismarck in his crusade to enhance the power of the state, both at home and abroad. This goal, in fact, can be seen as the primary object of German "National Liberalism" in the 1880s and 1890s, despite the fact that this preoccupation was accompanied by a withdrawal from social concerns not fully characteristic of the liberal tradition.

The particular liberal tradition and the specifically national characteristics of the German intelligentsia were uniquely represented in the political and intellectual group called the Verein für Sozialpolitik (Social Policy Association). Formed in 1872 by such men as Schmoller, Adolph Wagner, and Brentano, this organization formed the practical focus for the "historical" school of economics, an organicist, anti-instrumentalist approach to the study of the origins and processes of modern economic life. Because the members argued for the reform of German capitalism and for the amelioration of the condition of the working classes, they were called "socialists of the chair." Yet they shared the liberal weakness for state control, and their fear of political opposition led them to view Bismarck's nondemocratic state as the appropriate vehicle for instituting their reforms.[22] We may recall that Durkheim was strongly affected by these "moral economists" during his early trip to Germany, and it is not unimportant in comparing Durkheim and Weber to note that Weber was profoundly influenced by the same group. Yet as a leading member of the younger generation of the Verein, Weber also shared Durkheim's dislike of its statist ideology. Thus, while Weber was strongly influenced by the Verein, he withdrew from it in significant ways. Indeed, this dual attitude of incorporation and critique characterizes Weber's attitude toward German ideology and German intellectual life as a whole.

The position of German liberalism, the ideology of the German intelligentsia, and the specific imperatives of the historical school form the background for Weber's intellectual development, the soil from which he drew sustenance and the foil against which he rebelled. Weber never fitted completely into the nationalist liberalism that formed his paternal inheritance. Attracted to the "English style" of democratization, he was also committed to the spiritual values of the German nation. Sympathetic to the moral claims of the oppressed, he also supported the imperialist expansion of the German nation. As one of the group of brilliant social scientists that formed the younger generation of the Verein für Sozialpolitik, Weber, along with Sombart and Tönnies, refused to sympathize with the traditionalists' antagonism to modernity. Yet, at the same time, he and his coworkers have to be seen more as "accommodationists" than "modernists," for their attitude toward industrial society reflected more resignation and an acceptance of the inevitable than any genuine enthusiasm.[23]

Weber and his fellow accommodationists had an accurate sense of the crisis of German society. They knew that concessions must be made if the sting was to be taken out of industrialization and democracy, if the working classes were to be weaned from Marxism. They knew, moreover, that if urban and proletarian Germany were to be so incorporated into German society, the agrarian conservatism championed by the Junkers had to be defeated. Within the context of cultural pessimism and estrangement, then, Weber argued vigorously against the Prussian three-class suffrage. He justified his support for the imperial expansion of the German nation, in part, by arguing that the well-being of the industrial masses depended on a dynamic capitalism. He was friendly with Eduard Bernstein, the revisionist Marxist, and he dedicated his early research to demonstrating that Germany had to initiate fundamental economic and political changes that involved the elimination of the Junker class.[24†] In his participation in the Verein für Sozialpolitik, Weber followed the more liberal Brentano rather than Schmoller. Although he embraced the importance of noneconomic context and of industrial reform, like Brentano he was less confident than Schmoller of the beneficence of bureaucracy. He supported English-style trade unionism, and he joined with Protestant reformers in the effort to push German middle-class politics in a more "socially" liberal direction.[25†]

Weber's ideological orientation and intellectual inheritance, then, involved strong internal tensions. These strains, in turn, proved enormously fruitful for his scientific development, for they pushed him to try to embrace seemingly incompatible extremes—positions that neither Marx nor Durkheim were ever motivated to join together. On the one hand, Weber accepted the reality of instrumental "interest," not only coercive state power but class conflict and the industrial exigencies that produced it. On the other hand, Weber remained extraordinarily sensitive to spiritual questions, to *Geist*, to the play of irrational emotions vis- à-vis external events. In fact, before he had ever begun his serious scientific labor these sensitivities had firmly structured his intellectual position. This early formation is clearly demonstrated by Weber's reaction, at the age of twenty, to the writings of William Ellery Channing, the American Romantic Unitarian. He was impressed by, and took very seriously, the "unassailable loftiness" of Channing's sentiments. "The clear, calm idealism he draws from the observation of 'the infinite worth of the human soul' is so refreshing . . . that even those who do not share his way of looking at things . . . can be in no doubt that his views are universal and based on real needs of the spiritual life."[26] At the same time, however, Weber had no patience with what he viewed as Channing's "highly frivolous" pacifism and antimilitarism. Such an attitude, he believed, could "easily produce a rift in people's sentiments between the supposed demands of .*Christianity* and the consequences and conditions that are created by the social order of the states and the world." On these grounds, Weber concludes that Channing had wishfully allowed his spiritual concerns to nullify worldly pressures, and that his antiwar doctrine was not only "impractical" but actually "reprehensible."[27] It is this tense blend of idealism and materialism that laid the groundwork for Weber's first scholarly work.

2. THE INTELLECTUAL BACKGROUND FOR WEBER'S SYNTHESIS

There is no "early Weber" in the sense that there is an early Marx or early Durkheim. In Weber's early writings, we do not find a theoretical position that is crucial to the unfolding of the mature theory. His first works certainly became the basis for later refinements, but never the polemical reference against which the later work was defined. To be sure, there is a significant chronological watershed in Weber's writing, the fallow period of 1897–1902 that divides the works written between 1889 and 1897, before his nervous breakdown, from those begun after his recovery in 1902. There are, moreover, distinctive differences between the writings of these two periods. In the earlier work, Weber was more of a historical economist and legal historian than a sociologist, and though his research was often insightful and compendious, it was never conceptually brilliant and generalizing. Despite such empirical and conceptual variations, however, there exists no decisive presuppositional shift between the early and the mature work. Both manifest an important synthetic ambition, though one that is in marked tension, as we shall eventually discover, with a more instrumentalist bent. It is, in fact, precisely in terms of this shared emphasis that the early writings hold particular interest. Because Weber had not yet developed a conceptual scheme of his own, the elements with which he attempts to move beyond the traditions we have identified with Durkheim and Marx are more nakedly visible than in the more tightly woven web of his later work.[28†]

In his early writings, Weber drew, in the first place, upon the intellectual resources of the traditional intelligentsia, the peculiar combination of idealist Romanticism and Realpolitik which I have described as the legacy of the German middle classes. From Idealism, Weber learned a lesson forgotten by the later Marx—the hermeneutical sensitivity to subjective intention—and from it he learned also to comprehend the voluntaristic element in history. From the Protestant Reformation onward, hermeneutics had been cultivated in Germany as a method for the close interpretation of the Scriptures. Schleiermacher systematized the method in 1829, defining it as the reconstruction of the meaning of a text as the author meant it to be understood. Later in the century, Dilthey translated this hermeneutical tradition into a historical methodology, arguing that through *Verstehen* (understanding) the historian should grasp the individual meaning of a fact rather than try to explain it as the necessary instance of a general nature-like law.[29] From this idealist tradition in historiography Weber also developed an appreciation for the individual element in action—a voluntarism, the idealists held, that could occur only because individuals were inspired by a higher spirit and force. Friedrich Meinecke, in one of his early works, sympathetically describes the origins of this historicist tradition, the very one that Marx and Engels mocked in *The German Ideology*, as "the voyage of discovery which the German spirit undertook with such zealous enthusiasm in the realm of the individual." The approach is characterized, Meinecke writes, by "our sense of individuality even in the supra-individual groupings," a sense that reveals an "individuality, spontaneity, an urge towards self-determination and extension of power that is observable at every hand."[30]

Yet the normative sensibility that Weber derived from this Romantic dimension of German liberalism was never separated in his mind—as it came to be for the later Durkheim—from the tradition of Realpolitik. This represented the other side of German liberalism. Formed by the liberal defeat in 1848, such a "realistic" understanding of the significance of force in human history was made even more powerful by the emergence after 1860 of Social Darwinian ideas. Glorification of the state and its power as ends in themselves, as determinant forces sui generis, became characteristic of much of liberal historiography in the last decades of the century. Mommsen, once an idealistic liberal himself, summed up this doctrine in his adage, "Life is work, and work is struggle."[31] His *Roman Public Law* analyzed the Roman evolution from principate to empire in terms of balance of power and political struggle; his *Roman History* eulogized Caesar and condemned the "honest mediocrities" of the Roman Senate. In the face of the critical outcry against the apparent inhumanity of his "realistic" approach, Mommsen simply had replied that "when a government cannot govern, it ceases to be legitimate, and he who has the power to overthrow it has also the right."[32†]

To this double legacy of intellectual liberalism, however, Weber also brought a new intellectual force that had only recently emerged on the German intellectual scene: the economically "realistic" theory of Marxism. In his inaugural address upon assuming his professorship at Freiburg in 1895, Weber announced that his generation would add to the Realpolitik of the older leaders and scholars a strong social conscience and a commitment to improving the condition of the working classes.[33†] From an early age, Weber had identified with his mother's conscientious concern with the lower classes, and this sympathy was undoubtedly given further support by his critical reaction to the anti-socialist laws which were in force between 1878 and 1890. In the course of this period, the German Social Democratic labor movement increased in power and intellectual influence, and by the second half of the 1880s most of Marx's and Engels' major works had gained substantial circulation.[34†] When Weber joined the Verein für Sozialpolitik in 1888, Marxism was already a significant political-cum-intellectual issue. Schmoller, the leading spokesman of the Verein, dismissed Marx as a "Talmudic social philosopher"; arguing that Marxism lacked any scientific validity, he sought to justify its exclusion from the German universities.[35] Weber and his younger colleagues in the Verein argued against such a dismissal. They took Marx's conception of capitalism much more seriously. Indeed, the most important contemporary historian of the Verein has gone so far as to insist that this "younger generation made capitalism into their scientific main-problem and an interpretive scheme for the present."[36] When the third volume of *Capital* appeared in 1894, it initiated a thorough discussion of Marxism in German political economy, a debate which intensified after Engels' death in 1895 and with the appearance of Bernstein's revisionist writings in the years immediately following.[37] In 1904, when Weber, Sombart, and Jaffe took over editorship of the *Archiv für Sozialwissenschaft und Sozialpolitik*, their joint editorial stated that the journal would "treat all phenomena of the economic and total social life from the viewpoint of the revolutionary nature of capitalism."[38] Durkheim, too, had shared Marx's conscientious concern for the working classes and for social reform; this ideological commitment, however, never was expressed in theoretical terms so colored by Marx himself.

There is no certainty that Weber actually read the works of Marx during the period of his early work, although his relative sympathy with and political support for "Marxist" influences is evident. It is clearly established, however, that scholars who had a direct impact on Weber's early work espoused a quasi-materialist, if not Marxist, approach to history. In the course of the 1880s there had developed in Germany a reaction against excessively idealist historiography; this movement was eventually labeled *Kulturgeschichte*, a term which in the sense then used would be translated as "history of civilization" but in contemporary language might be identified as "social history."[39] There seems little doubt that Weber's teachers were influenced by this reaction. The supervisor of his first dissertation (1889), Levin Goldschmidt, had written about Roman history in terms of state power, economic exploitation, and class conflict; and August Meitzen, who supervised the second dissertation (1891), taught Weber, according to Weber's own testimony, that ideas and institutions must be studied in terms of their relation to material group interests.[40†] Weber was also strongly affected in his early work by the economic history of the conservative socialist Karl Rodbertus, whose one-sided analysis he defended as extraordinarily suggestive if not fully accurate.[41†] To Weber's contemporaries, at least, the impact on Weber's early writings of such materialist teachings and of Marxism more generally was unmistakable. Troeltsch observed that Marx "seems to have made a deep and lasting impression" on Weber; Baumgarten, referring specifically to the dissertation of 1889, noted "a viewpoint unmistakably oriented toward Marx."[42†]

As a springboard to the polemical reading of his later work, Weber's early writings have been labeled as Marxist, as idealist, and as perfectly multidimensional. Each of these assessments is partly true; each, considered as a whole, is false. Weber's intention is to avoid the dilemmas of either extreme. In this sense, I would agree more with Troeltsch than with Baumgarten. Marxism made a lasting impression on Weber, but he never completely surrendered himself to it. He sought a more synthetic perspective, combining elements from Marx not only with the political and legal orientation of Realpolitik but with the normative reference of German Idealism. Whether Weber could form a true synthesis from this combination is, however, another question altogether.

3. THE THEORETICAL ACHIEVEMENT: MULTIDIMENSIONAL ELEMENTS IN WEBER'S EARLY WRITINGS

In one important strand of his early writings, Weber asserts that the ruthlessness of capitalist economic conditions virtually eliminates the chance to maintain moral regulation. Modern action, in this understanding, tends definitely toward the instrumental, order toward the external and coercive. These presuppositions inform Weber's analysis of various institutional spheres. In writing about the stock exchange, for example, he insists that it "cannot be a mere club for 'ethical culture,' " since it must operate within an international economic environment disciplined by harsh exigencies which create a "relentless and ineluctable economic struggle for national existence and economic power."[43] The internal conditions of the modern stock exchange usually produce the same kind of pressure for instrumentalism. Because the exchange is based upon market mechanisms, anyone with money can participate; but the heterogeneous mass that results undermines any chance for the kind of stable traditions upon which ethical regulation would depend.[44] Weber applies the same kind of reasoning to the institution of the nation-state. Under conditions of modern capitalism, the destinies of national cultures depend largely upon the utilization of national power. "There is no peace in the economic struggle for power," Weber warns his countrymen, and he cites the force of critical external conditions to buttress his argument: "The gloomy threat of the population problem . . . is reason enough to prevent us from . . . thinking that there might be any other way than the fierce struggle of man against man, if the necessary elbow room is to be attained."[45] Group relationships, the most important of which is the relation of different social classes, are subject to the same kind of reduction. With the development of capitalism, Weber says, "there takes place a phenomenon of incomparable significance: the replacement of personal relationships of dominance by the impersonal dominance of class."[46] The ethical order of religious bonds can no longer have any effect, for the "personal relationship of responsibility" has disappeared. What has replaced it is the "objective hatred" of one class for another.[47]

Weber's first major application of this instrumental perspective was in his 1891 study of Roman agrarian history, which must be read in connection with his 1896 essay, "The Social Causes of the Decline of Ancient Civilization." In every study of Rome, Weber writes, the question arises, Who led the wars of conquest, and why?[48]† Immediately, he rephrases this question in terms of conditional exigencies and instrumental interest. The pertinent question must be: "Which social strata and economic interest groups politically formed the driving force, and, therefore, to which tendencies can the apparent displacement of the center of gravity of Roman politics be attributed?"[49] As this question implies, Weber has placed alongside his conception of the coercive state an analysis of the economic exigencies which influence it. The Roman politics of conquest, he insists, was not only an extension of the political-power position of the state, but represented at the same time a continuous expansion of Roman colonization and capitalistic cultivation of the defeated areas. "Probably never in the greater matters of state," he concludes, "has the political rule [*Herrschaft*] had such a direct value in money."[50]

In part, then, Roman expansion had an instrumental political purpose. Roman society had been marked by a fierce struggle between the plebs and other groups for the right to cultivate public land. In these terms, colonization must be seen as "a means for the Roman authority to deal with problems in the social body," as a way of dealing with "revolutionary unrest."[51] At the same time, however, Weber insists on the importance of more purely economic pressures. Although he refers to the luxury goods demanded by the "small stratum of the wealthy classes," he emphasizes an even more "Marxian" element as the secret instigator of Roman expansion: the massive reliance on slave labor. Slaves became vital to antiquity, he writes, for reasons of efficiency; the chronic warfare of ancient civilization made their labor cheaper than that of free workers.[52] Yet this very reliance on slavery introduced a tremendous inefficiency in the longer run, for slaves could not reproduce themselves as rapidly as economic expansion demanded. Once the entire area of ancient civilization had been conquered, therefore, the Roman economy faced an "acute shortage of labor"—in Marx's terms, a crisis in the reproduction of labor power. From this there could be no escape.[53] It was as a result of this crisis that there occurred the "transformation of the fundamental structures of society" that Europeans understand as the decline of the Roman Empire. As this economic and political infrastructure weakened, "the intellectual life of Western Europe also sank into a long darkness."[54]†

We can find the same base-superstructure logic, and the same understanding that the historical analysis of capitalism presupposes instrumentalism, in Weber's treatment of the problem of agrarian labor in Prussia. This was another major social-structural phenomenon which he studied in the early writings, and between 1892 and 1894 he devoted four different publications to it.[55]† Initially undertaken for the Verein für Sozialpolitik, Weber's assignment was to find out why Germans had gradually been replaced by foreigners as laborers on the estates east of the Elbe. In striking contrast to his coworkers on the project, Weber shifts analytical attention away from individual decisions and personalities to the collective pressures that ordered them. This order is, in crucial respects, external and conditional to the individual, the kind of order that assumes instrumental action. Weber is concerned with the "basic changes that can be detected in the social structure in the labor organization of the large landed properties of the east." He compares these to changes in the physical world, to "disturbances in the molecular structure of solids," for they "occur slowly but irresistibly" and they are "hidden from the eye."[56]†

Once again, Weber's instrumental orientation is applied to the relatively autonomous spheres of state and economy. The Prussian estates, he writes, were not merely economic units but also local political "centers of domination [Herrschaftszentren]."[57] Yet successful political domination, Weber insists, could not occur without the economic success of the estates themselves. Profitable estates provided the "material basis" for Prussian political dominance; the very wealth of the Prussians, in fact, made them more honest and trustworthy administrators of the lower-class interests.[58] The challenge to this stable situation, and this relation of trust, was created by drastic shifts in the world market for agricultural products. The Prussian ruling class, Weber writes, was "coerced by relations of exchange, which . . . were outside their control."[59] The result was an "unavoidable transformation" of agricultural relations, a transformation that produced the rationalization of economic life: "The necessity emerges of increasing the outlay of capital and farm management on business-like lines unknown to the traditional landlord of the east."[60] This new economic demand, in turn, creates changes in other external conditions. There are "reorganizations of farm management," then "alterations in labor relations."[61] Each enterprise, of course, reacts somewhat differently, but this variation is the result of similarly coercive conditions: "The necessary consequences for these enterprises differed according to the soil and climatic conditions."[62] In every case, economic rationalization undermines patriarchal trust between owners and workers. The wage system replaces both payment in kind and payment by profit sharing. Migrant workers become economically more "efficient" than the permanent German labor force, first because they are better adapted to seasonal labor, second because they will tolerate the inferior diet that the landlords have initiated as a costsaving device.[63]

From the immigrant's perspective, the "prime cause" for their movement is the relatively higher quality of wages they receive in Germany.[64] For old and new workers alike, the new situation is one of "proletarianization."[65] In the earlier, traditionalistic situation, the master-worker relation had been one of mutual trust, or at least mutual interest, a *Herrschaftsverhältnis* or *Interressengemeinschaft*. Now it is simply impersonal class-rule, *Klassenherrschaft*.[66†] In these "material conditions of life," the agricultural workers have become a proletariat, but whether they will become a successful and aggressive one is another issue. Weber asks the Marxist question: Will this objective class be able to become a class-for-itself?

> What will the result of this be? Will the struggle develop in a manner similar to that in industry? Is there a possibility that over a period the organization of workers will create a rural labour aristocracy as has emerged in England, whereby thorough proletarianization engenders in turn a movement made up of the highest level of workers?[67]

He answers this question in the negative. Like the peasants in Marx's *Eighteenth Brumaire*, the estate laborers lead an isolated existence. "Dispersed far over the land," they are engaged in a "struggle of interests" for which "they lacked the means of resistance."[68] From this material deficit, a certain consciousness will follow. "The rural proletariat," Weber concludes, are "able to develop an anti-landlord class consciousness . . . only in an isolated fashion against *individual* masters."[69]

These discussions certainly demonstrate the impact on Weber's early writing of the instrumentalist traditions of Marxism, Social Darwinism, and Realpolitik. Weber has sketched an antinormative portrait of modern society that stands as a self-sufficient, if relatively undeveloped, social theory. Yet he is not, in fact, content to let it stand alone. He has been receptive, we have seen, to other kinds of intellectual influences, and within his early work he sets alongside his "realistic" analysis references to factors that are of a more "ideal" composition. Capitalist order can, apparently, be strongly affected by moral commitments. Weber moves, in effect, from Marx to Durkheim, though in doing so he indicates an intention to interlink orders that Durkheim would never have allowed. In the midst of Weber's discussions of the stock exchange, for example, he insists that the "judgment" of speculators is an independent variable, not reducible to market constraints.[70] Members of the Hamburg exchange were actually subject to a strict code of honor, one upheld by effective traditions.[71] Such traditions can be maintained regardless of economic pressures, Weber believes, if organizational measures are initiated to create more homogeneity and privacy within the speculator group.[72] The same crucial reservations are expressed about a purely instrumental theory of state power. In the 1892 study of Prussian agriculture, Weber insists that whether in power or not, the old noble class will continue to exert pressure on the government simply through the "customs" that it established.[73] And in his earlier study on Roman agrarian history, Weber argued for the independent importance of legal regulation of the state. Roman constitutional and civil law had a definite "practical meaning" for the development of agrarian relationships.[74]

Finally, Weber argues at strategic points that even class relationships themselves—the group order which at other points in his early writings typifies the pure instrumentality of capitalism—cannot be seen as completely separated from moral and ethical concerns. Voluntary will and internal commitment become, in this way, critical factors in class analysis. Classes need "spiritual capital," not just economic resources.[75] They need "political intelligence," which can be gained only through the experience of "political education."[76] Moods are as basic to class action as interests; a class may be listless and unpolitical, or energetic and determined. Thus, a dominant class that is declining in objective power may still expect to maintain political leadership and a high standard of living, while a class that is rising economically may lack the political maturity to wrest state power away.[77]

Weber inserts these crucial qualifications of instrumentalism into his analyses of ruling and dominated class alike. It is not only the material base that sustains the Prussians' domination, but, in addition, "traditions" of rule have "accustomed" them to possessing it.[78] Similarly, the Junkers have rationalized their agricultural production not only because of external pressures from the world market but also because their "particular aspirations with respect to living standards" motivate them to compete for prestige and income with the rising German bourgeoisie.[79]

In parallel theoretical fashion, Weber similarly insists that lower-class agricultural workers did not submit to Prussian domination simply for utilitarian reasons. The relationship had significant "psychological supports," particularly the "apathetic resignation" of the workers.[80] Once economic rationalization had occurred, moreover, it too was supported by significant elements in the normative order: the migration that followed agricultural economies was willed, not just coerced. For the proletarianized workers, Weber writes, "homelessness and freedom are the same."[81] Proletarianization, in other words, must also be seen as internally motivated, and when he describes this motivation his debt to the idealist tradition is strikingly apparent. In the migration of agricultural workers he finds the "gloomy, half-conscious impulse [*Drang*] toward distant lands," an impulse within which "a primitive idealism is hidden."[82†] This desire for freedom is distinctly irrational, a form of "magic."[83] Irrationality, then, retains significance even as economic rationalization proceeds. In the behavior of classes there are still to be found nonefficient, even anti-economic elements.

> Such elementary movements cannot be calculated. It is the powerful and purely psychological magic of "freedom" which is expressed. Partly, it is a grandiose illusion, yet as is known, man, and therefore the farm worker, does not live "by bread alone." We recognize from the strivings of the farm workers that the "bread and butter question" is of secondary importance. Most importantly it [i.e., the immigration] is the chance to be the architect of one's own fate.[84]

Presupposing the possibility of such an ideal reference, Weber finds empirical facts that bear him out. Statistics show that migrants did not necessarily come from areas with lower standards of living and that they often traveled to areas where their objective position might be less secure. "The rural workforce," he insists, "forsakes positions that are often more favorable, always more secure, in a search for personal emancipation."[85] They do so because of "decisive psychological factors" that while "quite unconscious are all the more effective for it." These psychic desires attract the worker to the money wage as a symbol of the freedom he needs. "Just as money rent appeared to the medieval peasant as the most important sign of his personal freedom, so does the money wage appear to today's worker."[86]

In the midst of an otherwise apparently materialist analysis, Weber has asserted that the "subjective point of view of the labourer" is of crucial theoretical importance.[87] "The changes in the psychological needs of men," he now insists, "are almost even greater than the reorganization of the material conditions for life." Since both orders have such significant collective force, it would certainly be "scientifically improper to ignore them." Order cannot be understood in a purely instrumental way; indeed, with the modern worker, it is the "possibility of rising *beyond* [his] condition" that is critical. "Everything else," Weber writes, is "simply a means to that end [*Zweck*]." Conditions are not exclusively determinant. They are in tension with individual will, and means must be understood as mediated by willed ends, not just by conditions. As means refer to conditions, so do ends refer to developments in the normative order. The individual's drive for freedom, Weber asserts, is a "characteristic of the modern world which is the product of a psychological development of a general character." Only if the analyst presupposes this cultural rather than material element can he understand a critical empirical fact: the modern worker "has tasted *freedom* and he [is] increasingly incline[d] to sacrifice his material welfare in his aspirations toward this end."[88†]

One should note, in conclusion, that Weber discovered the same empirical facts in the midst of his analysis of the agrarian capitalism of ancient Rome. The critical inefficiency of slave-based agriculture, he asserts, was not caused by purely economic considerations. There was, indeed, a crisis in the reproduction of slave labor, but this occurred because Roman "custom" prevented male slave workers from having monogamous relationships.[89] It was because the slaves were "condemned to live in barracks" that they did not have enough children to reproduce themselves, and the link between these facts was psychological: "Man thrives only in families." True, unfree labor continued to be employed in post-Roman Carolingian times, yet this later feudal economy did not suffer from a reproduction crisis; to the contrary, it marked the earliest beginnings of modern economic life. The reason for this must be found in normative rather than instrumental facts; Carolingian slaves were able to maintain their own cottages and could lead a normal family life.[90] They were able to do so because of changes in the moral order. Ascendant Christianity, Weber writes, "surrounded their family life with firm moral guarantees."[91]

4. CONCLUSION: THEORETICAL UNDERDEVELOPMENT AND SOCIOLOGICAL AMBIVALENCE

Weber has initiated in his early writings an extraordinarily significant break with the one-dimensional traditions of sociological thought, a rupture that may even, in Hegel's language, be called "world-historical." I must stress, however, that this break was, indeed, only "initiated.'" We cannot read Weber's early work without realizing his multi-dimensional intention, yet neither can we read it without being struck by how this intention remains unfulfilled. Weber's analysis is unfailingly ambivalent. If he realizes that material and normative order should be interrelated, the realization is as often out of mind as in it. On the one hand, Roman agriculture is fueled by instrumental calculation and class struggle that operate within the terms set by slavery, itself a material fact produced by the cheapness of unfree labor; on the other hand, Roman economic conflict is "indeterminate" and slavery a psychological condition which depends upon moral regulations whose origins are unexplained. Prussian agriculture is undermined by the coercive and unstoppable forces of the market, and the lower wages that result are the primary force driving workers from their land; yet customs, values, and status concerns would lead the Junkers to rationalize agriculture anyway, and wages actually are secondary to the idea of freedom as the cause of the worker migration. The stock exchange is unethical because it operates according to market considerations; the exchange can be controlled if political organization is committed to moral ends. Nations fight in Darwinian fashion for their economic lives and they are led by classes whose power rests upon a material base; nations fight for cultural goals, and the material base of political power is less important than cultural self-consciousness. Class conflict is instrumental, devoid of religious hope or ethical control; class conflict depends on psychological and cultural supports, the outcome of spiritual not just material concerns.

It would not be entirely inappropriate to see the early Weber—in terms of theoretical logic, not actual history—as a "Durkheimian revisionist" awkwardly coupling powerful norms with efficacious interests, a sociological idealist with a bad conscience about the darker side that he knows only too well exists.[92†] Yet an analogy with Marxist revisionism would be even more to the point, for we can see in Weber's early writing significant signs of a theorist trying to escape from the Marxian dilemma. Though Weber is more purposefully multidimensional than most of Marx's revisers, and though he certainly has no loyalty to Marx himself, it is true that in his early writings he develops the material order much more systematically than the ideal. To escape his inheritance from the German Idealist tradition, Weber embraced instrumental kinds of theorizing, both in their Realpolitik and Marxian forms. He evidently found these modes more developed and easier to employ, for they occupied much more of his theoretical attention. The ideal moment is very much a presence in this work, but it usually is covered—as it is in the work of Marx's revisers—with a gauze of indeterminacy, both in terms of its own structure and in terms of its relationships to instrumental order. Sometimes Weber portrays subjective order as the reflection of instrumental changes: the psychological urge for freedom that follows from agricultural rationalization and, at a later point, assumes an independent role. Sometimes, in contrast, the orders are completely parallel in time: slavery constituted *simultaneously* a subjective and an objective barrier to reproduction. And at still other times subjective order precedes instrumental change and, in fact, is much more important: the desire for freedom is part of a long-term psychological development of a general character. Finally, it seems that when Weber invokes subjectivity most directly his analysis assumes its least systematic and determinate form. The drive for freedom and individuality becomes virtually unanalyzable, an elementary movement that cannot be calculated, a primitive, half-conscious impulse, a mysterious result of powerful magic.

Rebelling most of all against the ideology and presuppositions of German Idealism, Weber revises this tradition from an instrumental position. He will not, however, affirm an exclusive materialism, for he remains committed to strong elements of the very tradition he would like to overthrow. His indeterminacy toward normative elements reveals that he is uneasy with this intended reconciliation, for the indeterminacy is produced by theoretical anxiety that the two orders threaten each other in an analytical way, that to specify one makes it difficult to emphasize the other. Yet, ironically, the very indeterminacy of Weber's treatment of subjective facts confirms his continuing allegiance to the idealist tradition, for in German Idealism, as nowhere else, the normative is viewed as a mysterious confirmation of the freedom of personal will.

Interpreters of Weber's early writing either have denied his multidimensional intention or asserted his full competence to make this intention actually come true. Bendix presents the stock exchange analysis as if it were a "last instance" argument for the ultimate power of moral force; he contends, more generally, that Weber's early investigations are unambiguously multidimensional, that they indicated that "economic conduct was inseparable from the ideas with which men pursued their economic interests, *and* that these ideas had to be understood in their own terms."[93] But Mommsen paints early Weber simply as a Machiavellian instrumentalist, without reference to ethical control or the desire for freedom.[94] Dibble, with a similar animus, presents the early work as arguing only against German Idealism.[95] Löwith similarly equates the early Weber with Marx, pointing to his concern with the connection between forces and relations of production.[96] Parsons agrees, though he reads the early writings not as theoretically coherent but simply as "disconnected historical studies with a rather definite materialist bias."[97†] Mitzman takes this one-dimensional argument in the other direction. Psychological change, he believes, "is the key unifying theme of Weber's early work," and for Weber "the key forces in bringing about this change were not, as Marx might have put it, the development of the forces of production, but psychological motives among both rulers and ruled."[98†]

But all of these interpretations, no matter how illuminating, are polemical in their intention: they are grist for analyses that rationalize interpretations of the later and more important work. For Mommsen, the early writings provide contextual evidence for Weber's typically German Realpolitik; for Troeltsch, they offer evidence of his untypicality vis-à-vis the German tradition. Dibble and Parsons use the early "materialism" to highlight the contrast with the later "normative" emphasis; Mitzman emphasizes the early "idealism" to provide a reference for Weber's later declension to cynicism and despair. For Bendix, the early writings lay a solid foundation for a theoretical structure which gains power by virtue of its perfect consistency.

In the present treatment, I have tried to avoid these polemical objectives. Weber's early writings, it seems clear, demonstrate that he was open toward the traditions that motivated both Durkheim and Marx. Marx, of course, evinced a purely normative perspective in his early writings, and Durkheim, whose early work was more ambiguous, set a dichotomizing course of "either/or" in whatever direction he took. The mature Durkheim followed a one-sidedly normative approach in presuppositional terms, although he sharply departed from Romanticism and Idealism in empirical and ideological ways. The later Marx was just as consistently an instrumentalist. Weber, for his part, starts off much further down the road than either Durkheim or Marx, in their early or later work. In fact, Weber begins much where each of these other traditions ends—with the sophisticated self-consciousness of their ambivalent revisers. With strong reservations about either independent course, Weber would like to bring them back together. In this early work he fails to do so, partly because his intention is not completely resolved, partly because his theoretical logic is not fully developed. In order to effect this reconciliation in a way that is truly synthetic rather than simply combinatorial, Weber needs to become much more theoretically explicit. He must articulate his multidimensional ambition in a direct manner, and he must develop a presuppositional framework within which his intellectual intuition and empirical insight can more successfully be couched.

Chapter Two

THE LATER WRITINGS AND WEBER'S MULTIDIMENSIONAL THEORY OF SOCIETY

In addition to the debilitating theoretical confusion noted at the beginning of chapter 1, the interpretation of Weber's work has been beset by a problem which derives from the "strategy" of interpretation rather than from issues of theoretical logic. The one-sidedness that is encountered in most major readings of Weber has been justified by taking one or another segment of his prodigious output to stand for his work as a whole. These segments, needless to say, have been those that especially supported the particular interpretation. This tactic has often been legitimated, moreover, by reconstructing the chronology of Weber's publications so that a chosen segment appears as the final and culminating phase of his work.

Weber died in 1920, in his middle fifties. The process of "reconstructing" the segments of his corpus according to interpretive preconceptions set in before many years had passed. In *Kritik der Soziologie*, Landshut argued in 1927 that meta-methodological principles divided Weber's comparative studies in the sociology of religion, which in Landshut's view continued idealism's search for the "historical individual," from the more social and political writing of *Economy and Society*, which supposedly committed itself to a more materialist search for causal relations.[1] Three years later, Freyer made much the same argument.[2] This German interpretation of an internal dichotomy based on formal principles of analysis set the stage for the more substantive compartmentalization of Weber's work that Parsons established in his 1937 work, *The Structure of Social Action*, the most influential early interpretation of Weber in English.[3] Although Parsons overtly claims Weber as a synthetic theorist, and in fact offers some evidence for his claim, the focus of his attention is almost entirely the religious sociology. Parsons mentions the historical political sociology of *Economy and Society* hardly at all, and because he fails to do so he can present a picture of Weber as primarily a normative theorist. Parsons' covert message is that readers must choose between different Webers, that an interpretation placing equal weight on the whole of his work is impossible. It took almost a quarter of a century for a more inclusive analysis to appear, Reinhard Bendix's "intellectual portrait." Yet Bendix too leans toward one part of Weber's work. He argues that the sections in *Economy and Society* on the sociology of domination represent Weber's "most original" contribution, and he attempts to buttress this claim with a chronological rationale, which Parsons did not provide.[4] Locating the writings on religion in Weber's middle period, approximately between 1905 and 1917, Bendix contends that *Economy and Society* was the work upon which Weber was working in the later period immediately preceding his death.[5†] Abramowski's *Das Geschichtsbild Max Webers*, the most important German analytical work in the 1960s, follows Bendix's lead, arguing that *Economy and Society* is the "torso" of Weber's corpus, his "chief sociological work."[6]

But if Parsons erred by ignoring Weber's historical sociology of domination, Bendix is guilty of putting it in too much of a leading position. In fact, his chronological rationale may have backfired, for more recent historical research has revealed that Bendix confused the publication dates of Weber's work with the dates of actual composition.[7†] Although *Economy and Society* did not appear until after Weber's death, major sections were actually composed between 1911 and 1913; the comparative studies on world religion, therefore, although published during his lifetime, certainly cannot be seen as reflecting an "earlier" period in Weber's thinking. Yet if this bibliographic research throws doubt on Bendix's historical rationale, it does not in itself disprove his theoretical reading. Such disproof, however, is precisely what Nelson, Tenbruck, and Schluchter have tried to assert: they have utilized their more accurate chronology to rationalize a shift back toward the theoretical emphasis of Parsons' early interpretation. On the basis of its relatively early composition, for example, Tenbruck contends that in *Economy and Society* "little can be seen of the deep development of his [Weber's] sociology."[8†] The comparative studies of religion, because they were taken up later and in a more volitional way (*Economy and Society* was composed on assignment), are said to represent more accurately Weber's theorizing at the highest level.[9†]

Such historical and bibliographical argument makes interpretation appear more tactical and strategic than theoretical, for the truly fundamental issues at stake are not dealt with in an explicit way. Each of these interpreters has, in fact, engaged in substantive and illuminating theoretical argument. But these analytic contributions have been partly neutralized by their emphasis on selected segments of the Weber corpus and by their reference to purely historical considerations in justifying this choice. In what follows, I will consider the whole of Weber's later writings, giving special weight neither to the religious nor to the political work. In fact, I will demonstrate that they often interpenetrate, and that the crucial problems in Weber's later work must be seen in terms of analytical issues rather than in terms of any particular empirical referent. Chronological issues, I believe, are of no particular importance for the analytical problems which are the focus of our present concern. Just as we can find no "early" and "later" Weber in the contrast between the nineteenth- and twentieth-century phases of his work, we find no theoretical periodizations in the chronology of the later period itself.

Although Weber began his recovery from his breakdown with the religious sociology, in 1909—only four years after *The Protestant Ethic* appeared—he published his political and economic study on ancient civilization, a work that avoided comparative religious issues almost entirely.[10] In the year following, he made his final replies to critics of *The Protestant Ethic*, and in 1911 he began three years of intensive labor on the political and historical sections of *Economy and Society*. In the final year of this effort he had already begun sketching the first draft of the essay known in English as "Religious Rejections of the World and Their Directions," and his monographs on comparative religion appeared throughout the next four years. Throughout this final period of his most intensive work on religion, however, Weber was still writing political and economic essays. He gave his Vienna lectures on socialism and the state in 1918. The lectures that became the *General Economic History* were given in 1919, the same year as the revised essay on China was published. In 1920, Weber was adding new footnotes to *The Protestant Ethic* and reworking the essay on historical rationalization that forms the famous "Author's Introduction" to the volumes on comparative religion.

It should be clear, in other words, that the political and religious aspects of Weber's writings were, in fact, historically intertwined. Indeed, the best evidence that they should be considered so comes from Weber himself. With all the clarity one could wish for, Weber wrote in 1915 that the comparative studies on religion were meant "to appear at the same time as *Economy and Society* and to interpret and supplement its chapter on religion, but also to be interpreted by it in turn."[11] The interpretation of the meaning of Weber's later writings, then, cannot be made on historical and biographical grounds. It must be made in theoretical terms, or not at all. To begin such an analysis, we must return to the issues of order and action and to the theoretical legacy of Weber's early work.

1. THE SYNTHETIC APPROACH TO ACTION AND ORDER

Durkheim's most important early work included instrumental and normative elements in an ambiguous way, but in his later writings he abandoned this synthetic potential for his normative theory of social life. Marx similarly renounced the tendencies of his early writing and developed a mature theory that was equally one-sided. Weber, in contrast, maintains the multidimensional elements of his earlier work, and in critical respects he improves upon them. After the fallow years of his breakdown period, Weber is better able to articulate his alternative to the idealist and materialist traditions from which he has broken. This progress is particularly clear in his relationship to German Idealism: he is now able to describe normative order in a much more systematic and explicit way. On the basis of this normative reconstruction, and drawing also upon important innovations in his understanding of instrumental order, Weber achieves in his later work the first truly synthetic strand of sociological theory, a multidimensional analysis in which he is fundamentally reconstructing idealist and materialist theory rather than simply "drawing upon" them.[12†]

Although Weber is generally regarded as disdainful of explicitly nonempirical, abstract kinds of theoretical discussion, it is not irrelevant to our understanding of the role of generalized thinking in his sociology that his later work begins precisely with an exercise in such abstract and general argument. Between 1902 and 1905, Weber published a series of detailed discussions on the "logical problems" in the historical economics of two of his most illustrious predecessors, Roscher and Knies. He justified such explorations in the most generalized terms, pointing to contemporary theoretical conflict over the very nature of the empirical world itself. "Radical shifts" have taken place, Weber asserts, "in the points of view which constitute any item as an object of investigation." These "new 'points of view,' " he believes, "require a revision of the logic of scientific research that has hitherto prevailed within the discipline."[13] This is precisely the revision he now undertakes, and he takes as his primary focus not only the reworking of general methodological issues but the reconsideration of the most fundamental presuppositions of sociological theory.

In these first essays of his maturity, Weber effectively transcends the hesitant dichotomization of his earlier work. Instead of action that is "realistic" at one point in time, psychological at another, and cultural at still another, he portrays action in a generic sense as including all three modes as simultaneous reference points. Action refers to " 'external' constraints," to psychological "affect," and to cultural "ends" [*Zwecke*], but it cannot be defined in terms of any one of these alone.[14†] In this way, idealism and materialism have assumed an analytic rather than concrete state in Weber's work: empirical action can be defined by both analytic references at the same empirical moment in time. On this more sophisticated theoretical basis, Weber can now reject the element of unreconstructed idealism that still informed his earlier work, the notion that the voluntaristic aspect of action depends on the ineffability of human motivation. True, freedom does depend on the actor's relative autonomy from external conditions. But "freedom of will," Weber now insists, cannot be equated with "incalculability" or "irrationality" per se.[15] Free action depends upon a control that is achieved when individual purpose is formed over and against the barriers of both affect and conditions. "An actor's 'decision' is 'more free' than would otherwise be the case," Weber writes, to the degree it is "based more extensively upon his own 'deliberations,' which are upset neither by 'external' constraints nor by irresistible 'affect.' "[16] This kind of leverage can be provided only by the actor's reference to an overarching normative order. It is the "constant and intrinsic relation to certain ultimate 'values' and 'meanings' of life" that allow will and intentionality to come about: " 'Values' and 'meanings' . . . are forged into purposes [Zwecke] and thereby translated into rational-teleological action."[17]

The instrumental element of calculation must be considered part of every human act. "Every military order, every criminal law, in fact every remark that we make in conversations with others," Weber writes, ". . . depend[s] upon a calculability which is sufficient *for the purposes* [Zwecke] which the command, the law, and the concrete utterance are intended to serve."[18] On the other hand, subjective and nonpurposeful "ultimate" considerations pervade every calculation. Because of his reference to ultimate values, "the actor is more 'determined' in the selection of [his] means."[19] Voluntary action, then, involves reference to both means and ends,[20] and Weber uses this presuppositional position to make an ideological point. The Romantic, conservative conception of true personality as the effusive center of unrestrained freedom is incorrect; "personality" must be seen more in terms of the Enlightenment ideal of the culturally meaningful yet still substantively rational act.[21]†

Upon this reconstruction of the nature of social action, Weber builds in these first writings of his maturity a resolutely multidimensional understanding of collective order. He rejects out of hand the idealist notion that a metaphysical element, the *Volksgeist*, or "spirit of the people," is the ground from which all action simply "emanates."[22] Every action, to the contrary, also confronts the material order, an order associated with externality, with "means," and with struggle. "The satisfaction of our most ideal needs," he insists, "are everywhere confronted with the quantitative limits and the qualitative inadequacy of the necessary external means, so that their satisfaction requires planful provision and work, struggle with nature and the association of human beings." [23]† Just as the instrumental dimension accompanies every more idealized motivation, so does this material order permeate every dimension of normative constraint. "The indirect influence of social relations, institutions, and groups governed by 'material interests,' " Weber believes, "extends (often unconsciously) into all spheres of culture without exception, even into the finest nuances of aesthetic and religious feeling."[24]

Yet Weber rejects, just as strongly, the "materialistic conception of history," which "believes that the economic 'factor' is the 'real' one, the only 'true' one, and the one which 'in the last instance is everywhere decisive.' "[25] Order is multidimensional. Theory must distinguish between "economic" phenomena, in which action is directed toward a consciously economic end; "economically relevant" phenomena, which are not economic themselves but have indirect significance for economic life; and "economically conditioned" phenomena, which have little economic effect but which can be more or less strongly influenced by economic factors in their formation.[26] Historical events which do not have directly economic status, therefore, are hardly insignificant "accidents," and should not be treated only as residual categories.[27] Rather, these events must be linked to orders that have determinate significance in their own right. Because the "transcendental presupposition" of every social science is that "we are *cultural beings*, endowed with the capacity and the will to take a deliberate attitude toward the world and to lend it significance," every human action must be judged "from the standpoint of his [the actor's] values" as well as from the perspective of his external conditions.[28] Since values allow actors to lend "significance" to their acts, theory must treat action itself "as being (positively or negatively) meaningful." "Political, religious, climatic, and countless other non-economic determinants" which "are 'accidental' according to the economic interpretation of history actually follow their own laws" in relation to relatively independent collective arrangements.[29] As Weber puts it in a later work, there is an "internal and lawful autonomy" to the "individual spheres" of social order.[30] The noninstrumental laws of the spheres which are not economic define the actor's "cultural *interests*," interests which motivate him as surely as material ones.[31†]

This rich and complex analysis of presuppositional issues supplies a framework for understanding the more self-consciously systematic and abstract discussion of action that occurs in Weber's famous later analysis in *Economy and Society*. In the most important section of this analysis, Weber sets out to present the ideal types of "social action."[32] The ideal type, in Weber's terms, is a selective reconstruction of the empirical world, one that refers to a preexisting analytic interest. Four such selective reconstructions are made. *Zweckrational* action, which can be translated as purposively-rational or instrumental action, occurs when actors take into account the consequences of their acts so that they can pursue their ends more rationally and can better calculate their means. In contrast, action is *wertrational*, or value-rational, when it is determined by a conscious belief in an absolute value pursued for its own sake, independently of the prospects for success. Action is *affektuell* ("affectual") when it is determined by the actor's feelings, and *traditionell* ("traditional") when determined by ingrained habituation.

The theoretical controversy that this apparently simple fourfold division has generated can be stated as follows: According to what analytic referent have these ideal types been selected? Only if we understand that they actually have more than one analytic referent can the problems be resolved. In fact, Weber's action scheme actually refers to various levels of the scientific continuum at the same time. On the one hand, it functions as an empirical generalization that summarizes—as we will see shortly in the sections which follow—Weber's view of the course of historical development from earlier, more spontaneous society, to traditional life, and finally to more deliberate and rational institutions. Thus, shortly after introducing this typology, Weber writes that "one of the most important aspects of the process of 'rationalization' of action is the substitution for the unthinking acceptance of ancient custom, of deliberate adaptation to situations in terms of self-interest."[33] At the same time, and here I draw upon a point made above, this scheme must be seen in more general terms as a set of distinctions that refer to Weber's ideological evaluations of the relative freedom of different kinds of action. Traditional action, as an "almost automatic reaction," and affectual action, as "uncontrolled reaction," represent the prototypically unexamined behavior that Weber earlier rejected as unfree, as associated with conservative and idealist approaches to the problem of freedom.[34] *Wertrational* action, in contrast, is distinguished in Weber's mind by its "clearly self-conscious formulation" and the "consistently planned orientation" that it allows—an attitude that represents the kind of freedom that Weber himself upholds.[35] *Zweckrational* action, of course, simply comes closer to this normative standard, insofar, at least, as it involves the conscious choice of ends.

Finally, these ideal types clearly refer also to the most general presuppositions that inform Weber's argument. Here they must be seen as empirically concretizing the analytic references that Weber outlined in his discussions of 1902–1905. Affectual action recalls action guided by purely psychological considerations; *wertrational* emphasizes the relation of action to values; *zweckrational* underlines, particularly, the relation to external conditions.[36]† Of course, the concreteness of these conceptualizations of action means that this presuppositional association cannot be taken literally as a one-to-one correspondence. Weber is describing empirical acts, not simply analytical types of action, and each empirical act involves references to each of the analytical elements he referred to earlier: psychic impulses, external conditions, and values. It is for this reason that Weber goes out of his way to emphasize that each type of action is no more than a "limiting case."[37] For example, *Wertrationalität* may emphasize absolute values more than *Zweckrationalität*, but it must still be seen as conditioned by objective pressures; *Zweckrationalität*, similarly, should be viewed as referring to ends as well as means.

The concrete character of this classification, then, is somewhat de-ceptive, but it should not be seen only in a negative way. While it makes Weber's analytic intentions more difficult to understand, the fact that it is presented as generalizations about empirical action allows us to see how Weber utilizes his analytic presuppositions in empirical ways. It is, indeed, only when the issue is put in these terms—in terms of the tension between analytic and concrete reference—that a fundamental problem in Weber's conceptualization is revealed. The emphasis on conditions and consciousness in Weber's formulations of *Wert* and *Zweck* types of rational action demonstrates clearly that his empirical thinking avoids the idealist fallacy of unadulterated subjectivity. It is not so unequivocally clear, however, that in every instance he makes as fundamental a break with purely instrumental rationality. The difficulty occurs in Weber's understanding of the ways in which *Zweckrationalität* is purposive and goal-oriented. Just how far does the pragmatic weighing of means and ends go? Certainly the *zweckrational* actor is calculating about means—even *wertrational* action is calculating to that degree. But what about ends? Self-consciousness and calculation must extend to ends themselves if the rigid absoluteness of *wertrational* behavior is to be avoided. The *zweckrational* actor can, therefore, examine the "relations of the end to the secondary consequences" of his act and in doing so weigh the "relative importance of different possible ends."[38] It is in this second area that the ambiguity occurs. On the one hand, an actor can weigh the consequences of pursuing various ends "in terms of a rational orientation to a system of values."[39] In this case, action is still portrayed as multidimensional, referring to values and conditions; it is simply presented, within this context, as being as self-conscious as it can possibly be. On the other hand, Weber clearly states that the *zweckrational* actor may act without any reference to values at all. In this case the "orientation of action" is "wholly to the rational achievement of ends without relation to fundamental values."[40] What, then, do ends relate to? Apparently, simply to the actor's "subjective wants," to the instrumental advantages he can gain in each situation. Action, then, becomes guided by the economic principle of "marginal utility."[41]

The problem with this formulation is not that it distorts the empirical world, for certainly empirical action can be and often is so instrumentally rational. The objection, rather, is that in making this description Weber has slipped into an instrumental and materialist framework in more general, presuppositional terms. He has described empirically instrumental behavior not in a multidimensional but in an analytically more reductionistic way. To the degree that his theoretical understanding of action has been so reduced, Weber will be unable to include normative order in the empirical analysis of *zweckrational* behavior, and the voluntaristic element will drop out of this part of his work altogether.

This possibility becomes a manifest reality when Weber, in a section following his discussion of types of action, turns to the problem of order. "Within the realm of social action," he writes, "certain empirical uniformities can be observed, that is, courses of action that are repeated by the actor or (simultaneously) occur among numerous actors." These are "typical modes of action," and it is with such collectively ordered action that sociology is concerned.[42] The different kinds of order described here generally correspond to the types of action that Weber earlier laid out. Thus, "a uniformity of orientation may be said to be 'determined by self-interest' [*Interessenlage*] if and insofar as the actors' conduct is instrumentally [*zweckrational*] oriented toward identical expectations."[43] It is Weber's understanding that in many instances the order produced by such interest-position will involve no normative reference at all, that it would depend, in other words, on an understanding of *Zweckrationalität* that is anormative in turn. Thus, Weber writes that "many of the especially notable uniformities in the course of social action are not determined by orientation to any sort of norm which is held to be valid . . . but rest entirely on the fact that the corresponding type of social action is in the nature of the case best adapted to the normal interests of the actors . . ."[44] In this situation, the ends of action are reduced to the status of means; for example, "the dealers in a market thus treat their own actions as means for obtaining the satisfaction of the ends defined by what they realize to be their own typical economic expectations as to the prospective behavior of others."[45] Once again, Weber emphasizes not only that this "orientation to the situation in terms of the pure self-interest of the individual" is a theoretical possibility but that it actually represents one of the most frequent and powerful facts of empirical life.

> The more strictly rational [*zweckrational*] their action is, the more will [the actors] tend to react similarly to the same situation. In this way there arise similarities, uniformities, and continuities in their attitudes and actions which are often far more stable than they would be if action were oriented to a system of norms and duties which are considered binding on the members of a group.[46]

In terms of theoretical logic, order without reference to internal ideals is order from which the voluntaristic element of action has dropped out. In fact, in the very first section of *Economy and Society*, entitled "The Definition of Sociology and of Social Action," this is exactly the possibility that Weber lays out. In the midst of a methodological discussion of the difference between causal explanation in general and "lawlike" explanations of the natural-science type, Weber suggests that there is only one kind of social order where individual acts can be predicted in a lawlike way, and that this is an order based upon acts of a purely instrumental type.

> It is customary to designate various sociological generalizations, as for example, "Gresham's Law," as "laws." These are in fact typical probabilities confirmed by observation to the effect that under certain given conditions an expected course of action will occur, which is understandable in terms of the typical motives and typical subjective intentions of these actors. These *generalizations are both understandable and definite in the highest degree insofar as the typically observed course of action can be understood in terms of the purely rational pursuit [zweckrationale Motive] of an end* . . .[47]

This kind of purely instrumental situation eliminates voluntarism because, as Weber demonstrated in his earlier work, freedom depends on the tension between means and ends created by the actor's reference to an overarching normative order. If value-reference drops out, action can only assume a deterministic caste. "In such cases," Weber writes, "it is legitimate to assert that insofar as the action was rigorously rational [*zweckrational*] it could not have taken any other course because for technical reasons, given their clearly defined ends, no other means were available to the actor. . . . The choice of means was 'inevitable.' "[48]

What this discussion indicates is that Weber has not, in fact, fully resolved the difficulties of his early writings. He has not fully committed himself to translating the empirical impact of ideal and material facts into analytic dimensions of the same empirical act. Although he did achieve this theoretical breakthrough to a significant degree, he did not achieve it completely: he is willing to allow certain kinds of empirical acts to be related to one dimension of order alone. Indeed, he has suggested a reductionist orientation for the very mode of empirical action—*Zweckrationalität*—that is closest to his normative ideal of freedom and is most prototypically associated with historical modernity. At a later point in this book, we will discover that this analytic instrumentalism corresponds to a persistent reductionism in a wide range of Weber's empirical work. The point of the present discussion, however, is Weber's multidimensional accomplishment. We turn now to the methodological framework within which his empirical investigation of multidimensionality is pursued.

2. MULTIDIMENSIONAL THEORY AND COMPARATIVE METHOD

Observers of Weber's sociology have usually separated consideration of his methodological writings from the evaluation of his empirical and theoretical ones. Substantive discussion is separated from methodological; the latter investigations become specialized and a field unto themselves.[49] But while propositions and methodological assumptions are differentiated levels of the scientific continuum, they affect each other nonetheless. More importantly, both are informed by the most general level of theorizing itself. If we are to comprehend the full meaning of Weber's empirical investigations, we must understand that the methodological framework that guided this factual search is as vitally affected by his theoretical assumptions as is his perception of the facts themselves. Weber's methodology involves a double critique, one that is directed to the same issues as his multidimensional theory.

Since subjective meaning is a necessary part of action, Weber writes, sociology must be an interpretive science. But meaning for Weber is not located on an abstract metaphysical plane; it must be considered part of the natural world. Cultural elements are, therefore, "necessarily *concretely* determined," subject to "concrete causes and effects." In this way, the idealistic concern with meaning and interpretation is connected with the naturalistic concern with causality. "The only sort of 'interpretation' we are discussing here," Weber writes, "is the sort of 'interpretation' which produces knowledge of *causal* relations."[50] Sociology for Weber, then, is the following: "A science which attempts the interpretive understanding of social action in order thereby to arrive at a causal explanation of its course and effects."[51] When Weber further specifies this interpretive method, he similarly draws upon multidimensional assumptions. Because sociology is interpretive, it is concerned with reconstructing the meaning of action from the actor's point of view. Weber calls this the exercise of "understanding" (*Verstehen*). To "understand" action, we must "identify a concrete 'motive' or complex of motives 'reproducible in inner experience,' a motive to which we can attribute the conduct in question with a degree of precision."[52] Weber insists, however, that this very concern with describing inner experience must be seen as itself a repudiation of the "irrational" concerns of idealist thought. For the very possibility of precision about motive implies the possibility for clarity and self-consciousness about inner subjectivity that idealism denies. "Because of its susceptibility to a meaningful *interpretation*—and to the extent that it is susceptible to this sort of interpretation—individual human conduct is in principle intrinsically less 'irrational' even than the individual natural event." Indeed, Weber suggests that "incalculability" is no more than "the principle of the 'madman.' "[53] Only if action is utterly insane is it completely undetermined, and if it is so purely free from determination then interpretation itself is impossible.

The cultural context which is the object of understanding, then, must be conceived as a "determinant of behavior,"[54†] and interpretive methodology must be concerned with certainty. Weber identifies two bases for certainty in understanding, "rational evidence" and "empathic accuracy."[55] These modes of evaluation correspond to two distinct methods of investigation. Certainty can be derived from "direct observation" of the meaning of an act or from more indirect "explanatory understanding." Once again, this distinction must be understood in terms of Weber's concern for presuppositional synthesis. The distinction turns upon the following paradox: How can the simple observation of action be enough to achieve "understanding" if every action involves an internal component that is objectively invisible? The answer is that such observation is sufficient only when the ends of an action are so much like our own that we can understand its motive without any imaginative effort. The observational understanding of motive, then, provides rational evidence of motive on the basis of external behavior alone. This method is successful when an actor "tries to achieve certain ends by choosing appropriate means on the basis of the facts of the situation *as experience has accustomed us to interpret them.*"[56] For example, "we have a perfectly clear understanding of what it means when somebody employs the proposition $2 \times 2 = 4$ . . . that is when someone carries out a logical train of reasoning according to our accepted modes of thinking."[57] And if an actor were performing this kind of task, we could explain it on the basis of observation.

Lawlike processes in social life are especially susceptible to this kind of observational understanding, since social "laws" are, in fact, only "typical probabilities confirmed by observation to the effect that under certain given conditions an *expected* course of social action will occur, which is understandable in terms of the *typical* motives and *typical* subjective intentions of the actors."[58] Hypothetically, of course, any type of action could produce such lawlike order, but, in practice, the prototypical form of such action is *zweckrational*: "Generalizations are both understandable and definite in the highest degree insofar as the typically observed course of action can be understood in terms of the purely rational pursuit [*rein zweckrationale Motive*] of an end."[59] The existence of *zweckrational* action makes motive observationally understandable because the motivation and course of each action can be predicted solely on the basis of external conditions. It is, in other words, the very fact that voluntarism is eliminated from the "interest-order" that results from *Zweckrationalität*—the fact that "the choice of means was 'inevitable' "—that makes the motives which produce this order so directly comprehensible.[60] The laws of the market, like "Gresham's law," present the most common instances of this situation. "In such cases," Weber agrees, "it is legitimate to assert that insofar as the action was rigorously rational [*zweckrational*] it could not have taken any other course because for technical reasons, given their clearly defined ends, no other means were available to the actors."[61] Rational economic life, therefore, is usually studied in terms of observation.

In fact, of course, external conditions do not actually create motives even in the economic case; the focus on observable facts is possible only because we *assume* that the actor's motives are ones that we ourselves would have. Even *zweckrational* action is multidimensional, and if we can, because of familiarity, correctly perceive its meaning through observation we would still have to explain the source of this commitment by reference to independent values. If this is true for *zweckrational* action, it is even more true for motives which are further from our own typical life experience. Weber reminds us of the freedom of actors vis-à-vis the same conditions. "The actors in any given situation," he insists, "are often subject to opposing and conflicting impulses."[62] This freedom occurs, we recall, because actors can refer outside their immediate concrete situations to overarching value commitments. In many cases, then, "even though the situations appear superficially to be very similar we must actually understand them or interpret them as very different . . . in terms of meaning."[63] It is when this meaning complex is, indeed, different from our own expectations that we must employ the standard of empathic understanding and an explanatory rather than an observational method. Rather than simply observe and assume, we must place ourselves, empathetically, within the perspective of the actor himself. If we fail to do so, we will not only mistake the actor's true motive, but the very importance of motive itself may effectively disappear. Action may appear to be determined only by conditions, and the voluntary element nowhere to be found.

But if empathic understanding is partly inspired by Weber's critique of instrumentalism, it is also informed by his reservations about idealist thought. Weber insists that such explanatory empathy cannot be understood as simply reproducing the elements of direct experience, the "unarticulated 'feelings'" of the historical subject.[64] If action is never motivated solely by irrational impulse, then empathy cannot be directed to it alone. Since the actor's subjectivity is also affected by suprapersonal values, empathy must recognize the "determinateness of content," a specificity that "removes the object of the value judgment from the sphere of that which is merely 'felt.'"[65] Weber argues that the "relation of individuals to possible 'values' always implies that exclusively intuitive 'feelings' have been eliminated."[66] Empathic exploration of the pattern of meaning that orders action can be verified, he believes, by comparing this hypothetical action so motivated with the concrete course of events.[67] Only rarely, of course, can a truly controlled experiment be conducted. Similar control can be obtained, however, by "comparing the largest possible number of historical or contemporary processes which, while otherwise similar, differ in the one decisive point of their relation to the particular motive."[68] This "imaginary experiment," Weber writes, is "a fundamental task of comparative sociology."[69]

Insofar as Weber's sociology remains multidimensional, his empirical attention is devoted to empathic and explanatory understanding. Motive must be isolated, and its meaning cannot be assumed simply from external observation of the actor's situation. Actions cannot be objectively predicted from the context in which they occur, and the voluntary element of life experience is preserved. But if subjectivity remains crucial to action, it is a subjectivity determined by specific patterns of cultural meaning. Weber's later studies are devoted to exposing such particular patterns, and to defining the contexts within which they interact. He makes these studies comparative because this allows him to verify that such action often does not follow expected, "typical" motives. Economic action is the type that holds his greatest interest, and he demonstrates that it would be a mistake to assume that its motives are always *zweckrational*, that it is efficient simply because external conditions demand it to be so. In this way, and for these reasons, Weber's empirical sociology becomes a historical and comparative study of presuppositional rationality itself.

3. THE NORMATIVE DEFINITION OF RATIONALITY: RELIGION IN THE COMPARATIVE STUDIES

The founders of sociological idealism and materialism took antithetical attitudes toward instrumental rationality as an empirical fact. With Durkheim, such rationality is either reduced to a morality unsullied by merely efficient pressures and effects, or relegated to the residual status of the profane. With Marx, instrumental rationality is the fetishized epiphenomenon of external conditions alone. In the multidimensional aspect of his work, Weber steers a middle path. He accepts the condition-orientation of rationality as a decisively instrumental fact, but he insists that nonrational, normative elements are integral to even this most efficient orientation to conditions. Action, in other words, is explained as the product of different analytic orders. Weber demonstrates, through a series of crucial historical experiments, that economic motivation derives as much from value traditions as from external demands. In doing so he lays the groundwork for the truly multidimensional understanding of social life that Durkheim and Marx never achieved.

In his sociology of economic ethics and religion, Weber argues that the degree of rational efficiency which can be attained vis-à-vis the external conditions of action actually depends, in crucial historical cases, on the degree of "efficiency" achieved in the internal pursuit of religious grace. In terms of ideal types, *Wertrationalität* is a significant determinant of *Zweckrationalität*. To make an ironic theoretical point, as well as to generalize his empirical observation, Weber describes the problem of "religious efficiency" as the question of "religious rationalization." Rationalization can occur, in other words, in relation to a completely non-material order, and in describing this process Weber relates the empirical analysis of normative order to fundamental presuppositional issues. Rationalization occurs to the degree that the sacred achieves a transcendent and objectified position vis-à-vis nature and society, with the corresponding power to transform human life into a mere instrument for salvation. Weber argues, in other words, that the sensitivity to conditions which is taken to be the result of prototypically instrumental action is actually derived from a situation of systematic determination by normative exigencies.[70†]

In his comparative study of the great world religions, Weber constructs a continuum of degree of religious rationalization which in turn corresponds to the degree of *economic* rationalization—"instrumental efficiency"—achieved in the economic ethics of the civilizations of which these religions were a part. At the most rationalized end of the continuum, Weber analyzes the type of purely *zweckrational* action associated with modern economic life as the product of the highest degree of religious rationalization ever achieved. He describes this modern economic action, first, in a manner that emphasizes its subservience to external economic conditions and its reduction of ends to the status of means. In modern capitalism, Weber writes, "the earning of more and more money" is normally a means that has no relation to any broader ends, that is, it "is thought of . . . purely as an end in itself."[71] Yet Weber links this instrumentalism not to natural adaptation but to a deeper subjective discipline that is the product of profound cultural development. He demonstrates how this type of development in the "external" sphere relies on rationalization in the sphere of religion, in the modern case on the influence of Calvinist Protestantism. To simply observe modern economic action, then, is not enough. The comparative and empathic study of motivation is needed.

To establish this inner meaning behind outward appearance, Weber presses the ironic parallel between efficiency in the normative and material spheres of life. The most decisive fact of Calvinism, from which all else followed, was its conceptualization of the absolute transcendence of God. Through the hermeneutical investigation of meaning, Weber describes the rationalization of Calvinism in a manner that recalls the objectivistic determinism of materialist theory.

> The interest of it is solely in God, not in man; God does not exist for men, but men for the sake of God. . . . Everything of the flesh is separated from God by an unbridgeable gulf. . . . [God is] a transcendental being, beyond the reach of human understanding.[72]

It is, Weber insists, this very ideal transcendence that turns man's interest in salvation away from an other-worldly focus toward action in the material world. The particular content of normative order leads people to be more efficient and purposive in their dealings with order of an opposite type.

> The world for Calvinism exists to serve the glorification of God and for that purpose alone. . . . But God requires social achievement of the Christian because He wills that social life shall be organized only according to His commandments.[73]

Human desire for inclusion in the higher order is the desire for salvation. Yet in highly rationalized religions like Calvinism, "the concentration of human behavior on activities leading to salvation . . . require[s] the participation within the world (or more precisely: within the institutions of the world but in opposition to them)."[74] Weber calls such subjective rationalization "inner-worldly asceticism."[75] This combination of a total internal commitment to the force of God's will with a this-worldly orientation to material life led the Puritan to subordinate his life to systematic methodical planning—allowed him to *learn* the *subjective* attitudes that materialist theory considers the natural and automatic reflection of external demands.

> He could not hope to atone for hours of weakness or of thoughtlessness by increased good will at other times, as the Catholic or even the Lutheran could. The God of Calvinism demanded of his believers not single good works, but a life of good works combined into a unified system.[76]

Moral strictures created psychological strain, and the pressure created by such psychological necessity had, in its turn, new moral consequences: "The *moral* conduct of the average man was thus deprived of its planless and unsystematic character and subjected to a consistent method for conduct as a whole."[77] The result of this subjective development was discipline and predictability—strength of will and iron motivation—vis-à-vis the exigencies of the material world. In describing this result, Weber purposely plays on the typically economic term "rationality."

> The person who lives as an inner-worldly ascetic is a rationalist. . . . He rationally systematizes his own personal patterning of life. . . . The distinctive goal always remains the alert methodical control of one's own pattern of life and behavior.[78]

The invisible parallel between normative and material efficiency is now complete. Despite appearances, motivation cannot be taken for granted. It was the normative movement of religion that, in the first instance at least, created the *Zweckrationalität* that is the heart of modern economic life. "It is man's vocation," Weber writes of Puritanism, "to participate rationally and soberly in the various rational, purposive institutions of the world and in their objective goals [*Zwecke*] as set by god's creation."[79] Because of this orientation, the Puritan identified earthly conditions with the objectified will of God; that is, he viewed them as an external "condition" that imposed efficient and unalterable control over his life, the same kind of determinant power that accompanies *zweckrational* action in its economic form. "[In Puritanism,] the phenomenon of the religious sense of grace is combined . . . with the feeling of certainty that that grace is solely the product of an objective power."[80] The parallel is elaborated even further when Weber argues that this religious determinacy—like its economic counterpart—gives the appearance of dissolving the very intentional and voluntaristic qualities of action which it actually strengthened. It did so because it eliminated the self-conscious focus on "ends," allowing the impression that effective action was only a matter of "means."

> The ascetic, when he wishes to act within the world, that is, to practice inner-worldly asceticism, must become afflicted with a sort of happy ignorance regarding any question about the meaning of . . . his actual practice of a vocation within the whole world, the total framework of which is not his responsibility but his god's. For him it suffices that through his rational actions in this world he is personally executing the will of god.[81]

His subjective inferiority to God made the Puritan feel passive even in the midst of his heightened earthly activity. In this, once again, he provides the normative model for modern economic life.

> The feeling of certainty that . . . grace is the sole product of an objective power . . . destroys every possibility of the belief that this overpowering gift of grace could owe anything to [the Puritans'] own . . . achievements or [the] qualities of their own faith and will.[82] [To the Puritans] the meaning of our individual destiny is hidden in dark mystery which it would be both impossible to pierce and presumptuous to question.[83]

Finally, if the modern economic actor's instrumentalism and passivity is, beneath the surface, more a product of normative order than conditional necessity, the same empathic insight is certainly valid for his vaunted "individuality." Once again, Weber finds proof for this assertion by examining the historically prior impact of Calvinism on the capitalist spirit. The Puritan was the first "economic man," but his isolation was produced by his voluntary subordination to a religious order. "The sharp condemnation . . . of all dependence on personal relations to other men," Weber writes of the Puritan, "was bound unperceived to direct this energy into the field of objective (impersonal) activity."[84†] The transcendent and impersonal qualities of the Puritan's god made individual responsibility the key to salvation; as a result, the brotherly love characteristic even of early Christian religion was lost.[85]

At the other end of the continuum of religious rationalization, Weber places not the other-worldly mysticism of Hinduism or Buddhism, which were still religions of radical salvation, but the almost completely this-worldly religious orientation of Chinese Confucianism. The latter makes a particularly appropriate theoretical contrast to Puritanism, for in purely observational terms it gives the impression of encouraging a completely utilitarian and efficient ethic. "We shall designate both of them as rationalist in their practical turn of mind,"[86] Weber writes of the Confucian and the Puritan, and he notes "the watchful and rational self-control and the repression"[87] that marked the Confucian way of life, along with its "calculating mentality and self-sufficient frugality of unexampled intensity."[88] To purely external observation, this practicality would imply efficient economic motivation and the determination of action by condition. Yet Weber insists, to the contrary, that the attitude of the Chinese toward the economic conditions of life fell far short of the purely efficient relation of means and ends which characterizes modern economic action.

> It is very striking that out of this unceasing and intensive economic ado and the much bewailed crass "materialism" of the Chinese, there failed to originate on the economic plane those great and *methodical* business conceptions which are rational in nature and are presupposed by modern capitalism.[89]

The Chinese were oriented to external conditions and self-interest, and in this sense they were materialistic; they were not, however, efficient and methodical in this orientation. Action can never be explained by external conditions alone. The reason for Chinese inefficiency, according to Weber, was the low level of rationalization found in the Chinese religion: economic rationality has nonrational dimensions.

The true explanation for Chinese action must be traced to the ordering power of Confucian values. Confucianism did not achieve a high level of "efficiency" in the pursuit of grace because its conceptualization of the sacred remained at a relatively low level of transcendence. In the first place, the Confucian's image of his god was not sufficiently objectified. As Weber writes in the chapter on "The Confucian Life Orientation" in *The Religion of China*: "God, according to him, must not be conceived in anthropomorphic terms."[90] And this was accompanied by a relative lack of differentiation between god and man. Because "God is a 'body,' a shapeless fluid into which the essentially similar human spirit merges at death," it retains little power to coerce the individual in one direction or another. As a result, "any religious idea differentiating a 'state of grace' was absent."[91] What followed from these two theological facts was a general indifference in Chinese religion to the problem of salvation from earthly life. The lack of normative rationalization actually made Confucianism too this-worldly.

> In Confucianism there prevailed . . . an absolutely agnostic and essentially negative mood opposed to all hopes for a beyond . . . and the absence of any other eschatology or doctrine of salvation, or any striving for transcendental values and destinies.[92]

Because a strongly defined focus of orientation on the "other" world did not exist, the Confucian was not compelled to control his life systematically in this one, that is, to become efficient in the modern sense. In the final chapter of *The Religion of China*, comparing Puritanism and Confucianism, Weber first restates the relation that existed between transcendence and the methodical and instrumental control of life manifested by Puritanism. "A true prophecy," he writes in reference to Puritanism, "creates and systematically orients conduct toward one internal measure of value. In the face of this the 'world' is viewed as material to be fashioned.[93] In contrast, for the Confucian "life remained a series of occurrences" because "it did not become a whole placed methodically under a transcendental goal."[94] The Confucian had no freedom from external conditions—no "personality" in the Enlightenment sense—because he could not refer to strong values that could control them. He was, in Weber's terms, a "well-adjusted man [who,] rationalizing his conduct only to the degree requisite for adjustment, does not constitute a systematic unity."[95]

Because of the relatively unrationalized character of his Confucian religion, the Chinese could not act in a rationalized, objective way in the social world. Because the religious sphere did not demand strict subordination to an external transcendent goal, the Chinese did not view earthly "conditions" in an objectified manner, as being identified with the other-worldly impersonal will of God. The Confucian, therefore, remained responsive to the affective pressures deriving from immediate personal ties. "Whereas Puritanism objectified everything and transformed it into rational enterprise," Weber writes, "all communal action [in China] remained engulfed and conditioned by purely personal, above all, by kinship relations."[96] The Confucian and the Puritan both obeyed collective order, but for the former obedience involved a decidedly noneconomic sense. "The Puritan ethic," Weber writes, "amounts to an objectification of man's duties as a creature of God . . . to appraise all human relations—including those naturally nearest in life—as [an] expression of a mentality reaching beyond the organic relations of life." He contrasts this with the "religious duty of the pious Chinese," which "enjoined him to develop himself within the organically given, personal relations." The "duties of a Chinese Confucian always consisted of piety towards concrete people."[97] The affective and unrationalized character of normative order meant that the Confucian could not calculate his relation to external conditions in the purely efficient terms of self-interest. While for Puritanism, "trust in men, and precisely in those closest to one by nature, would endanger the soul," the economic ethic of Confucianism could not tolerate this individualism.[98]

> It hallowed alone those human obligations of piety created by inter-human relations . . . .[99] It tended to tie the individual ever anew to the sib members and to bind him to the manner of the sib, in any case to "persons" instead of functional [*sachliche*] tasks.[100†]

This personalism made economic life less responsive to external exigencies than to familial ones: "The strength of the truly Chinese economic organization was roughly coextensive [with] these personal associations controlled by piety."[101]

Weber has argued that normative rationalization, or the lack of it, is the source of rationalization in the material sphere.

> For the economic mentality, the personalist principle was undoubtedly as great a barrier to impersonal rationalization as it was generally to impersonal matter of factness.[102]

The Confucian "gentleman," unlike the Puritan "saint," did not reduce himself to the status of a religious "means." "The fundamental assertion [of Confucianism], 'a cultured man is not a tool,' " meant, in Weber's view, "that he was an end in himself and not just a means for a specified useful purpose."[103] Because this normative model of instrumental rationality was lacking, the motivation for such behavior did not exist. Confucian ethics, therefore, "rejected training in economics for the purs of profit,"[104] and Confucian organizations could never assume th personal form that allowed the instrumentally efficient respor ss to conditions that inspired Western economic life. "To a striki gree," Weber writes, the Confucian Chinese "lacked rational mat factness [*rationale Versachlichung*], impersonal rationalism, an ature of an abstract, impersonal purpose association [*Zweckver harakter*]."[105†]

4. BEYOND DURKHEIM'S IDEALI DUCTION: THE NORMATIVE AND INSTRUME DETERMINATION OF RELIGIOU LUTION

By describing the impact of exes of meaning which are not directly observable, Weber's com ative study of the religions of the great world civilizations establish ne independence of the voluntary, "motivational" element in soci order. If Weber's work had not gone beyond this point, it would have amounted to a substantial elaboration on the historical level of the theoretical position outlined in Durkheim's work. This, however, is far from being the case. True, Durkheim's work has itself been described as a crucial experiment designed to demonstrate the significance of normative order, and Weber's comparative studies perform, according to his own methodological account, an experiment of a similar kind.[106†] Yet Weber's experiment, we must remember, was designed to demonstrate a method which he developed to oppose idealism as much as to expose materialism. The very specificity of Puritan and Confucian cultural patterns, in Weber's mind, proved that the idealist notion of purely internal and irrational impulse was wrong.

The entire focus of Weber's comparative studies on economic ethics indicates this multidimensional ambition. Whereas in Durkheim's later work economic and religious actions are treated concretely as empirically separated activities, for Weber the normative religious actor—the Puritan, for example—is at the same time the utilitarian actor, and vice versa. The theoretical assumption underlying Weber's entire analysis of cultural rationality is that *all* action is conditioned by external conditions; in fact, it is the necessity for channeling these impinging exigencies that makes the very question of normative rationality so significant. Thus, although the conclusion of Weber's experiment is that action is *not* determined exclusively by external considerations, there is also an implicit corollary conclusion that without this element of conditional determination the influence of values would be impossible to assess. Orientations to normative and conditional order, spatially and temporally separated by Durkheim and Marx, are now divided only by analytic considerations.

This multidimensional focus becomes explicit in other phases of Weber's studies of religion, for upon closer examination it becomes clear that these writings represent far more than simply an experimental comparison of different forms of cultural rationality. They also include a complex historical explanation of varying religious origin and development. Taking off from his synthetic conceptualization of social order, this historical discussion analyzes the interaction between the cultural patterns which supplied the "ends" of the different forms of rational action and the economic and political forces which constituted their "conditions." The most successful example of this multidimensional historical writing on religious rationality is Weber's developmental study, *The Sociology of Religion*, which was published posthumously in *Economy and Society*. Weber's theoretical point of departure in this work is his assertion about the "anthropological" independence of instrumental and normative needs. He relates the latter to an inherent need for man to establish meaning on an abstract level, to the "metaphysical needs of the human mind as it is driven to reflect on ethical and religious questions, driven not by material need but by an inner compulsion to understand the world as a meaningful cosmos and to take up a position toward it."[107†] And although man's "material need," which is at the source of the influence of rational exigencies, is nowhere so explicitly defined, its existence is clearly an operative assumption throughout Weber's analysis. Each of these fundamental needs, of course, provides the basis for his insistence on the determinate power of different kinds of orders.

The first chapters of *The Sociology of Religion* describe how the interaction of these two forces produces increasingly rationalized religious ideas, a process that occurs as a development from magic to pantheistic religion and eventually to the type of ethical religion of salvation whose formulations of the sacred were the subject of my preceding discussion. The historical base point of this analysis is magic, in which, according to Weber, some "abstraction [has] already been carried out."[108] Yet magic is still relatively unrationalized; the image of its governing spirit is "indeterminate," "invisible," "nonpersonal."[109] The movement toward the more rationalized conceptualization represented by a pantheon involves further development of the impetus toward normative systemization and differentiation. In the pantheon, the image of the sacred becomes increasingly concretized.

> Gods, too, were not originally represented in human forms. . . . They came to possess the form of enduring beings . . . only after the supression of the purely naturalistic view . . . . The gods frequently constituted an unordered miscellany of accidental entities . . . . But as a rule there is a tendency for a pantheon to evolve once systematic thinking concerning religious practice has taken place.[110]

At the same time, however, for a pantheon to evolve there had to be simultaneous developments toward rationalization in the conditional elements of action. Although Weber specifically says that no economic preconditions were necessary for the emergence of magic, he believes that material conditions were of decisive importance for the origins and form of the pantheonistic development.[111] "Gods and demons," he writes, "have [also] been shaped directly by the economic situation . . . of different peoples."[112] That is, in addition to the influence of increasing rationalization of the "subjective reflection about them," "the increasing objective [*objektiv*] significance of typical components and types of conduct . . . [also] leads to functional [*sachlich*] specialization among the gods.[113†] The "typical components" and orders to which Weber is primarily referring are the structures of political association in a given community. "If an association is to be permanently guaranteed," he writes, "it must have such a [pantheonistic] god."[114]

The types of political associations for which pantheonistic rationalization is a necessary correlate—and which decisively influence the structure of the pantheon itself—are various forms of traditionalistic political authority. Weber notes first the impact on religious rationalization of patriarchal political structure.

> The importance attributed by the group to its cult, which is performed by the head of the house or *gens*, is quite variable and depends on the structure and practical importance of the family. A high degree of development in the domestic cult of ancestors generally runs parallel to a patriarchal structure of the household, since only in a patriarchal structure is the home of central importance for the men.[115]

Subsequently, Weber adds another link to this multidimensional causal chain by describing how the pantheonistic symbolic product of this interaction between conditional political structures and the movement of religious rationalization has, in turn, a formative impact on the structure of the traditional political structures themselves. "Where the power and significance of the domestic cult and priesthood remain unimpaired," Weber writes, "they naturally form an extremely strong personal bond, which exercises a profound influence on the family and the *gens*, unifying the members firmly into a strongly cohesive [and exclusive] group."[116]

> This cohesive force also exerts a strong influence on the internal economic relationships of the households [*Hausgemeinschaften*]. . . . It is largely to this religious motivation that the Asiatic (Chinese and Japanese) family and clan, and that of Rome in the Occident, owe the maintenance of the patriarchal structure throughout all changes in economic conditions.[117]

The limited degree of normative rationalization of the pantheonistic "product" is, in fact, a major factor in limiting the types of more rationalized political arrangements which can emerge from patriarchal organization.

> Wherever such a religious [i.e., pantheonistic] bond of the household and kin group exists, only two possible types of more inclusive associations, especially of the political variety, may emerge. One of these is the religiously dedicated confederation of actual or imaginary kin groups. The other is the patrimonial rule of a royal household over comparable households of the subjects, in the manner of an attenuated patriarchalism.[118]

This new material "product," in its turn, effects the content of the normative abstraction of the pantheon itself. "Wherever the patrimonial rule of the royal household developed," Weber writes, "the ancestors and personal gods, the *numina, genii* or personal gods at the most powerful household took place beside the domestic gods belonging to subject households."[119] Although Weber concludes by asserting that this development "thus lent a religious sanction to the position of the ruler,"[120] it should be clear from the preceding discussion that he never conceptualizes the instrumental exigencies of political structure as creating, in themselves, the religious impulse toward abstraction. They are described, rather, as a vigorous independent force that channels the direction of that normative impulse.

The major transition in religious development beyond the pantheonistic stage was the emergence of universalistic monotheism which finally culminated, in ancient Israel, in the creation of an objectified and anthropomorphic god fully capable of efficiently regulating human life. On the one hand, this religious development, which according to Weber adumbrated the ultimate rationalization of Puritanism, was the result of the continuing search for meaning that proved to be such a significant impetus for earlier religious rationalization. "Every consistent crystallization of a pantheon," Weber writes, "followed systematic rational principles to some degree," and "reason [*ratio*] favored the primacy of universal gods. . . . As reflection concerning the gods deepened, it was increasingly felt that the existence and nature of the deity must be established unequivocally and that the god should be 'universal' in this sense."[121]† Yet, Weber emphasizes that these religious changes were themselves related to developments in the material sphere, developments which facilitated such an increase of the "efficiency" of religious orientation. "The ascension of celestial or astral gods in the pantheon," he writes, "is . . . assisted by a rationalized system of regulated subordination of subjects to their overlords." For example, "the growth of empire in China, the extension of the power of the Brahmin caste throughout all the varied political formulations in India, and the development of the Persian and Roman empires favored the rise of both universalism and monotheism."[122] At another point he states this parallel even more directly by stressing that the economic and political factors conducive to religious "efficiency" were ones which themselves increased the element of "calculation." Material pressures for calculation and efficiency mounted with increases of territorial size and population; they accompanied similar pressures from the normative order: "Increased ethical [i.e., monotheistic] demands were made upon the gods by men, parallel with . . . the increased importance of an ethical attachment of individuals to a cosmos of [earthly] obligations."[123] Weber specifies these calculation-promoting material developments as "orderly legislation," increasingly complex "economic activity," the "increasing regulation of ever new types of human relationships by conventional rules," and the "growth in social and economic importance of the reliability of the given word—whether of friends, vassals, officials, partners in an exchange transaction, debtors, or whomever else." It was such a combination of pressures that finally made "it possible to calculate what the conduct of a given person may be."[124]

The emergence of this universalistic monotheism produced the intensive religious interest in salvation which, in turn, allowed religious prophecy to determine with such decisive influence the relative rationalization of religious life. Although Weber outlines the historical development of this arbiter of the final stage of religious rationalization in the fourth chapter of his *Sociology of Religion*, his most extensive treatment of the interaction of instrumental and normative in the determination of prophetic rationality occurs in the eleventh chapter of *Ancient Judaism*. A representative sample of this analysis is Weber's treatment of the origins of the prophetic idea that God's transcendent judgement of Israel was manifest in the hostile activities of foreign powers. This belief, Weber writes, was clearly linked to conditional aspects of Israel's situation, conditions that were external not simply because they were foreign but because they represented the military force of enemy nations. "Prophecy developed," Weber insists, "only with the rising external danger to the country and to the royal power."[125] In one sense, these political developments determined the very content of the prophetic message. Thus, "except for the world politics of the great powers which threatened their homeland and constituted the message of their most impressive oracles, the prophets could not have emerged."[126] Weber emphasizes, however, that such external considerations do not fully explain the motivational element of prophetic action. Observational explanation must be supplemented by empathic understanding. Although "the prophets were objectively political and, above all, world-political demagogues and publicists," nonetheless, "*subjectively* they were not political partisans."[127] In order to provide a more complete picture of the causal structure of prophecy, reference also must be made to normative, religious dimensions of the prophetic situation. What were the actual motives of the prophets? In fact, Weber insists, "the state and its doings were, *by themselves*, of no interest to them." "Their question was absolutely religious, oriented toward the fulfillment of Yahweh's commandments."[128] Without the overriding normative commitment to the covenant with their transcendent god, Jewish intellectuals and leaders would have had no reason to attach a prophetic meaning to their external conditions. Every action must refer to both internal and external elements. Their ineluctable interpenetration in this empirical instance can be illustrated by the prophetic position on foreign alliances. Though considered by many to be an efficient calculation in the light of Israel's external exigencies, they were, nonetheless, proscribed by the prophets because such foreign commitments would have inhibited the normative pursuit of religious grace. "The idea gained currency," Weber writes, "that the political aspirations of Israel would only be realized through a miracle of God, as once at the Red Sea, but not through autonomous military power, and, least of all, through political alliances."[129] This "idea," Weber emphasizes, derived from normative considerations, regardless of the instrumental advantages the alliances were thought to provide.

> The basis of the opposition was again religious. . . . Israel stood in the *berith* [covenant] with Yahwe. Nothing must enter competition with the *berith*, especially not trust in human help, which would bespeak of godless disbelief and evoke Yahwe's wrath.[130]

5. BEYOND MARX'S MATERIALIST REDUCTION: THE MULTIDIMENSIONAL ANALYSIS OF SOCIAL CLASS

Weber's comparative sociology of religion supports and amplifies Durkheim's critique of the materialist tradition while embracing the importance of instrumental order, and significant elements of Marxist theory, in a way that Durkheim would have found inimical to his sociology. The elegance and sureness of this strand of Weber's mature sociological history makes the synthesis seem simple enough, yet his achievement presented the most profound departure from the antinomies of classical sociological thought. Indeed, few contemporary theorists fully understand the nature of Weber's accomplishment or the analytical reasoning upon which it is based. Weber's sociology directly articulates what the best followers of Marx and Durkheim dearly wanted, but what they were never able to achieve.

But the true depth of Weber's "*Aufhebung*," his dialectical transcendence of the "abstract negations" of one-dimensional thought, can nowhere be seen more clearly than in the application of his multidimensional theory to the prototypically instrumental order of social class. In the enormous literature that has developed over the question of Weberian versus Marxist approaches to stratification, empirical precision has too often been achieved at the expense of more generalized understanding. Discussions of whether Weber is or is not a "Marxist" have hinged upon the propositional differences between Marx's emphasis on productive position and property ownership versus Weber's reference to market position and consumption style. When the argument has become more general, it has usually focused on Weber's empirical distinctions between classes and status groups or parties and classes.[131]† Neither of these debates, however, strikes at the theoretical heart of the question, which must be the presuppositions with which Weber approaches the study of class itself.

The question is not simply what criteria demarcate a class from other groups, or what kind of commodities give a class power once it is formed. The central problem, quite simply, is the nature of the collective order of which any class is composed. Here is where Weber's greatest originality lies. Even if class is accepted as based on property or productive grouping, even if economic groupings are accepted at the expense of status considerations, Weber insists that the economic grouping represented by social class can never be merely economically defined. For Weber, class itself is a multidimensional concept. How, he asks, is a hierarchical position defined: What is the relation between a stratum's instrumental location and its ideology?[132†] The interest of the members of a class is coded by ideology, but is this ideology created from purely instrumental pressures or does the perception of class interest involve independent normative components as well? The answer that Weber gives follows ineluctably from his most general presuppositions, from his critique of materialist and idealist thought. To comprehend correctly class interest is, in Weber's terms, thoroughly to transcend any one-dimensional frame of reference. This answer constitutes, in part, a normatively inspired critique of Marx's theory of reflected or instrumental class consciousness. Yet the very existence of Weber's theory of class gives the lie, at the same time, to the idealizing tendency in Durkheim's work, the normative inclination that made him overlook this solidary grouping in the collective order which so forcefully demonstrates differences in material experience.

Weber's essays on classes—principally "The Social Psychology of World Religions" (more accurately translated as "Introduction to the Economic Ethics of World Religions"), "Castes, Estates, Classes and Religion," and "Religion of Non-Privileged Classes"—reorganize the instrumental and normative determinants referred to in the preceding section. Weber regroups them according to the strata with which they are associated and indicates, thereby, how his wide-ranging discourse on their causal interaction can be interpreted as an analysis of the relation between the "material" and "ideal" components of a given stratum. His general formulations on the determination of social class, then, become a strategic rephrasing of the multidimensional approach outlined in the comparative and historical discussion of religious evolution. They remind us of Weber's closeness to Marx, yet they recall, just as forcefully, how Weber tried to combine Marxism with elements from the idealist tradition.

Like Marx, Weber insists on the vital importance of the conditional determination of class ideology, linking each of the world religions with a stratum's distinctive economic or political position. He writes of the "strata which are decisive in stamping the characteristic features of an economic ethic [i.e., a world religion]," and describes Confucianism, for example, as "the *status* ethic of prebendaries."[133] This material connection has, unfortunately, led some observers to equate Weber's analysis of class ideology with Marx's.[134†] Yet in the very same writings, Weber emphasizes that the religious superstructure has an important element of autonomy from the base. "However incisive the social influences, economically and politically determined, may have been upon a religious ethic in a particular case," Weber insists, "it receives its stamp primarily from religious sources, and, first of all, from the content of its annunciation and its promise."[135] The symbolic formulation of the sacred makes an independent contribution to the perception of class interest: "The nature of the images of God and of the world, have under certain conditions had far-reaching results for the fashioning of a practical way of life."[136] "Interest," in other words, has no substantive content even if its parameters are structured by a stratum's social position. Certainly a stratum's members are affected by their material environment, but they have ideal, metaphysical needs which must also be satisfied. Material environment can become significant only as a datum of experience, an experience which remains to be interpreted.

Throughout most of human history, the master idea through which such interpretation has occurred is spiritual salvation. Members of every stratum have an "interest" in salvation, and the image of divinity formulated by religious intellectuals and specialists which rationalizes their religious interest must be considered a significant normative contribution to class behavior. The empirical independence of this critical theological idea is formulated by Weber in different ways: it is the cultural legacy of the older generation to the younger one; it is the "promise" articulated by the upper-class prophet that molds the aspirations of the lower strata.[137] The most abstract formulation is Weber's famous assertion about the theological "tracks" along which ideal and material interest must run. "The meaning as well as the intended and actual psychological quality of redemption," Weber writes, "has depended upon . . . a world image."

> Not ideas, but material and ideal interest, directly govern men's conduct. Yet very frequently the "world images" that have been created by "ideas" have, like switchmen, determined the tracks along which action has been pushed by the dynamic of interest. "From what" and "for what" one wished to be redeemed and, let us not forget, "could be" redeemed, depended upon one's image of the world.[138†]

Although Weber's substantive writings on social class include discussion of the impact on the religious ethic of such conditional factors as the peasant's closeness to nature,[139] the arbitrary quality of the feudal orientation,[140] and the matter-of-fact work life of the intellectual-bureaucrat,[141] his most extensive discussion—and, from the standpoint of our present concern with instrumental rationality, the most interesting—is reserved for his analysis of the origins of the religious ideology of the bourgeois middle class of Western society. In regard to external exigencies, Weber writes that an urban location is essential for producing a "calculating" life orientation. Here Weber relates the connection he drew between normative and material rationalization—which I discussed in section 3—to the specific problem of class interest. "It is clear," he writes, "that the economic foundation of the city man's life has a far more rational character, viz., calculability and capacity for purposive [*zweckrational*] manipulation."[142] But this material location must be viewed as an input, or facilitating condition, rather than as an exclusive determinant. Among civic or urban strata, Weber writes, "there has always *existed the possibility*—even though in greatly varying measure— of letting an ethical and rational regulation of life arise." If a rational ethic is so linked to "technological and economic rationalism," then "the preferred religious attitude *could become* the attitude of active asceticism."[143] As these passages indicate, in sharp contrast, for example, to Engels' famous "Letter to Bloch" (see vol. 2, ch. 10), the vocabulary Weber employs, and the rhetorical form of his statements, clearly reinforces his presuppositional intention and empirical propositions. He writes at another point, for example, that merchants "lead economic existences which *influence* them to *entertain*" certain rationalized viewpoints, and that "small traders and artisans are *disposed* to accept a rational world view."[144]

To underscore the open-ended quality of the influence of this stratum's material position, Weber describes the extremely wide range of religious orientations that have been associated with various "civic strata" in the course of world history.[145] In his view, civic religions are never exclusively determined by conditional position: "The mere existence of artisans and petty-bourgeois groups has never sufficed to generate an ethical religiosity even of the most general type."[146] "On the contrary," Weber writes, "as is easy to see, the determination is very often the reverse."[147] The collective patterns of the normative order must be taken into account: How rationalized is the pursuit of grace? If it is not sufficiently rationalized, the person who is a proto-bourgeois in terms of material circumstance will not have the independent leverage against his material world that will allow him to be a bourgeois in spirit. Thus, Weber writes, "in China the great importance of the ancestral cult and clan exogamy resulted in keeping the individual city dweller in a close relationship with his clan and native village." And in India, "the religious caste taboo rendered difficult the rise, or limited the importance, of any soteriological congregational religion in quasi-urban settlements."[148] Weber concludes, indeed, that if urban location provided the general context for the creation of the ideology of the bourgeois class, it was the specific normative content of the Protestant "promise" that constituted its final cause.

Partly, the social environment exerted an influence, above all, the environment of the stratum that was decisive for the development of such [ascetic] religion. Partly, however—and just as strongly—the intrinsic character of Christianity exerted an influence: the supra-mundane God and the specificity of the means and paths of salvation as determined historically, first by Israelite prophecy and the thora doctrine.[149]†

Although Weber's primary focus in this discussion of urban class ethics is the incipient bourgeoisie, he maintained the relevance of this theory for the formation of the revolutionary proletariat as well. He acknowledges freely the fundamental importance of material conditions for the industrial working class and, in addition to urban situation and reified labor he expands the conditional determinates of the proletariat's situation to include the factor of "material disprivilege." Yet Weber argues, at the same time, that revolutionary socialism must be viewed as a secular variant of this-worldly asceticism and that, as such, it is subject to the same multidimensional explanation. Although the direct polemic in this context is against Nietzsche's concept of "resentment," this notion that proletarian ideology promises salvation from earthly suffering can also be compared to Marx's analysis of religion as an opiate. The proletariat's suffering, Weber insists, is contentless in itself; in his opinion, the specifically ideological "promise" of socialist intellectuals is of pivotal significance.[150]

The perspective generated by this analysis of Weber's theory of class formation provides a new framework for understanding his monograph on the Protestant ethic. We must take seriously Weber's insistence that he intended there to outline only one side of a more complex causal chain. Instead of being considered simply as the "experimental" demonstration of the normative element in history, the work can now be viewed as one part of Weber's multidimensional explanation of urban middle-class ideology, the strongest empirical case in Weber's larger study of the normative dimension of world history. In the historical context provided by his work as a whole, it becomes clear that Weber views the Reformation as having created a distinctively modern normative component, or ideology, for a class whose instrumental "base" was itself highly significant and the result of independent developments.[151] In his "Author's Introduction" to *The Protestant Ethic and the Spirit of Capitalism*, written almost fifteen years after the initial publication, Weber presents just such a perspective on that earlier work. "In terms of cultural history," he writes, "the problem is that of the origin of the Western bourgeois class and of its peculiarities, a problem which is certainly closely connected with that of the origin of the capitalistic organization of labour, but is not quite the same thing." He insists that "the bourgeois as a member of a class existed prior to the development of the peculiar modern form of capitalism, though, it is true, only in the Western hemisphere."[152]† In a footnote, Weber goes so far as to suggest that the material dimension of modern capitalism may actually have been first established by a different segment of the bourgeoisie entirely, by the commercial aristocracy or "upper bourgeoisie." These material accoutrements were then taken over and utilized in a truly modern capitalistic manner only by the spiritually reformed lower bourgeoisie, the class which later created industrial capitalism. As, Weber writes, "the assumption is thus by no means justified *a priori* that . . . on the one hand the technique of the capitalistic enterprise, and on the other the spirit of professional [or vocational] work which gives to capitalism its expansive energy, must have had their original roots in the same social classes."[153]

In fact, although the greater part of the *Protestant Ethic* focuses on different patterns of religious salvation, Weber never loses touch with the other, material facets of class development with which these patterns had to interact. This, indeed, is the rationale for his entire argument. In discussing the transformation of the putting-out system in the history of the textile industry, for example, he underscores the voluntaristic quality of the nascent Calvinist capitalists by reference to the constancy of the pressure of material conditions. "The form of organization was," he insists, "in every respect capitalistic," but it was still a traditionalistic business "if one considers the spirit which animated the entrepreneur."[154] Observation, then, is sufficient to reveal the material elements of the capitalist's situation, but by itself it is not enough. Weber insists that often "this traditionalistic leisureliness was suddenly destroyed . . . without any essential change in the form of organization."[155]

6. NORMATIVE ORDER AND EMPIRICAL CONFLICT: THE MULTIDIMENSIONAL ANALYSIS OF URBAN REVOLUTION

Weber, I have argued, is vitally concerned with the problem of order: the desire to produce a new, more multidimensional understanding of collective order informs his analysis of comparative rationality, historical development, and class ideology. The perspective on order presented here, I would emphasize, could not be more different from the perspective of "conflict theory," which reduces Weber's concern with order to his emphasis on empirical conflict rather than equilibrium. The most decisive confrontation between these perspectives can be made with reference to Weber's essay *The City*. I will try to demonstrate that here too the most important part of Weber's analysis derives from his generalized concern. It is the presuppositions Weber brings to the study of conflict, not the fact of his reference to conflict itself, that marks this essay as a monumental contribution to the historical understanding of social change.

The City is about the origins of modern revolution, and the urban class is, once again, the principal historical actor whose behavior is subject to explanation. Weber's discussion of the city details certain crucial political and economic challenges to order—in the empirical sense of social stability—that typically occur in the course of urban development. His central argument is that the reactions to these challenges differ according to the nature of the "civic strata" of which the city is composed. This analysis, then, hinges on the multidimensional analysis discussed earlier, on Weber's transcendence of an instrumental definition of rationality and a purely instrumental conceptualization of social class. Weber insists that the changes in the city's economic and political spheres were not perceived simply as "external" developments but were, in fact, filtered through the normatively structured expectations that were institutionalized differently in the urban areas of different civilizations. It is through this interaction of external and internal elements that a multidimensional conceptualization of empirical order emerges: the conflict that results from the attempt to resolve the changing economic and political situation occurs within a general context of internalized religious symbolization.

In presenting this Weberian position on conflict, the first point to establish is his multidimensional understanding of the environment in which it occurs, that is, of the city itself. For Weber, the city is more than simply an area of dense population in which economic and political regulation occurs, although these are certainly essential conditions and Weber's contribution to their exposition is original in itself. He suggests, in this regard, the same expansion and pluralization of the instrumental sphere that he offers in other segments of his work. The city, Weber believes, must be understood to include political-territorial aspects as well as economic-market ones. For the Western city, this addition turns out to be particularly important, for the absence of imperial bureaucracy allowed it to achieve an autonomous military position unprecedented in comparative terms.[156] This military independence was vital in allowing citizens to defend their rights—after they had been aroused by their violation. But what made urban dwellers citizens, and what gave them expectations of such rights in the first place? These questions point to the really crucial innovation in Weber's treatment, namely, his understanding of the different subjective and communal ties that bind inhabitants of the same geographic and political area.

To explain these ties, Weber brings his analysis of normative development—the uneven result of material change, religious rationalization, and prophecy—to bear on a new empirical sphere. The cities of the great civilizations differed according to the degree they were successful in creating "fraternization," truly universalistic associations rather than collections of small particularistically-oriented groupings. "The fully developed ancient and medieval city," Weber writes in a manner that emphasizes the internal factor, "was above all constituted, or at least interpreted, as a fraternal association."[157] This interpretation could not be made, Weber believes, unless the urban actors had intellectual access to "the concept of the *burgher* (as contrasted to the man from the countryside)," unless, in other words, they could conceive of themselves as having a separate status, that of citizen, from the peasant who may have migrated from the countryside.[158] In contrast to the Western city, in India, Japan, and China "the very concept of an urban burgher and, in particular, a specific status qualification of the burgher was completely lacking." For this reason, "there existed no association that could represent the commune of burghers as such."[159]

The results of this failure to develop the burgher, or citizenship, concept are the same particularistic groupings that Weber pointed to in his discussion of comparative economic development. "The Chinese townsman was legally a member of his sib kin group and his native village, where the temple of his ancestor-cult stood and with which he carefully upheld his association," and "the Indian townsman was . . . a member of his caste."[160] The particularism of these groupings meant that even capitalistic economic forces—usually thought to be carriers of purely abstract ties—could not create widespread association of a universalistic kind. Thus Weber writes of the Indian case that "although several merchant castes and very many craft castes with innumerable subcastes existed (and still exist), they cannot be equated as a group with the Occidental burgher estate, nor could they themselves combine to form something corresponding to the medieval craft-ruled city, for caste barriers prevented all intercaste fraternization."[161] Economic classes, not castes, could be formed in Western cities—classes composed of burghers, or citizens—only because the focus on particularistic group filiation that characterized Eastern development was replaced by the abstract legal definition of a universal bond between individuals. The urban dweller's "personal membership in the local association of the city," Weber writes, "guaranteed his legal status as a burgher, not his tribe or sib."[162]†

In Weber's view, the roots of this difference in urban communal bonds can be traced not to economic but to comparative religious rationalization. The more personalistic and unsystematic theodicies of Eastern religions allowed only "competencies or factual powers of a *particular* association with respect to *particular* issues touching on its concrete group interests."[163] In China, the cult of ancestor worship provided a cultural rationale for clan organization that "impeded confraternization in a city corporation."[164] The greatest barrier to fraternization, however, was the caste organization of India.[165†] Hinduism's lack of transcendental reference, its emphasis on the practical techniques of ritual and magic and on the sacredness of blood made Indian religion extraordinarily exclusive.[166] For Hinduism, Weber writes, "there was no universally valid ethic" but rather "only a strict status compartmentalization of private and social ethic."[167] Because "there was no 'natural' order of men and things in contrast to positive social order," Hinduism could apply different ethical standards to different strata. Rather than being "in principle equal"—equal, that is, in terms of the idealized 'natural' order—Hinduism declared that in principle men were "forever unequal."[168] In this religious situation, it is easy to understand why "the concepts 'state' and 'citizen,' even that of 'subject' did not appear." In fact, the very conception of "common 'rights' [was] obviously out of the question."[169]

The contrast with Western Christianity could not be more marked, for the abstraction and transcendence of Western religious theology meant, in principle, that a solidary religious community could be established over and against narrower ties of blood or economic status. Weber cites the "universalism of Paul's mission" at Antioch, and he argues that this first eucharist, by abolishing "all ritual barriers of birth for the community," represented "the hour of conception for the occidental 'citizenry.' "[170] Western religious association, he believes, remained the model for later city life, in which "full membership in the ecclesiastic community was the prerequisite for urban citizenship."[171†] Christianity deprived the sib, or kin group, of its particularistic power, "for by its very nature the Christian congregation was a religious association of individual believers, not a ritual association of clans."[172]

Only after he has established the variations in normative rationalization that have accompanied the same urban, middle-class instrumental interest does Weber embark on his long analysis of the dialectic between interest and value commitment in the social change that created the Western city.[173] It is here that an understanding of empirical order informed by multidimensional theoretical order clearly emerges, for Weber views the history of the Western city as the history of revolutionary conflict. In each of the two principal revolutionary periods, the actions by lower strata were motivated by the interaction of developments in the conditional spheres with the peculiar normative ideals Weber has associated with the "burgher" of Western urban development.

The Western city, according to Weber, first emerged as an institutionalized entity in the twelfth century. When the economic and political interests of the urban merchant-burghers began to clash seriously with the interests of the governing lord's manorial orientation, the former gained their autonomy through political and military struggle. Weber's account of this process emphasizes that the conflict of interest was so powerful a trigger precisely because it was perceived through the filter of the normative bond of the legal "rights of citizenship" that defined the Western type of urban community. His statement that the burghers had achieved a "revolutionary usurpation of rights" in effect combines these two faces of this early "coniuratio" movement.[174] Weber also emphasizes that the revolutionary political and military organizations by which the *"coniurationes" defended* these perceived interests—and which proved to be the seeds of the oath-bound confederations that formed the first true "cities"—were themselves possible only on the basis of the Christian definition of universal community. "For the development of the medieval city into a burgher association," Weber writes, it was of central significance "that at a time when the economic interests of the burghers urged them toward institutionalized association this movement was not frustrated by the existence of magic or religious barriers."[175] Where these barriers did exist, as in Asia, "the strongest common economic interests of the city inhabitants enabled them to achieve no more than transitory unification."[176]†

The second great period of revolution and reconstitution was also triggered by conflicts of instrumental interest induced by changes in external conditions, changes that arose because the burghers of the earlier period had used their new civic power to try to consolidate their positions in an exclusive way. "There developed in many of the . . . European urban settlements, where originally internal political equality of the settlers and free election of the municipal officials had obtained, a stratum of *honoratiores* . . . monopolizing the municipal offices by virtue of their economic independence and power."[177] This new situation, Weber emphasizes, involved powerful forces of instrumental interest and calculation. "Any individual," he attests, "who was unable to share in the burden of the collective tax guarantee and paid the royal taxes only from assessment to assessment—thus primarily anyone not wealthy—was *eo ipso* excluded from the stratum of active burghers."[178] Yet this material situation generated revolutionary conflict only because it also violated the Western city's normative principles of associational equality: "As a rule the movement was triggered by the often far-reaching denial of legal rights to commoners."[179] In fact, Weber insists that "the patrician families monopolizing the council seats could everywhere maintain closure easily only as long as no contrast of interests arose between them and the excluded part of the citizenry."[180]

Because of the normative egalitarianism of the Western city in other words, any sharp divergence of interest was bound to stimulate internal demands for change. And, "once the self-esteem of the outs . . . had risen to a point where they could no longer tolerate the idea of being excluded from power, the makings of new revolutions were at hand."[181] The crucial fact, indeed, was that those excluded defined themselves subjectively as citizens, and they were even tentatively acknowledged to be such by their oppressors. Thus, the agents of this second round of revolutionary change, Weber writes, "were once again sworn burgher unions."[182] The religiously defined conception of normative order allowed these rising groups to measure the status quo against a higher, transcendent authority; the result was that they constituted "the first *deliberately nonlegitimate and revolutionary* political association."[183]

7. CONCLUSION: ON THE GENERALIZED AND ANALYTIC INTERPRETATION OF WEBER'S ACHIEVEMENT

In 1918, Weber offered a series of lectures on comparative economic ethics under the title "A Positive Critique of Historical Materialism." By identifying his alternative to instrumental theory in this way—as a "positive" critique—Weber clearly intended to signal to his audience that he was offering, in Hegel's terms, a concrete rather than abstract negation of Marx's theory: he would dispense with materialism as the definition of order itself, but he fully intended to include material conditions as one part of the analytic environment of action. If the political atmosphere of postwar Germany had been different, Weber just as easily could have offered these lectures under an apparently quite different title: "A Positive Critique of Historical Idealism." For Weber's work revealed the same kind of concrete negation of idealist thought. On the one hand, he transcended its limitation by refusing to consider it as constituting the primary dimension of collective order. On the other hand, he had included it, for he recognized normative force as the other major environment of the individual act. Weber had always had a multidimensional intention. This was obscured by the awkward concreteness of his early writing, but in his mature writings Weber gained more theoretical clarity. I have tried to demonstrate in this chapter that a multidimensional achievement is, in fact, at the heart of Weber's most successful later work.

The hidden polemic of Weber's historical sociology of religion is a presuppositional attack on the notion that action is inherently instrumentally rational. He demonstrates that the most efficient type of action, economic action, actually varies in its efficiency, and that this variation can be explained only by the fact that rational action is mediated by normative order. Still, Weber accepts the implacability of external conditional pressures. Although an actor's rationality is filtered by internal commitments, what these commitments contend with are the pressures for efficiency produced by external conditions themselves. In a concerted attack on the "Durkheimian" solution to rationality, Weber demonstrates how the normative strictures on efficient action must themselves be viewed as the product of a complex interaction between political power, economic constraint, and a gradually rationalizing cultural life. Yet when he applies this multidimensional historical theory to the phenomenon of class, he produces just as strenuous a critique of the materialist tradition. If class exists only as a moral community in Durkheim's work, and even in that instance hardly at all, for Marx it is the prototype of instrumental order itself, the very embodiment of external, hierarchical control. Weber shows that class cannot, in fact, be understood by examining only the conditions that are external to a stratum's actions; the members of a class are also concerned with the meaning of life, and their understanding of this meaning is strongly affected by the normative tradition within which their lives are embedded.

Although Weber's theoretical achievement is enhanced by its empirical richness and specificity, by its sophisticated blend of hermeneutical and explanatory methods, by its open acknowledgement of conflict and change, and by its driving ideological concern for freedom and individual control, the most basic source of its greatness is a more generalized one. The most fundamental and ramifying theoretical commitment Weber makes is to a multidimensional understanding of action and order. Certainly his famous typology of action generalizes from his empirical findings about the course of historical change; so, too, does it formulate these generalizations in terms of his hierarchical evaluation of freedom and control. But the most significant fact about this typology, and about the more abstract speculations on freedom and determinism that inform it, is the presuppositional moment itself. Weber transformed the two major sociological traditions from sui generis concrete explanations into analytical variables; rather than invoking either/or solutions to order, they could now constitute different parts of the environment of every act. The same argument must be made for Weber's explorations in methodology and social conflict. Weber made extremely important methodological distinctions, and he used these distinctions to guide his empirical study. But the broader purposes of these distinctions, their daring combination of causal explanation and empathetic understanding, can be understood only by reference to the synthetic ambition of his more general theoretical intention. Finally, if Weber's achievement is not derived from method, much less can it be seen as derived from his sensitivity to the empirical phenomenon of conflict. Certainly Weber was no more sensitive to conflict than Marx, yet it is the striking differences between their understandings of class conflict and revolution that must draw the most serious theoretical attention.

The analytic focus in the interpretation of Weber's work must, therefore, be shifted toward more generalized concerns. I hope that the discussion in this chapter will contribute to that shift. I hope also that it has illustrated the poverty of the more specific interpretive strategy mentioned at the beginning of the chapter: the tendency to identify different empirical foci in Weber's work with different periods in his life. Weber's theoretical achievements, I have tried to demonstrate, cannot be concretely delimited through either periodization or an exclusive focus on one empirical point of his attention. The preceding exposition of his multidimensional theory, which draws from the earliest works of his maturity, from those composed in the last years of his life, and from the middle period as well, indicates the essential continuity between these chronological periods in terms of Weber's most generalized theoretical concerns. This discussion has drawn, moreover, upon the religious as well as on the political writings, on the sociology of urban life and social classes in *Economy and Society*, on the comparative history of religious traditions in *The Religion of China*, and on the most purely normatively-oriented work, *The Protestant Ethic and the Spirit of Capitalism*. None of these works, we have seen, corresponds to exclusively religious or political concerns. The *Sociology of Religion* segment of *Economy and Society* discusses at great length the nature of patriarchal authority, and it also analyzes the ideology of political and economic classes, combining structural analysis with the insights of religious history. The "structural" essay on *The City*, also in *Economy and Society*, relies heavily on the variable of comparative religious development, an insight drawn from the comparative studies in economic ethics. For Weber, the political analysis of revolution involved the cultural analysis of religion, and the analysis of religion demanded the understanding of polity and economy. In the best of his later sociology, these interconnections are made within the context of the same "political" or "religious" work, and the necessity of their interrelation is clear and manifest.

I have outlined what I consider the heights of Weber's achievement. We will discover in the chapters which follow that he does not always maintain such theorizing in a consistent way. With this discovery, we will understand better the sources for the contradictory quality of Weber interpretation and, indeed, of Weberian sociology itself.

Chapter Three

THE RETREAT FROM MULTIDIMENSIONALITY (1)

Presuppositional Dichotomization in the "Religious" Writings

The great theoretical achievement of Weber's maturity was derived from his ability to conceptualize material and ideal determination in an analytic way. Weber converted the traditions of instrumental and normative analysis which he had inherited from German intellectual history into precisely defined analytical moments of the same theoretical tradition—the "Weberian" one. It is upon this presuppositional accomplishment that every exercise in multidimensional theorizing must rest, whatever its more specific empirical, methodological, or ideological concerns. In his early writings, we have seen, Weber was unable to effect this translation of the German legacy. In the first place he conceptualized different kinds of determinants in a concrete way. In the second place, his very intention was open to doubt; in fighting against German Idealism, it seems clear that he permitted more play to economic and political elements than a truly synthetic attempt should allow. Even in the later writings, we will now see, this intention was still not completely resolved, though by this time the theoretical tools for multidimensionality were firmly in place.

In our analysis of Weber's famous typology of action—which was as close as he ever came to a formalization of his later presuppositional stance—we found in the interstices of his analytic treatment a strand of awkwardly dichotomistic and reductionistic thinking: *Zweckrationalität* is sometimes pragmatic, self-conscious rationality about ends, yet it is also presented at times as an instrumentalism devoid of any normative reference at all. It would be surprising if this presuppositional ambivalence did not manifest itself in Weber's more substantive sociology. In fact, when we consider his later sociology as a whole, we find that Weber has not by any means fully transcended the theoretical problems of his early work. There are strong tendencies toward concrete and nonanalytical thought, in which Weber's sociology falls back from the heights of his theoretical achievement. Rarely is this reduction presented in a purely one-dimensional form, for it reflects the ambivalence of the larger work. Yet it is clearly evident nonetheless, and the generalized failure ramifies throughout every level of his work.

Weber's theoretical synthesis conceptualized instrumental and normative pressures as having an a priori, epistemological status, the search for meaning and the responsiveness to external scarcity being "dimensions" of all human existence. In these terms, every concrete element of empirical reality is the *product* of the interaction of both dimensions. Religious ideas, though ostensibly normative, are produced by a complex interaction between religious abstraction and political-economic pressure; social class, formally conceived as an instrumental force, actually affects social life only as the product of the interaction among economic, political and religious constraints. In purely theoretical—not chronological—terms, Weber's more instrumental and concrete theorizing may be conceived as breaking this analytic synthesis down in two stages, corresponding to the "religious" and "political" segments of his work. In certain sections of Weber's comparative sociology of religious history—which, in reality, deals with political and economic as well as cultural institutions—the dual emphasis on instrumental and normative remains, but the two forces are no longer fused: they are separated and, by interacting as independent concrete entities, they in effect constitute self-sufficient explanations of the same empirical facts. In Weber's formally political sociology, however, the dual emphasis hardly occurs even in this truncated form. What reference to normative factors remains has a largely residual status; explanation hinges principally on political-economic variables, the motivational element becomes unproblematic, and order assumes a distinctly deterministic cast. In the present chapter, we will explore this theoretical ambivalence in Weber's "religious" writings. In so doing, we will learn more about what sociology must do to become multidimensional, and what it must not.

1. THE NEGATIVE CASE OF *THE RELIGION OF CHINA*

We have seen that Weber's studies of religion are hardly simply that: they actually explain political, economic, and cultural relationships in entire civilizational complexes. Yet it is precisely because they provide one of the principal examples of Weber's greatest theoretical achievement that they also provide the most striking introduction to what occurs when the synthetic logic of his work breaks down. Nowhere is the impact of instrumental reduction more acutely visible than in his monograph

The Religion of China. Social class and political authority, which in the works analyzed in the preceding chapter were two primary illustrations of synthetic theorizing, are here the object of strikingly dichotomous interpretation. Earlier, I referred to passages in *The Religion of China* to illustrate the autonomy of the normative element. It now becomes apparent that the very same book takes this autonomy away and manifests a strongly materialist bent. Still, we must read Weber as he is, not as we wish him to be or as he could be at other times. The cause of more synthetic theory is served, indeed, as much by understanding Weber's failure as his success.

In the formal conceptualization that forms the first major sections of *Economy and Society*, Weber defined sociology as an interpretive science and insisted that the observational understanding of action would often mistakenly take others' motives for our own. It is ironic that part 1 of *The Religion of China* is entitled "Sociological Foundations," for its failure lies precisely in its inattention to motivation: Weber develops an instrumental explanation for the traditionalism of Chinese political authority and class structure that is based on what "reasonable men" would do when faced with Chinese external constraints. In regard to political authority, Weber turns first to the instrumental motives involved in China's relatively antitraditionalist movement from feudal to bureaucratic authority. It was China's geography, Weber believes, that prevented economic development under feudalism. Indeed, he writes that it was such external, geographic pressures that presented the "main counterweight" against the continuation of feudalism,[1] for the rational interest in more efficient river regulation presented a strong external inducement for the creation of "an autonomous bureaucratic management by the prince."[2] Such inducement naturally produced instrumentally rational action, and there ensued a struggle for power between the warring feudal dynasties intent on usurpation of national power. "The princes," Weber writes, "had to struggle against the stubborn resistance of their subvassals who threatened them with a fate identical to the one which they had prepared for their own feudal overlords."[3] In response to this rational fear, they established new conditional structures and a normative order to rationalize them. "Princely cartels against subinfeudation were formed and ... principles [were established] according to which inheritance of office was ritually offensive." The Chinese bureaucracy, then, partly resulted from this instrumental political conflict—"bureaucratic administration displaced the administration of vassals"—but there were also important economic conditions involved, for "competition of the Warring States for political power caused the princes to initiate rational economic policies."[4]

Yet this bureaucratic authority retained, to a significant degree, a traditionalistic orientation, and Weber insists that the patterns of external order can explain this failure of development as well. Just as the original impulse for political rationalization hinged on the political struggle for external control, so its abatement was related to political pacification. "Just as competition for markets compelled the rationalization of private enterprise," Weber reasons, "so competition for political power compelled the rationalization of state economy and economic policy."[5] But once this had occurred to a significant degree, "the stimulus was gone." Since efficient action evidently responds only to external stimulus, the newly emergent "absence of competition prostrates rational management in administration, finance, and economic policy." With changed conditions, motivation changes too: "The impulse toward rationalization which existed while the Warring States were in competition . . . no longer [occurred] in the world empire."[6]

To explain the further undermining of bureaucratic power, Weber points to other external impediments on action, action that is, in itself, assumed to be perfectly rational. He cites the primitive systems of communications, transportation, and money which made it objectively impossible for the central authority which did exist to gain further power through a more efficient organization. The "farflung" geographical terrain of the Chinese state made the "undeveloped techniques of communication" particularly critical, and "when successive attempts at monetary centralization failed, patronage privileges—except for some supreme provincial offices—together with almost the entire system of finance were relegated to the provinces."[7] "The tremendous transportation difficulties . . . also always watered this wine," with the result that "the empire resembled a confederation of satrapies under a pontifical head." Impersonal bureaucratic authority, for these purely external reasons, existed only on paper: "The power lay formally—and only formally—with the great provincial officials."[8]

Weber called this personalized blend of bureaucracy and feudalism prebendary patrimonialism, and the most immediate and forceful opposition to rationalization lay in the structuring of the Chinese official's "prebend," his official income. "It was thoroughly in keeping with the nature of patrimonialism," Weber writes, "to have considered the official's income from administering a provincial district as his prebend, from which his private income was not really separated."[9] Political rationalization, or the lack of it, now has reference to the structuring of rational interests alone: "[the most] important result of this prebendal structure was its extreme administrative and politico-economic traditionalism."[10] Weber inverts his multidimensional explanation of the traditionalism of Chinese familial sibs in the same way. "The rationalism of the bureaucracy," he writes, "was confronted with a resolute and traditionalistic power" not only by prebends but "by the most intimate personal associations."[11] The strength of the impulse to reform external conditions now can be predicted simply by observing external conditions alone: "One can estimate the complete hopelessness of reform because of the vast material interests opposing it."[12]

Weber has produced an explanation of Chinese political traditionalism that rests solely upon external considerations—an explanation devoid of any reference to the impact on authority of the type of normative factors discussed in chapter 2. His description of Chinese class structure proceeds in an equally one-sided manner, a strategy that similarly contradicts the synthetic approach to class discussed above. Weber focuses on the stratum of literati, the officials who staffed the prebendary positions in the Chinese bureaucracy. He explains the emergence of this group in purely instrumental terms by referring to their decisive role in the feudal struggle for power which produced the bureaucracy itself. The literati, he writes, were the "scriptural scholars whose services the princes utilized in rationalizing their administrations for power purposes."[13] They achieved their triumphant class position, therefore, by their ability to produce the most efficient means for the princes' political ends. The literature produced texts that "usually indicated rather Machiavellian means for overwhelming neighboring princes by war and diplomacy"[14]—texts, in other words, that had no particular normative significance. Because these textual means were efficient, they advanced the literati's self-interest, apparently their only end: "Success fell to the literati whose rational administrative and economic policies were again decisive in restoring imperial authority."[15] The literati, then, were instrumental in establishing the Chinese bureaucracy.

Just as the burgher class incorporated the crucial peculiarities of Western modernity, so could the antireformist, antirational traditionalism of this Chinese structure be traced to the character of the literati. And just as the multidimensionality of Weber's account of the burghers reflected his broader theory of Western development, so does he now insist that the class traits of the literati can be fully accounted for by the instrumental interests that accrued to their role in the external bureaucratic structure. Because "any intervention in the traditional economy and administration impinged upon the unforeseeable and innumerable interests of this dominant stratum in its fees and prebends," Weber believes, "officialdom stood together as one man and obstructed as strongly as the tax payer every attempt to change the system of fee, custom, or tax payments." The literati were conservative, in other words, simply because their naturally instrumental motives were structured in this way: "In general, any innovation endangered either the present or future interest of each official in his fees."[16]

The extent of this mechanistic reduction of the prebendary class can be fully appreciated only by examining Weber's treatment of the ethic associated with it. For Weber discusses the Confucianism of the literati as if it were a direct reflection of their prebendary position in the materially pacified empire.

> The traditional view held by Confucius is that caution is the better part of valor and that it ill behooves the wise man to risk his own life inappropriately. The profound pacification of the country, especially after the rule of the Mongols, greatly enhanced this mood. The empire became an empire of peace.[17]

No reference is made here to the interaction of these political inducements with a movement toward abstraction in the nonrational sphere.

Nor is the religious ethic the only element to fall victim to Weber's now reductionist approach to the normative component of group interest. His treatment of law suffers in a like manner. Whereas his multidimensional treatment in *The City* emphasized the connection of legal rights to the particular religious formulations of the urban stratum, Weber's discussion of Chinese patrimonial law in *The Religion of China* makes no such internal reference, delineating only the law's relation to the instrumental interests of the literati.

> The dictum was: Power prerogatives [*Willkür*] have precedence over common law. . . . No "fundamental freedoms of the individual" were guaranteed. . . . When the question was discussed among the stratum of literati a minister of the state of Ch'in successfully objected: "If the people can read, they will despise their superiors." The charismatic prestige of the educated patrimonial bureaucracy seemed endangered and those power interests never again allowed such an idea to emerge.[18†]

Finally, although his principal discussion of class in this monograph refers to the prebendary literati, this instrumental revision also informs Weber's brief consideration of the stratum which was the focus of his extensive synthetic treatment of class noted above, namely, the middle class of urbanites. In his explanation of why the Chinese urban class never achieved the independent position of its Western counterpart, Weber now concentrates exclusively on the factor of military power. "The *legal* foundations beneficial to the development of petty capitalism in occidental medieval artisan crafts," Weber believes, "were absent in China because the cities and guilds had no politico-military power of their own."[19] While in his multidimensional account of urban strata presented above, this military element was carefully coupled with the impact of the religious definition of community, it is here considered sufficient in itself. There is no reference to the significance of religious rationalization, and this class development can refer only to China's peculiar material conditions: "[It] is explained by the early development of bureaucratic organization."[20]

In the first part of his monograph, then, Weber has provided an ex-planation of Chinese state and class structure which he apparently con-siders to be empirically sufficient but which remains completely within the boundaries of instrumental action and deterministic order. We know, however, that this cannot represent the totality of Weber's explanation, for our discussion in chapter 2 disclosed another, quite antithetical cur-rent of analysis in this very same monograph. Indeed, despite the logic of his discussion of the "sociological foundations" of Chinese society, it is apparent that Weber does not consider these material factors, so directly visible to the scientific observer, to be sufficient in themselves. The second half of *The Religion of China*, in fact, is replete with passages pleading the causal significance of the normative *at the expense of* the objective. This tendency culminates in the final chapter, "Confucianism and Pu-ritanism," which, as pointed out above, utilizes the methodology of em-pathic understanding to demonstrate the singular importance of normative order in Chinese development.

This "second version" of Weber's analysis of Chinese development is framed by two passages, the conclusions of parts 1 and 3. In the latter instance, he explains the significance of his argument by insisting that, in fact, the material conditions open to direct observation may not actually have been sufficient to explain the course of Chinese action: "Many of the circumstances which could or had to hinder capitalism in China simi-larly existed in the Occident and specifically right at the time of the con-clusive formation of modern capitalism."[21] And in detailing such now relatively uncompelling "circumstances" he lists the very same material facts which in the first half of the book he had forcefully described as in themselves sufficient to maintain Chinese traditionalism: "the pat-rimonial traits of occidental rulers, their bureaucracy, and the fact that the money economy was unsettled-and undeveloped."[22] From this asser-tion Weber reasons that the principal factor cited in the preceding dis-cussion, the material pacification of imperial China, cannot in fact explain Chinese traditionalism. Although "the pacification of the Empire explains, at least indirectly, the non-existence of political capitalism," it "does not explain the non-existence of modern, 'purely economically ori-ented' capitalism in China."[23]

In the conclusion of his monograph, then, Weber directly contradicts the explanatory rationale of the first part. This ambivalence helps us to understand how, in the concluding sentences of that first part, he could make a claim which the substance of that argument had thoroughly be-lied, namely, that it is religion, not political or economic factors, that most effectively accounts for the Chinese situation. Weber now urges his readers to look beneath the material facts—facts he himself has pre-sented—to the ordering of actors' motivations. "Rational entre-preneurial capitalism, which in the Occident found its specific locus in industry, has been handicapped not only by the lack of a formally guaranteed law, a rational administration and judiciary, and by the ramification of a system of prebends, but also, by the *bases* of a particular mentality." He now asserts, in fact, that, above all, modern capitalism was "handicapped by the attitude which found its place in the Chinese 'ethos.' "[24] In effect rewriting the actual import of his initial discussion, Weber now insists that the analysis of this ethos is the "main theme" of the monograph.[25†]

In the first pages of part 2 of *The Religion of China* Weber moves to redefine the central concepts of political authority and social class in more normative terms. The changes in his explanation of class first occur in his discussion of the education of the literati. In the first few pages of the section entitled "The Typological Position of Confucian Education," in the first chapter of part 2, Weber still explains the instruction of the stratum in terms of the instrumental factors involved in its political and economic position. Whereas in India education was "underpinned by cosmogonic as well as religious-philosophical speculations," in China the literati "developed rational systems of social ethics." The key fact, he writes, is that "the educated stratum of China simply has never been an autonomous group of scholars, as were the Brahmans, but rather a stratum of officials and aspirants to office."[26] Here Weber offers a historical sketch of Chinese education that notes only political pacification, the external factor that had been central to his earlier discussion.

> Higher education in China has not always had the character it has today. The public educational institutions (Pan Kung) of the feudal princes taught the arts of the dance and of arms in addition to the knowledge of rites and literature. Only the pacification of the empire into a patrimonial and unified state, and finally, the pure system of examinations of office, transformed this older education.[27†]

Up to this point, the explanation is perfectly consistent with the instrumental structure that informed Weber's discussion in the first section of the book. The departure is made, however, in the very next page, when, for the first time in the entire monograph, Weber offers a consistent argument for nonrational cultural phenomena as an independent social force. The peculiarities of the literati's education, he states, appear to have been, in part, "a result of the peculiarity of the Chinese script and of the literary art which grew out of it."[28] He then proceeds to assign to the particular nature of this cultural fact a large responsibility for the traditionalism of literati education: "The script retained its pictorial character, and was not rationalized into an alphabetical form."[29] And after explaining in some detail how this pictorial characteristic led to the "lack of all training in calculation" of the type which would have been necessary for the direction of a rational bureaucracy, Weber concludes with a general observation on the ramifications of script for the nature of the class ethos of the literati. "Chinese thought," he writes, "has remained rather stuck in the pictorial and the descriptive." As a result, "the power of *logos*, of defining and reasoning, has not been accessible to the Chinese."[30] Motivation has once again assumed center stage, and Weber reconnects the possibilities for material rationalization to the possibilities for subjective reason allowed by normative order.

Following this revision of his analysis of class, Weber attempts in the first pages of the following chapter, "The Confucian Life Orientation," to restructure his explanation of the traditionalism of Chinese political authority in a similar way.[31] For example, whereas throughout the preceding pages he had described the all-important emergence of imperial pacification purely as the result of instrumental factors involved in the feudal struggle for power, he now emphasizes the independent significance of the "pacific" quality of Chinese Confucianism. And he ascribes the origins of this latter condition to specifically religious developments: "Patrimonial bureaucracy was spared the competition of an autonomous hierarchy . . . because the Chinese 'soul' has never been revolutionized by a prophet."[32] The parallel with Weber's multidimensional civilizational history is finally brought to the surface. Because China had "no independent religious forces with which to develop a doctrine of salvation or an autonomous ethic," it never produced an independent religious stratum that could use ideas to challenge the status quo.[33] In these terms, the success of imperial pacification can be seen as depending partly on voluntary will, not on external control alone. "The [Chinese] official," Weber writes, "had to prove his charisma by the 'harmonious' course of his administration."[34]

Weber has offered explanations for his principal empirical categories, political authority and social class, which are in the most direct kind of theoretical confrontation. The question that naturally presents itself is how does he reconcile these two analyses? The answer is that he does not. As presuppositional positions, they are inherently irreconcilable, and Weber has presented them as independent, sui generis positions. Because of his concrete, dichotomizing logic, Weber cannot describe the interaction of instrumental and normative in an analytical way. What he does, instead, is simply to manifest his theoretical ambivalence, listing two opposing explanations side by side.

This self-defeating attempt to resolve contradictory theoretical perspectives is illustrated clearly in Weber's efforts to come to grips with the more normative revisions he has introduced into his explanations of class and authority. After his initial description of the independent cultural importance of Chinese script in the education of the literati, Weber does not, in fact, move to develop a third, more synthetic formulation of the origins of class education. Rather, as in his early writings, his explanation remains at the level of unresolved thesis and antithesis: the materialist and idealist traditions remain concrete and unreformed. Weber simply lists both of the factors which he has described.

> Chinese education served the interest in prebends and was tied to a script. . . . The very concept of logic remained absolutely alien to Chinese philosophy, which was oriented purely toward the problems and status group interests of the patrimonial bureaucracy, was bound to script, and was undialectical.[35]

The unsatisfactory, ad hoc quality of such an unmediated resolution is obvious. Weber is asserting that, on the one hand, the traditionalism of literati education is a product of instrumental motivation as structured by the economic and political situation, and, at the same time, that it is a result of the literati's voluntary, internal commitment to the cultural values embodied in Chinese script. Informed by epistemologically different presuppositions, these two propositions are incompatible. If ideal and material factors are to be combined, as our discussion in chapter 2 tried to indicate, rational action itself must be redefined to show its normative referent; external economic and political conditions affect action only as they are filtered through the internal element of motivation. Only in this manner can instrumental and ideal propositions be combined in the same theoretical framework.

The same kind of unresolved dualism appears in Weber's subsequent attempt to specify the reasons for the literati's Confucian rather than feudal and Western sense of honor. In "The Status-Honor of the Literati" (pt. 2, ch. 5, sec. 4), he cites the unstable conditions under which the literati worked, a situation caused by the vastly superior political power of their patrimonial rulers. Thus, in spite of the literati's privileges, Weber writes, "the development of feudal ideas of honor was impossible."

> These privileges were precarious because they were immediately voided in the case of demotion, which frequently occurred. Feudal honor could not be developed on the bases of . . . possible degradation, corporal punishment during youth, and the not quite infrequent case of degradation even in old age.[36]

Yet in the section immediately following Weber seeks to explain the literati's conception of honor by pointing, in a strikingly different way, to the influence of the ideal notions embodied in Chinese religion.

Rather than external fear, the status ethic is now seen in terms of the order that structures will and motivation. "The peculiar spirit of the scholars," Weber writes, "was intimately connected with the basic presuppositions from which the orthodox and also, by the way, nearly all heterodox, Chinese theories proceeded." Their idealization of etiquette and placidity derives from the following religious facts: "The good spirits ... are those who protect order and beauty and harmony in the world. To perfect oneself and thus to mirror this harmony is the supreme and the only means by which one may attain such power."[37]

It should not be surprising that this ambivalent alternation of presuppositional orientation extends also to the key issue of the literati's opposition to any attempt at antitraditionalist political reform. At first, Weber completely reverses his earlier position on this matter, stating that the literati's opposition stemmed from an internal commitment to religious ideas. "The Confucian aspirant to office, stemming from the old tradition," in Weber's view, "could hardly help viewing a specialized, professional training of European stamp, e.g., the type of training that induces reform, as anything but a conditioning in the dirtiest Philistinism."

> This was undoubtedly the locus of much of the important resistance to "reform" in the occidental sense. The fundamental assertion, "a cultured man is not a tool," meant that he was an end in himself and not just a means for a specified useful purpose. The all-round educated Confucian "gentleman" ... supported a status ideal of cultivation that was directly opposed to the socially oriented Platonic ideal.[38]

Soon after, however, Weber explains an incident of antitraditionalist suppression solely in terms of external economic exigencies. Writing about the Han dynasty's return to orthodox Confucianism in a period of intense social change, Weber writes with a deterministic tone that "a patrimonial officialdom, finding itself in a position of absolute power and monopolizing both the official and priestly functions, could indeed have none but a traditionalist mentality regarding literature."[39]

Precisely the same theoretical ambivalence ensues following Weber's introduction of his normative explanation of Chinese political authority. In the final paragraph of his discussion about the causal significance of Confucian religion, which was noted above, Weber observes that the Chinese view of the individual represented "a view which characteristically followed upon the absence of supra-mundane deity," a reference to the independent process of religious rationalization, or the lack thereof.[40] Yet in the very next sentence he concludes the section with a statement which, while intended apparently merely to reinforce this analysis, actually expresses the very opposite. "These ideas," he writes, "moreover, were a reflection of the status conditions in the patrimonial state."[41] And in the following sections on the absence in China of conceptions of rational law and natural science, an absence integrally connected to the traditionalism of Chinese religion, he reverts to the reductionist approach to political authority of his earlier discussion.[42†] The fact that "the very word 'liberty' was foreign to the language," he asserts, "can readily be explained" simply by noting "the nature of the patrimonial state." As for the absence of natural science, this occurred because "under the conditions of patrimonial bureaucracy," according to Weber, "the context of the ruling stratum was discharged entirely into competition among prebendary and degree-hunting literati" rather than into competition that challenged "economic and technological interests" of a rising bourgeoisie.[43] This disposition toward the instrumental is then abruptly reversed by three sections which focus on the sui generis religious sources of the bureaucracy (ch. 6, pts. 4–6), only to be reinstituted, once again, by a discussion that finds the roots of Chinese filial piety, one of the basic tenets of Confucianism, in the intrinsic power interests of the bureaucratic class.

> In a patrimonial state where filial piety was transferred to all relations of subordination, it can be readily understood that an official—and Confucius for a time was a minister—would consider filial piety as the virtue from which all others issue. Filial piety was held to provide the test and guarantee of adherence to unconditional discipline, the most important status obligation of bureaucracy.[44]

The problems which we have discovered in Weber's monograph on China are not related to the empirical facts themselves. Other sections of his comparative sociology of religion, and even certain passages in this discussion of China, succeed in placing these same facts in a more successful synthetic framework. The problem rather is on the level of theoretical logic itself, in Weber's inability to conceptualize the relation between the facts which he has observed or, more generally, to presuppose an understanding of action and order that would allow this conceptualization to develop. The difficulties in this monograph indicate that the possibilities for reduction we discovered in Weber's formal definitions reflect a fundamental irresolution which extends deeply into his substantive work—that they exist, indeed, in the most fundamental presuppositions of his sociology. In the terms of that conceptual discussion, what we find in *The Religion of China* is, in effect, the frequent separation of instrumentally rational action, or *Zweckrationalität*, from any reference to normative order at all. This is the source of Weber's frequent reduction to concreteness and dichotomization, for such *zweckrational* action so defined is action that stands completely on its own. If rational action is so concretized, then nonrational action must be separated in the same way. *The Religion of China*, then, institutionalizes the dilemma of the materialist-idealist debate instead of transcending it.[45†] The influence of political and economic pressures can now be expressed only through describing actions as concretely economic and political, and

vice versa, the effects of religious patterns can be described only by referring to explicitly religious behavior. As we will see, Weber's "political"
sociology is merely this problem of misplaced concreteness writ large.

2. *ANCIENT JUDAISM* AS THE MULTIDIMENSIONAL ALTERNATIVE

Before examining how this "declension" emerges as a full-blown instrumentalism in Weber's so-called political sociology, we will return for
a final time to the multidimensional segment of Weber's comparative sociology of religion. This reconsideration will allow us to contrast Weber's
synthetic and reductionist approaches to culture more directly than was
possible before the China case had been discussed. For this purpose, the
monograph *Ancient Judaism* presents the most convenient point of reference, both because its multidimensional character has already been
discussed and because its structure of argument is formally parallel to
the structure employed in *The Religion of China*.

In *Ancient Judaism*, Weber apparently organizes his presentation in a
similarly dichotomous way, for an analysis of the "social structural" conditions of ancient Israel precedes a typological description of its religious
commitments. We will see, however, that this formal organization is de-
ceptive. As in *The Religion of China*, Weber describes in *Ancient Judaism*
the "material basis" of an entire society at two different points in time,
measuring the impact of this temporal change on the extant religious
ethic. In the one, the Chinese feudal situation of warring principalities is
described as eventually giving way to a pacified bureaucratic empire. In
the other, Weber recounts the steps by which an agrarian society of
armed peasants, herdsmen, and patriarchal rural princes evolved into
an urbanized kingship.[46] Despite these formal similarities, however, the
descriptions differ radically in terms of the theoretical logic within
which these empirical observations are couched. In the one, Weber describes the initial disposition between the warring princes, feudal vassals, and emergent literati as motivated by purely instrumental action,
and as ordered only by the distribution of material resources. In the
other, he carefully documents how the groups engaged in class struggle
and the contest for political authority were bound by normative integuments as well.

The first thirty pages of *Ancient Judaism*, entitled "The Social Structure and Its Setting," mention only the external factors that conditioned
social change in ancient Israel: the economic ownership of land and the
military control of power. The monograph therefore at first appears simply to duplicate the approach in *The Religion of China*. In the sections
immediately following, however, Weber introduces modifications that
systematically alter this instrumentalist portrayal, describing how the

economic and political struggles among peasants, herdsmen, and ruling powers were affected by legal and political principles. As Weber writes of the impact of landlessness on the lower-class herdsmen, or *gerim*, "Whatever his position with respect to the ownership of land, the sources regularly mean by 'ger' a denizen who was not only under the private protection of an individual [and given] the religious protection of guest right, but a man whose rights were regulated and protected by the political organization."[47]

In direct contrast to his treatment of legal relationships in *The Religion of China*, Weber elaborates this "right" of the Israelite lower class in a manner that is consistent with the multidimensionality of his essay on the city. He emphasizes that although the *gerim* were "without land of their own," and therefore in strictly material terms without any power vis-à-vis other groups, "all gerim nonetheless had a fixed legal relationship to the settled population."[48] This relationship included, in addition to "contractually-fixed meadow and traverse rights,"[49] another privilege that ran even more directly against the strictly instrumental conception of economic position: the *gerim* were legally entitled to debt remission.[50†] Finally, Weber makes the normative reference of these rights perfectly clear by relating them directly to the historically unique Judaic conceptualization of the religious *berith*, or covenant, between the Jews and their God. "The very name of the oldest law book," he writes, was the "Book of the Covenant," and he explains that "all gerim, including the patriarchs, are in their legal situation through berith."[51] This normative order interpenetrated with the hierarchical structure of conditional relations. Thus, Weber maintains that "the 'covenant' concept was important for Israel because the ancient social structure of Israel in part rested essentially upon a contractually regulated, permanent relationship of landed warrior sibs with guest tribes as legally protected metics . . ."[52]

The earlier rationalistic explanation is further modified by Weber's description of how the class struggle in ancient Israel also was mediated by the political manifestations of this religious *berith*. Weber relates the existence of the Israelite tribal confederation to the enforcement of the rights discussed above, for, as he stated at the outset of his more multidimensional analysis, such rights could be regulated and protected only through political organization.[53] Accordingly, he insists that political power could be, in principle, and often was, in fact, in the service of normative ends: "Grave violation of metic rights, which every Israelite enjoyed in every other tribe, under certain circumstances was revenged by the confederacy."[54] Instead of discussing the origins of this central political authority simply in terms of the need for external self-protection—the conceptualization advanced in his discussion of state origins in *The Religion of China*—Weber now connects this confederation to communal bonds of brotherhood created by the religious *berith*. Although simple observation would conclude that the *gerim* were completely defenseless, empathic understanding would reveal that they were not completely so: "An Israelite, including a member of another tribe, who stood only in the relation of a *ger* to one spoken to, nevertheless addressed him as 'brother.' "[55] And it is not surprising, given this normative reference, that Weber describes this political community as an "*oathbound* confederation," a "*coniuratio*,"[56] using phrases that directly parallel his account of the oathbound urban leagues that helped create the Western city.

As in that other analysis, which contrasted the Western city with its economic and political counterparts in the Orient, Weber compares the Israelite confederation with other groups that were exposed to similar external situations but which nonetheless differed in their religious orientations. In the present case, the common issue is the lack of stability in the political life of landless peasant groups, an instability which the Arab Bedouins shared with Israelite peasants: "All political organizations among Bedouins and [*gerim*] stockbreeders were quite unstable due to their [external] life conditions."[57] Weber contrasts this objective instability, however, with the "extraordinary stability of a definite type of organization to be found precisely among . . . the Israeli unsettled strata: namely, the religious order or 'cult' organization of similar pattern."[58] This normative order presented a significant mediation to objective pressures, for "apparently only such a religious organization provided [a] solid basis for permanent political and military structures."[59†] Finally, Weber goes out of his way to make explicit the generalized reference within which this discussion is couched, a position that recalls his analysis of the ideology of the urban classes rather than the reductive approach to class and ideology assumed in the monograph on China. "The point at issue," he writes, "is not that the life conditions of the . . . semi-nomads had 'produced' an order whose establishment could be considered as something like the 'ideological exponent' of its economic conditions"— the very formulation, indeed, of the China monograph. To the contrary, "this form of historical materialistic construction is here, as elsewhere, inadequate." Weber insists on putting the causal relationship into a more analytical, multidimensional context: "The point is, rather, that *when* such an order was established, then it had, under the [economic and political] life conditions of these strata, by far the greatest chance to survive in the selective struggle for existence against the other, less stable political organizations." The Darwinian struggle takes place within a normative as well as material context, and only this subjective context allows motivation to be understood. "The question, however, whether such an order emerged at all was dependent on quite concrete religious-historical . . . circumstances."[60]

It should be clear, then, that Weber's analysis of the first stage of Israel's development—in which the groups competing were peasants, herdsmen, and patriarchal rural princes—occurs within the framework of a synthetic multidimensional theory. In sharp contrast to his analysis in *The Religion of China*, the relative autonomy of the religious element is never in doubt. First, and most importantly, this is true because the initial "structural" discussion in *Ancient Judaism* has turned out actually to be couched in multidimensional terms. Second, the concentration on textual and typological analysis that characterizes the latter part of *Ancient Judaism*, although formally parallel to the presentation of argument in the China monograph, is never compromised, as that discussion was, by presuppositional ambivalence about the "real" determining role of exclusively instrumental factors. For both of these reasons, the lengthy discussion Weber initiates in the latter half of the book about the ideas formulated by the Judaic covenant represents the logical fulfillment of his earlier analysis of Israel's political and economic situation rather than an alternative to it. His most significant assertions, that the Judaic conception of God produced a unique sense of ethical obligation and an unprecedented definition of "peoplehood" within the Jewish tribe,[61] present a detailed elaboration of the normative resources for the specific phenomena of contractual right and political confederation that were the subjects of the first part of the work.

It is within the context of this conceptualization of Israeli social life that Weber describes the conditional changes that constituted the "second stage" of the development of ancient Judaism. As in the discussion of imperial pacification in China, he portrays the movement toward proletarianization and urbanization in Israelite society as "developmental tendencies" arising from what appear to be strictly instrumental motives.[62] However, whereas the reductionist argument in the China monograph conceives of political bureaucratization as directly producing its own normative justification, in *Ancient Judaism* the religious development corresponding to the later stage of bureaucratic monarchy is conceived as a product of the interaction of these conditional changes with the religious ethic that arose in the earlier situation. Only because of this theoretical difference can an empirical possibility be described that actually proved to be of ultimate significance for later Israel: Israel's political bureaucratization did not, in fact, produce a correspondingly "bureaucratic" religious ethic. To the contrary, because the Israelites remained internally committed to the particular ideas of covenant religion, Israel's bureaucratization produced its normative antithesis. In the face of conditional changes which facilitated economic exploitation and political hierarchy, the egalitarian thrust of early Judaic ideology was sharply illuminated. Religious mythology came to glorify the lower classes, and voluntary opposition to bureaucratic centralization, on the individual and group level, became a central ideological focus.[63†] Weber writes, for example, that despite the "demilitarization of the peasant strata" which occurred in the course of Israel's political development, the autonomy of the religious ethic ensured that, nonetheless, "one knew full well that the ancient confederacy and its army had once had a different social appearance."[64] Alongside this material development, therefore, there emerged a religious mythology in which the peasants and herdsmen of the earlier society were transformed into "the champions of the truly pious heroism, 'inspired' by the war god of the covenant."[65]

Weber emphasizes that the critically-oriented religious ethic of this second period derived from the long-standing cultural patterns of communal authority and legal right. Thus, the new mythology reflected the familiar "hallowing of the ancient social right, above all, of the social debt rights of the Yahwe confederation."[66] New material challenges were vital to its development but were not sufficient in themselves, for the one theme basic to all criticism of the newly stratified society was "the time-honored 'law' of the ancient Israelite confederacy, as the critics understood it." Critics measured the present against the normative order of the past. "To them," Weber writes, "the source of all evil was the transformation of the state into a liturgical rather than confederate state."[67] In these new conditional circumstances, moreover, another critical aspect of Israeli religion emerged, one that further contributed to the voluntaristic opposition to external bureaucratic control. The juxtaposition of the powerful and impersonal Judaic god—product of the long-term religious rationalization described above—and the disorderly challenges of new social conditions produced for the first time a strong conception of collective "social sin." This new product of the search for meaning created the psychological desire to discover the sources of Israel's guilt and the possibilities for absolution. "The question inevitably arose," according to Weber, as to "whence [came] this unfavorable development of the political and military situation of Israel."[68] Because of the Jews' "peculiar relationship to Yahwe," he concludes, "when Yahwe was angry and failed to help the nation or the individual, a violation of the *berith* with him had to be responsible for this."[69]

It was the interaction of these three ideal factors—the notions of communal authority, legal right, and social sin—with new economic and political developments that provided the general context for Judaic prophecy. The content of the prophetic vision reflected the religious myths that arose in the second stage of Israel's development;[70] the prophets made sense of an unstable world in terms of abstractions about order that were deeply entrenched in the history of the people.[71] A product of multidimensional pressures, prophecy was an invocation of higher normative order that altered the subsequent course of Israel's, and the world's, social development. It serves the same theoretical function in the Judaism monograph as the second wave of oathbound urban confederations served in Weber's analysis of the Western city. Both demonstrate the role of normative order in creating radical critique and social change.[72†]

3. CONCLUSION

The contrast between the monographs on China and Israel upon which this chapter turns demonstrates, once again, how impossible it is to identify the different theoretical thrusts in Weber's work with his "religious" or his "political" sociology alone. *The Religion of China*, part of the comparative studies of religion that often have been identified as Weber's more "idealist" work, slides on frequent occasions into a one-dimensional, materialist mode of thought. Indeed, as we have seen in the preceding chapter, the *Sociology of Religion* segment of *Economy and Society*, purportedly the most political and "realistic" work that Weber produced, interpenetrates material with normative order in a much more consistent way. *Ancient Judaism*, on the other hand, the other work examined here from Weber's series on religion, resembles, in theoretical terms, the segment of *Economy and Society* more than the volume on China, its companion in the religious series.[73†] In fact, the logic employed in it is the same that informs Weber's "political sociology" of the city and social class.

Only after these issues of general theoretical concern have been firmly separated from any specific empirical referent can we turn to the most drastic strand of Weber's retreat from multidimensionality. Although Weber's political sociology is not in any sense inherently instrumental, it is only in aspects of the political sociology that the difficulties we have discovered in *The Religion of China* assume the status of the typical.

Chapter Four

THE RETREAT FROM MULTIDIMENSIONALITY (2)

Instrumental Reduction
in the "Political" Writings

A belief that has attained almost axiomatic status in modern social science is that Weber's political sociology successfully introduced the recognition of normative variables into political analysis. Weber did so, it is believed, through his general concept of legitimation and, more particularly, through his commitment to describing political life in terms of the different forms of legitimation that have characterized the course of history. Considering the work we have previously examined, such an argument is rather easily constructed. Suffering and salvation are certainly problems for political, not just religious, life; political ideology must, therefore, address the same problems of meaning as conventional theodicy. If traditional society is fettered by the personalization of religious ideas, this limitation might well affect its political life as well. The universalism provided by Western religion could, in this way, lead to the legal rationality of Western politics, and the transformation might be effected by political leaders assuming the same spiritual mantle as the prophets of old.

It is my contention in the present argument, however, that, with the exception of the works examined in chapters 2–3, Weber's sociology of politics generally fails to make this kind of link between normative order and political life. Certainly the formal discussion of legitimation does occur, as does the periodization of history—so temptingly cultural in appearance—into charismatic, traditional, and rational-legal forms. There are even occasional passages of normative analysis in the substantive empirical work. Yet no matter how cleverly and imaginatively they are "read," these definitions, classifications, and empirical references in themselves add up to very little, for they are encapsulated in a presuppositional framework that is decidedly, even aggressively, instrumental.

76

Weber's "political" sociology can be read as synthetic only by those who misunderstand the requisites of theoretical logic, or by those whose theorizing is tied to some polemical intent. I will suggest, to the contrary, that the major thrust of this political sociology elaborates the declension from multidimensionality that we first perceived in the China monograph. Weber's political sociology "concretizes" this approach to theoretical explanation, particularly in regard to the purposely instrumental action he calls *Zweckrationalität*, and while his method continues to be comparative, he is increasingly satisfied with observation rather than empathic understanding. Weber consistently portrays political life as a Hobbesian situation of Realpolitik, in which the exigencies of political power and economic class impose themselves on actors as purely external force. With the focus shifted to such external controls over action, the motivation of political actors loses its significance. The political sociology, therefore, makes little reference to religious systems and "meaning complexes," the very elements Weber established as central to a voluntaristic understanding of society in other parts of his work. Finally, the portrayal of conflict itself, which achieves such a subtle multidimensional treatment elsewhere, here becomes identified with the disposition of instrumental interests alone. In this aspect of his work, then, Weber joins Marx as a founder of "conflict sociology." Within the thoroughly instrumental logic of his political analysis, Weber's sociology reverts to the unresolved problematic of his early work.

1. THE EVOLUTION FROM "LEGITIMATION" TO "DOMINATION" IN THE FORMAL WRITINGS

The primary source of the misperception of Weber's political sociology is to be found in his famous definitional discussion of the role of legitimation in political action. It is to these formal concepts, not to the actual empirical and historical studies, that contemporary social thinkers have turned in the course of establishing their own propositions about the normative element of political life. And they have apparently done so for good reason, for no matter what the course of Weber's empirical analyses of political history, there can be no argument about the fact that "legitimation" is a central concept in the formal conceptualization that begins *Economy and Society*. Whether the problem of legitimacy lends itself, in principle, to a synthetic approach is, however, not the issue. The question of concern here is whether or not this concept is utilized in such a manner in Weber's actual treatment of political authority. This exacting standard of *actual* treatment—not the hypothetical possibility that a synthetic discussion *could* take place within some vaguely defined "Weberian" framework—will be applied not simply to the empirical and historical analyses, but to the formal definitional discussions as well.

In the beginning of the formal analysis in *Economy and Society*, the segment first translated independently as *The Theory of Social and Economic Organization*, Weber carefully connects the issue of political authority to the critique of instrumental order discussed earlier. He links his method of *Verstehen*, that is, the method of interpretive or hermeneutic understanding, to the notion that action has an important nonrational dimension. "The interpretation of action," he writes, "must take account of a fundamentally important fact."[1] Structures of power, he insists, have an internal subjective reference: "Collective entities which are found both in common sense and in juristic and other technical forms of thought, have a meaning in the minds of individual persons." These institutions, then, exercise power only partly by virtue of "something actually existing"; they also order action "partly as something with normative authority."[2] The fact of this moral authority links political institutions to the complexes of ideas which are so much a part of Weber's other analyses. Because "actors . . . orient their action to them," Weber writes about institutions with normative authority, "ideas have a powerful, often a decisive, causal influence on the course of action of real individuals."[3] Weber concludes by linking politics to "belief." "One of the most important aspects of the existence of a modern state," he insists, "consists in the fact that the action of various individuals is oriented to the belief that it exists or should exist."[4]

Subsequently, Weber relates this nonrational dimension of action to the existence of a nonrandom and noncoercive order, a concept which lies at the heart of a multidimensional theory. Normative order exists, Weber writes, only if the voluntary, normative element comes into play: "The meaningful content of a social relationship [will] be called an 'order' only if action is approximately or on the average oriented to determinable 'maxims'."[5] It is within the context of this presuppositional framework that Weber introduces the specific concept of legitimacy. "Order" exists if action is oriented to rules. Legitimate order exists only if these rules are thought to be binding: "An order [will] be called 'valid' if the orientation to these maxims occurs, among other reasons, because it is in some appreciable way regarded by the actor as in some way obligatory or exemplary for him." An order which is so voluntarily obeyed, Weber writes, "enjoys the prestige of being considered exemplary or binding," and "legitimacy," he believes, is only another expression for the same thing.[6] Thus, the order that guides legitimate action has the same status as the order that guides religious belief. "Action, especially social action which involves a social relationship, may be guided by the *belief* in the existence of a *legitimate order*."[7] In a series of contrasts that emphasize the presuppositional issues at stake, Weber compares the concept of legitimate order with a situation in which ordering is achieved without any such reference, that is, purely on the basis of the instrumental and efficient calculation of interest. "A uniformity of orientation," he writes, "may be said to be 'determined by self-interest,' " but such self-interested order must be based upon purely rational action. It can occur, that is, "only if and insofar as the actors' conduct is instrumentally oriented [*zweckrational*] toward identical expectations."[8] Weber illustrates such an order, one that has no reference to legitimation, by referring to the ideal-typical form of utilitarian action: the economic situation in which ends are treated not as normatively determined but simply as means to be reached by efficient calculation, where other actors are regarded not as interpenetrating individuals but merely as external conditions.

> Many of the especially notable uniformities in the course of social action are not determined by orientation to any sort of norm which is held to be valid ... but entirely [by] the fact that the corresponding type of social action is in the nature of the case best adapted to the normal interests of the actors as they themselves are aware of them. This is above all true of economic action .... The dealers in a market thus treat their own actions as means for obtaining the satisfaction of the ends [*Zweck*] defined by what they realize to be their typical economic interests, and similarly treat as conditions the corresponding behavior of others.[9]

Weber has made a brief for the normative reference of political action, its voluntary quality, and the belief systems that regulate it. Political legitimacy, in these terms, is only empirically different from religious sacralization. The stage is set for the integration of Weber's "religious" sociology with his formal political analysis, the Marxian emphasis on interest and struggle for power with Durkheim's understanding of the religious dimension.

Yet Weber never moves on to the drama itself. At this point in his formal analysis, his conceptualization of political order begins its descent toward instrumental reduction. In fact, the first seeds of this shift can be discerned in the very midst of the multidimensional analysis just presented, for even here Weber intimates that the existence of a legitimate order could be a matter of external appearances only, a behavioral, observational fact rather than an intentional, empathic matter. For example, immediately following his fundamental definition relating legitimate order to belief, he writes: "The probability that action will actually be so oriented will be called the 'validity' of the order in question."[10] Shortly thereafter he illustrates the ways in which the action of a civil servant "is not determined by ... self-interest alone,"[11] and among these ways he points to several actions which are themselves guided not by internal normative commitment but by rational-efficient calculation. The civil servant's action is "determined by the validity [*Wertrational*] of an order," Weber writes, not only because " its violation would be abhorrent to his sense of duty," but also "because disobedience would be disadvantageous to him."[12] The problem here is not, of course, Weber's insistence that a civil servant may uphold an order only because he fears the disadvantages of punishment. It is, rather, that Weber has introduced such a purely rational motive in the context of purportedly presenting an alternative to an order that is "determined by . . . self-interest alone."[13] But if this fear of punishment presents an alternative to "self-interest," it can only be an alternative at the level of order, not action. Purely self-interested order may, in Weber's view, imply individualism: if so, disadvantageousness implies an external collective force. Yet such collective order leaves the instrumental motive of self-interest intact. Weber has raised the paradoxical possibility that a legitimate order may have no internal referent at all.[14†]

Having opened up his definition of legitimate political order to different presuppositional interpretations, Weber primarily pursues the second, more instrumental understanding in the remainder of the long discussion of "Basic Sociological Terms" that comprises *Economy and Society's* first chapter. In section 8, "Conflict, Competition, Selection," order assumes significance not as an orientation reflecting the actor's belief in a system of ideas but only as an external condition that defines the structure of opportunities within which a process of social selection occurs. "All typical struggles and modes of competition which take place on a large scale," Weber writes, will lead "in the long run . . . to a selection of those who have in the higher degree, on the average, possessed the personal qualities, important to success." What structures these qualities and, hence, the course of this Darwinian movement has little to do with internal expectations defined by normative patterns. Rather, "what qualities are important depends on the *conditions* in which the conflict or competition takes place."[15] The ordering quality which Weber still considers essential to social action is now reduced to a matter simply of non-random "regulation" of the type that characterizes the collective order of Marx: it is an external control that directs individual atoms by making a given act more or less costly to perform. Weber claims that a "competitive process is 'regulated' competition to the extent that its ends and means are oriented to an order."[16] If this minimalist, one-dimensional understanding sounds like a return to the kind of theoretical logic employed by Marx, in which economic order becomes a prototype of society, this is exactly what Weber himself has in mind: "A classic example of conventional regulations [is] the competition for economic advantages in exchange relationships, bound as that is by the order governing the market."[17] In section 12, "The Organization," the ambiguity now associated with this conception of political order is further reinforced by Weber's connection of the concept to "enforcement" by an administrative staff. Order has now become simply a hierarchical directive, an object to be manipulated by those in positions of power without reference to supra-individual normative belief. For Weber, administrative hierarchy embodies instrumental order much as class hierarchy embodied it for Marx. "For organization to exist," Weber insists, "it is sufficient for there to be a person or persons in authority . . . whose action is concerned with carrying into effect the order governing the organization."[18] Organization, the quintessential order of group life, is, therefore, defined in merely behavioral terms. Hierarchical power is "decisive because it is not merely a matter of action which is *oriented* to an order, but [one] which is specifically directed to its *enforcement*."[19] To match this new instrumentalism, Weber's method is now purely observational, not empathic. "For purposes of definition," he writes, "it is indifferent what 'order' is the basis of the relevant expectation."[20]

This movement toward defining an alternative, Realpolitik version of the order problem is finally formalized with Weber's introduction, in the conclusion to his analysis in chapter 1, of the concept of political authority, or, a concept which he employs in a synonymous way, political domination [*Herrschaft*].[21†] Certainly one purpose of this analysis is empirical and conceptual, namely, to distinguish the "power" that is achieved by simple superiority of economic interest from the "authority" that is the result of intentionally-issued command. Indeed, in terms of any complete evaluation of Weber's political sociology, this distinction between political and economic control is a vital one, for it differentiates Weber's analysis of power from that of Marx.[22†] Our present concern, however, is at once a more particular and a more theoretically generalized one: we wish to know whether Weber's analysis of power differs from Marx's in its presuppositional referent. For, after all, whether or not political power is defined as an independent variable vis-à-vis economic interest is a question of the kind of model employed. The relationship of both variables must still be defined vis-à-vis normative and material order in a more abstract sense, a question that involves more general, presuppositional issues. In this theoretical context, the identification of authority with command must be viewed in terms of the evolution of the discussion of order that preceded it. The generalized purpose of this emphasis on the "command" aspect of power is clear: it elaborates a conceptual apparatus for studying the imposition of collective order by the application of external political coercion. Weber has now applied to political authority a thoroughly behavioral definition. Authority exists, he contends, quite simply when the order represented by a "command" is obeyed. Thus, he defines authority or "domination" as "the probability that a command with a given specific content will be obeyed by a given group of persons."[23] And in direct contradiction to his earlier normative criterion for the existence of legitimation, Weber now insists that an actor's subjective commitment is not a criterion for measuring successful exercise of authority, or, indeed, its very existence. " 'Obedience' will be taken to mean that the action of the person obeying follows in essentials such a course that the content of the command *appears* to have been followed for its own sake." External compliance is all that matters; the scientist needs only observation, not understanding. As Weber continues, "the fact that it so appears is referable *only* to the formal obligation, without regard to the actor's own attitude to the value or lack of value of the content of the command as such."[24†] Internal motivation, in other words, is irrelevant. All that matters is whether an outsider could—in his own terms—conceive of some motive that might be adequate after the fact. The voluntary acquiescence to political authority has now been redefined as, for theoretical purposes, identical with the operation of instrumental political interest.

Because of the tendency to focus on Weber's empirical concepts divorced from their larger framework, and also because of the strong bias toward viewing Weber as masterfully consistent, scholars of his work have generally overlooked the problems our discussion has revealed. The most important interpretations of the "multidimensional Weber," those of Parsons and Bendix, find no basic inconsistency in his formal analysis. As indicated by Parsons' awkward translation of *Herrschaft* as "imperative control," his reading, with a few important exceptions, emphasizes the continuity of the subjective definition of legitimation with Weber's analysis of political authority, and although in the translation dispute Bendix emphasized more the coercive aspects of the *Herrschaft* concept, he too asserts a clear line of continuity.[25†] In the interpretive tradition that sees an "instrumental Weber"—the picture articulated by Dahrendorf and "conflict sociology"—Weber's theory is also taken to be thoroughly consistent: the conflict school's understanding of authority as command is taken without any reference to the earlier, more subjective understanding of legitimacy.[26†] Finally, the few interpreters who have actually recognized some ambiguity in Weber's treatment have attributed this to problems in the empirical observation of authority itself, not to more generalized difficulties.[27†]

The interpretation I offer is very different. It recognizes the split in Weber's general work, and gives it a generalized, theoretical meaning. In the course of Weber's formal analysis of political power there has clearly been a shift of emphasis from a synthetic attempt to include reference to normative order—which Weber identifies with the problem of legitimacy—to a concentration on order as an externally imposed phenomenon, conceptualized as the problem of authority or domination. The issue is not whether social life actually involves both of these collective forces, not whether the commands of organization constitute a significant datum for sociological analysis. It is certainly the purpose of multidimensional thought to be inclusive of both. The question that does arise, however, is why the logic of Weber's analysis of these two forces has evolved in such a dichotomizing fashion: Why does the discussion of authoritative domination occur in isolation from any reference to the concept of legitimacy as previously described? Such dichotomization recalls the awkward splitting that occurred in the course of Weber's writing on religion, the fall away from the analytic reconciliation of materialism and idealism that is foreshadowed in his ambivalent formal treatment of *zweckrational* action. The organization of Weber's classificational and definitional argument about the nature of political life marks a shift of emphasis back toward an instrumental resolution of the problem of collective order. It is, in fact, precisely this resolution that informs the sociology to which we now turn. Legitimacy, with its "Durkheimian" connotation, has become a hollow shell. Weber proceeds to discuss the "real" determinants of political domination upon which it is based.

2. THE ELABORATION OF INSTRUMENTAL DOMINATION IN THE SUBSTANTIVE POLITICAL HISTORY

In the heart of *Economy and Society* we find a dense historical analysis that, while rarely discussed, is, nonetheless, paid great theoretical homage as the ultimate "empirical demonstration" of the synthetic nature of Weber's political sociology.[28†] Yet as Weber's own Introduction to this empirical analysis of political history makes perfectly clear, it is not intended to be a study of the "types of legitimation" if we understand this term in anything like a normative way. To the contrary, drawing on the distinctions established in his earlier, formal analysis, Weber indicates that the principle significance of legitimation for his empirical studies derives from its utility as a reliable indicator of the types of domination: "For a domination, this . . . justification of its legitimacy is much more than a matter of theoretical or philosophical speculation; it rather constitutes the basis of very real differences in the empirical structure of domination."[29] Weber concludes his Introduction on exactly this point, employing "legitimation" simply as a means for emphasizing the types and structures of instrumental domination. The three principal "forms of domination," he writes, "*correspond* to . . . three possible types of legitimation."[30]

> *Rationally* consociated conduct of a dominational structure finds its typical expression in *bureaucracy*. Social conduct bound in re-

lationships of *traditional* authority is typically represented by *patriarchalism*. The *charismatic* structure of domination rests upon that authority of a *concrete individual* which is based neither upon rational rules nor upon tradition.[31]

Weber's political sociology, then, is a study of the different conditions under which corporate groups, or organizations, have tried to enforce obedience to their commands. It does not address the effects of different types of belief systems on the minds of men, or measure the social impact of these legitimate beliefs, or elaborate the ideational patterns from which they are constructed. Charismatic, traditional, and legal forms are not, for Weber's political sociology, the vehicles for studying, respectively, "faith," "inherited mores," or "rational thought"; rather they are considered as distinctive external frameworks for the play of relatively invariant instrumental self-interest. Even on the rare occasions when legitimation as a problem of internal meaning is mentioned, it is separated from any connection to ideational rationalization in the search for meaning—a process which in his multidimensional work Weber placed on an equal level with the struggle for power—and reduced to a factor that is responsive solely to the rationalization of power as such.[32†]

2.1. CHARISMA AS A FRAMEWORK FOR DOMINATION

Because of the fact that charisma refers to the subjective "interpenetration" among actors that occurs through an affective attachment, it would appear to be an ideal vehicle for conceptualizing the cultural impact of ideas on an actor's relationship to political authority, and the "routinization of charisma" would appear to be the perfect connection between Durkheim's theory of structure as the crystallization of emotion and the "realistic" theories of Marx. Such a relationship between normative and instrumental aspects of political authority was, in fact, a primary focus in the multidimensional studies we examined above—for example, in Weber's analysis of the role of the Mosaic covenant in the formation of the Israeli political confederacy. And while "charisma" certainly was not the central theoretical vehicle through which the impact of religious rationalization was conceptualized—as certain theorists have claimed it to be—Weber does discuss prophecy in terms of charismatic power, and his scattered references to the connection of charisma with religious process suggest the potential for a broad multidimensional application.[33†] Nevertheless, when "charisma" is introduced by Weber into his explicitly political analysis, its ideational implications are for the most part eliminated.

In Weber's political sociology, charisma is utilized as a vehicle for discussing the ramifications for the instrumental struggle for power of a specific type of domination, namely, the short-lived, unstable type of domination derived from the personal allocation of power to a particular individual. Weber asserts that the insecurity generated by such a situation for the other participants in the struggle produces a succession of "efficient" strategic innovations that result in the depersonalization, or routinization, of that charismatic form. The motor of this development is not, for Weber, the mercurial qualities of intense affect or the search for meaning by increasing numbers of people, as an insistence on linkage to the religious studies would imply. Nor does Weber consider this development to be the diffusion, or "institutionalization," of the charismatically communicated ideas. Rather, the process of routinization of charisma is said to be fueled by the peculiar insecurity of this particular type of domination; the effect of routinization, therefore, is simply to provide a more assured and stable form of power. And when, infrequently, Weber does refer to charisma as a form of legitimacy rather than domination, it is to specify an external condition which those involved in this power struggle must take into account, not to describe a belief through which the participants in the struggle are motivated.

"Charisma is self-determined and sets its own limits."[34] At the very beginning of his analysis, Weber establishes the framework for all that follows by emphasizing how this internally generated quality makes authority unstable by making it unpredictable, both for the followers of the charismatic leader and for the leader himself. Because, frequently, "charisma abhors the owning and making of money," Weber writes, it "always reject as undignified all methodical rational acquisition, in fact, all rational economic conduct."[35] But the political consequences of this form of domination are even more significant: "Charisma knows no formal and regulated appointment or dismissal, no career, advancement, or salary," and "no permanent institutions . . . which are independent of the incumbents."[36] In the section of his analysis of charismatic domination which follows this discussion, Weber refers to this instability of power as the prime impetus for the routinization to which all charisma is subject. Thus, he describes the motivation of those involved in this routinization as proceeding from an instrumental motive for possession of a valued means, from the "desire to transform charisma and charismatic blessing from a unique, transitory gift of grace of extraordinary times and persons into a permanent possession of everyday life."[37] Although this statement in isolation could perhaps be understood as denoting the need to maintain a more permanent relation to a valued context of meaning, its actual reference to the previously described exigencies of political and economic instability is clear from an assertion that follows in the same paragraph. The routinization of charisma is the achievement of a stable and privileged status by the group, or staff, whom the individual charismatic leader had originally dominated. "The turning point," Weber in-

sists, "is always reached when charismatic followers and disciples
become privileged table companions, as did the *trustis* of the Frankish
king, and subsequently fief-holders, priests, state officials, party officials,
officers, secretaries, editors and publishers, all of whom want to live off
the charismatic movement, or when they become employees, teachers
and others with a vested occupational interest, or holders of benefices
and of patrimonial offices."[38] The results of the struggle for routinization
match the various instrumental motives that propelled it. Routinization
is the "efficient" goal pushed by the self-interest of the staff, a staff, we
recall, that is the backbone of all authority because of its power to
enforce demands. With routinization, the staff can be certain that such
enforcement will bring them economic and political benefits.

The discussion of routinization which follows this section is in two
parts, which differ according to the degree to which the depersonalization of charisma has been carried through. The first part concerns the
phenomenon of leadership succession, in which the disciples attempt to
assert their own authority after the departure of the charismatic leader.
It is essential to understand that Weber couches his explanation of the
succession issue in terms of the *framework for struggle*, in terms, that is,
of the threat to self-interest created by the external condition of unstable
charismatic power. If the charismatic leadership "wants to transform itself into a perennial institution," Weber writes, "the first basic problem is
that of finding a successor to the prophet, hero, teacher, or party
leader."[39] Not only do the disciples, as those next in power, have a rational interest in succession, but, according to Weber, their proximity to
the charismatic leader has given them the power to direct it. Because
charisma is based upon intimate personal qualities, only those physically
close to the original leader will have effective access to power. The external fact of instability creates the necessity for action—if, of course, instrumental motives are assumed—and the peculiar intimacy of personal
power determines the form this action will take. Any efficient action, of
course, demands access to means: "Since the disciples have in fact complete control over the instruments of [charismatic] power, they do not
find it difficult to appropriate this role as a 'right.' "[40] And in a crucial
passage, Weber asserts that it is because of this instrumental and conditionally ordered process—the preservation of power by expropriating
control over selection of a successor—that the "routinization of charisma" actually occurs.

> In all originally charismatic organizations, whether prophetic or
> warlike, the designation of a successor or representative has
> been a typical means of assuring the continuity of domination.
> But this indicates, of course, a step from autonomous leadership
> [*Herrschaft*] based on the power of personal charisma toward le-
> gitimacy derived from the authority of the "source."[41]

Finally, Weber discusses several ways in which this selection by disciples may occur, most of which involve acclamation by the ruled. Instead of some social-psychological process, or some cultural dynamic like socialization, Weber's description of these strategies underscores the dominant, instrumental role of the interested disciples. "Designation by the closest and most powerful vassals and acclamation by the ruled," he writes, "is normally the end product . . . of choosing a successor."[42] And although the process of selection does occasionally pass power over to the ruled, Weber emphasizes that it generally results in a consolidation of domination by the disciples: "Acclamation by the ruled recedes increasingly behind the charismatically determined right of prior election by clerics, court officials or great vassals, and ultimately an exclusive oligarchic electoral agency comes into being."[43†]

The second, more complete form of routinization occurs with the depersonalization signified by the emergence of "lineage charisma" and "office charisma." In regard to the former, Weber develops his framework, once again, in terms of the instability of such a purely individualistic form as charismatic domination. Referring not at all to the nonrational aspects of the process by which legitimacy is transferred from an individual to a group focus—an aspect that would involve attention to motive and to complexes of meaning—Weber writes quite simply that it is through the limitation of charisma to a given lineage that disciples can become assured of political authority and economic privilege. Rather than cultural process, this is actually just another strategic development, the result of proto-economic calculation. "The closing of the rolls of nobility, the tests of ancestry, the admission of the newly rich only as *gentes minores*, and similar phenomena," Weber insists, "are all equally products of the attempt to increase status by making it scarce."[44] This reduction from multidimensional structures toward the easy assumption of pragmatic motivation now becomes very direct: "Economic motives are not only behind the monopolization of remunerative offices or of other connections with the state, but also behind the monopolization of the *connubium;* noble rank provides an advantage in the quest for the hands of rich heiresses and also increases the demand for one's own daughters."[45]

The association of charisma with office occurs, according to Weber, when for various empirical reasons the disciples and followers have organized an institution rather than a lineage. In such a situation, their power can be preserved only by maintaining the special charismatic quality of an "office" rather than a group. Action is the same, efficient and rational; the only difference pertains to the external conditions. Thus, "depersonalization was the means whereby an hierocratic organization mechanism was grafted upon a world which perceived magical qualifications everywhere."[46] The movement of Christianity from personal to impersonal religious structure is, for Weber, an example of this logic: "The bureaucratization of the church was possible only if the priest could be absolutely depraved without endangering thereby his charismatic qualification; only then could the institutional charisma of the church be protected against all personnel contingencies."[47] Nowhere does Weber connect this analysis to the insights of his religious history. Nowhere, for example, does he refer to the role of the specifically religious idea of universal brotherhood that allowed charismatic authority in the West to attach the sacred to an abstract and impersonal church office, even though precisely this consideration was pivotal in his multidimensional analyses of the subject.[48] Here the explanation is solely in terms of the preservation of institutional power.[49†] In fact, in the course of this entire discussion of the role of charisma in political life, reference to charisma as a force relating political power to normative considerations occurs only once. In a single anomalous paragraph in the midst of the analysis of office charisma, Weber compares the "anti-idolatrous" attitudes toward office in countries under Puritan influence to the "more purely emotive" attitude manifest in Lutheran Germany.[50†] This isolated association of charismatic legitimation with ideal elements sharply illuminates the reductionistic quality of the discussion which surrounds it, in which the focus on the structure of domination has superceded any serious consideration of the structure of charismatic belief.

2.2. THE INSTRUMENTAL STRUGGLE FOR TRADITIONAL DOMINATION AND ITS TRANSITION TO A RATIONAL-LEGAL FORM

The best known Weberian definition of the traditional period of political development occurs in terms of its particular form of legitimation. In opposition to charisma's spontaneity and legal rationality's impersonality, traditional political life ensures "that which is customary and has always been so and prescribes obedience to some particular person."[51] In the first pages of Weber's lengthy historical analysis in the later sections of *Economy and Society*, it appears as if this normative element is to be a major part of the discussion that follows. Patriarchal domination is introduced as a *"belief"* in authority"[52] that depends on voluntary obedience, that finds its "inner support in the subjects' compliance with norms."[53] And Weber proceeds to elaborate some of the voluntaristic components in the relationship between patriarchal ruler and subject that emerge because of the reciprocity involved in the shared commitment to traditional belief. On the one hand, "custom prescribes that the subject support his master with all available means";[54] on the other hand, "piety toward tradition . . . also constrained the master."[55] "Even if it constitutes at first a purely one-sided domination," Weber writes, "this relationship always evolves from itself the subjects' claim to reciprocity, and this claim 'naturally' acquires social recognition as custom."[56]

Such an approach, if continued, presumably could involve reference to the larger meaning complexes in which such internal elements are imbedded. Ultimately, it would have to refer to the independent role of religion in shaping the will to patriarchal and patrimonial domination and, more generally, to the relationship between religious abstraction, or the lack thereof, and the relatively particularistic orientation of the traditionalist to political authority. Weber did, of course, consider both of these issues in other sections of his work. The discussion of his multidimensional writing in earlier chapters elaborates these aspects of his analysis of traditionalism, and they have been the subject of a vast array of purportedly "Weberian" political sociology. This multidimensional path, however, is not the direction that Weber's political sociology actually takes.

In a pattern that follows, instead, the reductionist strain of his Chinese monograph, Weber's discussion of traditional authority soon departs from the framework of multidimensional theory. In the section in *Economy and Society* which immediately follows the more normative analysis I have just discussed, Weber indicates that his intention is to consider traditionalism in its dominating rather than legitimating aspects, to analyze the traditional ruler not as an object of belief but rather as an object of power. The situation of internal habitual obligation, he now asserts, was merely temporary, a first historical stage. From a situation of "voluntary material support of the ruler and the absence of any patrimonial obligation to surrender fixed tributes," there ineluctably develops the period in which "a very powerful lord will tend to force even the 'free' subjects to meet the costs of his . . . appropriate upkeep."[57] The true perspective on patrimonial rule is the Hobbesian one. Traditionalism is now defined purely as the political situation that results from the struggle for power between the coercive patrimonial ruler and those on whom he must rely to carry out his will, that is, the officials of his apparatus. "Wherever the ruler creates typical and lucrative offices," Weber writes, "he must face attempts at monopolization by certain strata" whose "powerful interests" attempt to promote decentralization through the "legally autonomous sodality."[58] Particularistic, personalistic practices are a logical and efficient response to this challenge: "Wherever possible the ruler attempts to avoid such monopolization of offices by status groups . . . by appointing hereditary personal dependents or aliens who are completely dependent upon him."[59]

It is this "continuous struggle" between the ruler and his erstwhile "officials," Weber asserts, "which pervades the history of the patrimonial state."[60] Why is there "traditionalism"? Because these peculiar external conditions create constraints on the attempt by the ruler to further centralize his power, constraints that are either much too great or else not great enough. If in the course of this struggle the ruler retains his position of unlimited power, traditionalism results because the arbitrariness of his power position promotes irrational personalistic direction. "The completely discretionary power of the lord in areas in which this appropriation of offices has not occurred," Weber writes, "permit[s] him to appoint his personal favorites especially to administrative tasks and power positions."[61] If, on the other hand, the decentralized monopolization of office is actually effected, traditionalism ensues because of the stereotyping power of these local vested interests, a situation just as particularistic and even more resistant to change. "As the appropriation of offices progresses," Weber writes, "the ruler's power ... disintegrates into a bundle of powers separately appropriated by various individuals by virtue of special privileges [which] cannot be altered by the ruler without arousing dangerous resistance from the vested interests." Those local interests prevent rationalization: "This structure is rigid, not adaptable to new tasks, not amenable to abstract regulation."[62]

What determines the course that traditional domination actually takes? The decisive factors concern the conditions of action, the resources available to wage the struggle for domination. In part, these means are purely political. If the ruler is to succeed vis-à-vis his local officeholders he must obtain a complete monopoly on military power. "The more technically developed the ruler's own patrimonial position," Weber writes, "and especially his patrimonial military power on which he could rely ... against his political subjects, the more easily the ... total dependency [of the officials on the ruler] could prevail." Ultimately, however, this military factor involves the matter of economic exigencies, the prototypical means for *zweckrational* action.

> There is a decisive economic condition for the degree to which the royal army is "patrimonial," that means, a purely personal army of the prince and hence at his disposal also *against* his own political subjects: the army is equipped and maintained out of supplies and revenues belonging to the ruler. The more this condition prevails, the more unconditionally is the army in the ruler's hands.[63]

Weber analyzes the sources of traditional political authority, then, exclusively in terms of the impact of certain conditional factors, relying not at all on order of a normative kind.

In Weber's concrete and dichotomous approach to the traditionalism of China's patrimonial bureaucracy, military and economic factors were also pictured as determinants. Yet at least that analysis was "shadowed," very awkwardly to be sure, by independent reference to cultural patterns that, in Weber's words, "also" were decisive in different historical outcomes. Yet we find not even this ambiguous reference in Weber's magisterial analysis of traditional societies in *Economy and Society.* The heart of his discussion of traditionalism focuses, appropriately enough, on the disposition of the struggle between patrimonial ruler and officials in the different world civilizations, elaborating in detail the calculative strategies that evolved for preserving power and the external conditions that proved decisive in carrying them out. Turning first to historical instances of the successful defense of patrimonial exclusivity, Weber starts by listing the numerous political devices to which the rulers had recourse.[64] However, the main thrust of the analysis—of Ancient Egypt, the Chinese empire, and various satrapies and divisional principalities[65]—emphasizes the general factors which provided the ruler with the necessary support. In each case, Weber's explanation follows the theoretical logic of instrumentalism. For example, concerning Egypt, he writes:

> The army . . . was patrimonial, and this was decisive for the pharaoh's power position. At least during wartime the army was equipped and provisioned out of the royal magazines . . . . Career opportunities and the dependence upon the royal magazines were apparently sufficient to preclude an extensive appropriation of benefices.[66]

The army, in other words, served a web of instrumental interests. Soldiers were obedient to leaders because service supplied them with the means to live. The army obeyed the prince because without his ammunition they could not fight. Means became ends, and each end another means. Motive itself is never at issue. Weber's analysis here closely follows his instrumental account in *The Religion of China*, even down to the residual reference to the conceptual issue of Chinese calligraphy.[67]

The remainder of Weber's analysis focuses on the other possible resolution of the struggle for traditional domination, namely the decentralized appropriation of offices which eventually resulted in the formation of estates and in feudalization.[68] In regard to the latter, Weber insists, once again, that the object of investigation is the structures of domination, not legitimation. "Fully developed feudalism," he writes, "is the most extreme type of systematically decentralized domination."[69] The subjective sense of honor associated with feudal position, in fact, is merely a means in the struggle for power, the "price" for further control: "The quite considerable guarantee of the ruler's position through the vassal's knightly honor is acquired at the price of a great decline of his power over the vassals."[70] Here again, various strategies of the officials are cited first—Weber does not argue that in a purely instrumental collective order free will and contingency no longer exist—but as in the discussion that preceded it the focal point of his analysis is the external conditions with which these actions must contend. For Persia, for England, and for Russia—as in the cases of successful patrimonial rule he had earlier analyzed—Weber describes military and economic factors as decisive, though in this instance they have served to limit rather than to

facilitate centralized rule. As Weber writes about this Western development generally, "in the Occidental monarchies of the Middle Ages the
claims of the local seigneurial powers proved much more effective" because "their rulers were not supported by the standing army."[71] This external condition determined within strict limits the consequences of
monarchical acts, for the "monarchy could not avoid making compromises with the seigneurial lords, as long as it was not in a position to establish its own army and bureaucracy and to pay both from its own
treasury."[72†] The goal for each group is power, and in the search for an
efficient means this contentless end becomes no more than a means itself.
Weber never relates power, on either side, to a more general context of
meaning. Although he rarely employs the term, it is *Zweckrationalität*
(goal-rationality) in its most instrumental form, not *Wertrationalität*
(value-rationality) and certainly not "traditional" action normatively understood that characterizes the motives of Weber's principals in this description of "traditional" society.

The principal thrust of Weber's study of traditional authority, then, is
to establish the variation that occurs in the Hobbesian struggle to assert
patrimonial power. He has created a systematic explanation, where the
disposition to act "reasonably" creates, in the face of observable exigencies, certain predictable outcomes. This account of precapitalist society
is empirically rich and complex, closer to the realities of the empirical
world than Marx's account. Yet the theoretical logic that informs it is
much the same.[73†] On the few occasions, moreover, when the subject of
legitimate belief does become a focus for analysis, Weber considers it not
as an independent variable with references to complexes of meaning but
rather as a reflected offshoot of the structure of domination itself. For
example, in his discussion of the feudal ethos, Weber links the qualities of
heroism and the sense of personal honor exclusively to the political conditions which characterized the decentralized appropriation of power
by the officials. It was, after all, only because the feudal lords had successfully opposed the attempts to bind them in a bureaucratic network
that they could realistically be characterized, in Weber's view, as
"bearers of a peculiar, personal sense of dignity whose root was *personal*
honor, not only the prestige of office."[74] The ethic of heroism is similarly
linked directly to the military power, the external condition that sustained the movement toward decentralization. "The typical feudal
army," Weber writes, "is an army of knights, and that means that individual heroic combat, not the discipline of a mass army, is decisive."[75†]

But the most significant instance of the kind of reductionist approach to meaning involved in Weber's analysis of traditional domination occurs in relation to the issue of religious rationalization. Probably
the most basic tenet established in the multidimensional sections of
Weber's work is that the culturally inspired rationalization of Western

religious ideas played a highly significant independent role in the creation of modern economic and political life. Yet, in his efforts as a "political sociologist" to tie all the elements of the traditional era to the struggle
for domination, Weber actually ends up by challenging this very hypoth-
esis. He begins, in the discussion entitled "Hierocratic Rationalization
and the Uniqueness of Western Culture," on what is apparently familiar
ground by noting the central relationship between rationalized Christianity and Western capitalism.[76] Weber writes of "the more favorable
constellation for capitalist development that Occidental Catholicism offered," contrasting it with the "Oriental religions [which] preserved the
unrationalized charismatic character of religiosity.[77] He also notes particularly the nature of Western science and law in contrast to their counterparts in the Orient. At this point, however, the multidimensionality of
Weber's sociology ceases, for he attributes these developments not to the
development of religious abstraction but rather to the objective independence of the Western church, an autonomy that allowed it to engage in
the unhampered exercise of its authority. Because of this institutional
freedom, he contends, the Western church was able to succeed in what
comes naturally to any structure of domination, that is, in the rationalization of its power.

Weber now writes about the failure of non-Western religious rationalization in a manner that relies exclusively on the instrumental
structure of his analysis of traditional domination, citing the "conse-
quence of the purely historical fact that not they [i.e., the non-Western
churches] but the secular powers, whose paths they crossed, were the
carriers of spiritual and social culture, and that they always remained
subject to caesaropapist control."[78] Religion in the non-Western world, in
other words, remained unrationalized for a political reason, a situation
that did not require empathic understanding to be recognized: patrimonial power had completely triumphed in these societies, and it had,
thereby, eliminated the chance for autonomous centers of power to
emerge. In the West, by contrast, the conflict engendered by traditional
domination had been resolved in the opposite direction. The attempts at
appropriation of power by the estates had succeeeded, with the result
that separate centers of domination were allowed to exist. "In the Occident," Weber writes, "authority [*Herrschaft*] was set against authority, legitimacy against legitimacy, one office charisma against the other."[79]
This resolution of traditional struggle, then, merely led to a new stale-
mate: "Occidental hierocracy [i.e., the church] lived in a state of tension with
the political power and constituted its major restraint."[80] It is purely in
terms of the results of such independent churchly *power* that Weber now
explains the emergence in the Western world of rationalized law and science. The former developed, he asserts, as a mechanism of social control
to protect the church's organizational interest. The normative referent

of the church's motivation is irrelevant, for it acted, in Weber's view, in terms of external constraints and with purposive, instrumental rationality. "[Outside the West] there was no rational judicial system of the kind established by the Occidental ecclesiastic apparatus. The [Western] church created a trial procedure—inquisition—in order to obtain evidence in a rational manner, primarily for its own purposes [*Zwecke*]."[81] Similarly, it was the Oriental church's inability to defend its own interest, according to Weber, that prevented it from developing the powerful ideological weapon represented by the type of rationalized philosophical thought which facilitated the creation of Western science. The absence in the Orient of an "infallible doctrinal authority," Weber writes, "impeded the rise of rational philosophical thought evolving out of theology."[82]

Weber's analysis of Western traditional domination provides an explanation for the emergence of the modern economic and political orders that can be couched in purely instrumental terms. The conditional structures of Western traditionalism, Weber believes, established a framework of external resources and sanctions that could provide rational actors with the means and inducement to create modern life. Weber's point here could not be more clear: it was because of its decentralized estate patrimonialism that the West provided an unfettered political environment for the rise of the bourgeois class. Eastern patrimonial power, in contrast, quashed any incipient movement toward economic independence just as it had eliminated any attempt at appropriation by officials. It was power and material conditions that produced the uniqueness of Western development. Ideal interests are unimportant, let alone the ideational "tracks" along which they, as well as their material counterparts, are supposed to run in the multidimensional strand of Weber's work. Christianity is still important, but it is not treated as a set of ideas at all. Rather, "the more favorable constellation for capitalist development that Occidental Catholicism offered," Weber writes, "was primarily due to the rationalization of hierocratic domination."[83]

In *Economy and Society*, this for the most part implicit contention receives explicit formulation only once, when Weber examines the English case in his discussion of the antipatrimonial alternative that characterized Western traditional development. The fact that the first great bourgeois breakthrough occurred in England is here attributed to the feudalization of its political power, not to the normative impact of the Puritan ethic. In England, Weber writes, the "minimization of administrative activity . . . gave almost completely free rein to economic initiative."[84] And behind this crucial political factor of the "distribution of power"[85] Weber points to the influence of the economic variable, the possession by the English lords of great economic leverage vis-à-vis the state. For in contrast to the "benefice holders and aspirants to benefices" of the

Chinese empire, he writes, "in England the core of the gentry was a free status group of large landowners."[86†]

According to this understanding, then, the only further developments necessary for the expansion of Western commercial development were the external economic incentives necessary for triggering bourgeois action—factors like the increase in world trade and the discovery of precious metals. According to this analysis, a shift of motivational attitude is not theoretically or empirically necessary, and any reference to the internal matter of the cultural preconditions of bourgeois economic rationality is avoided. The prior existence of such rationality, indeed, is the assumption upon which the emphasis on political conditions is based. What was crucial for Western development was the structure of external sanctions that guided this rationality, a form of motivation that, in itself, is theoretically without interest. The same theoretical reduction informs the manner in which Weber relates his analysis of the struggle for traditional domination to the origins of the modern Western state. He now describes the latter simply as the princely bureaucracy which arose in self-defense—as well as to perform certain administrative tasks—against the coalition that was formed by the feudal estates (the "*Ständestaat*") to further ensure their appropriation of power.[87] The modern state is a pure power state, and the Western political tradition is virtually unmediated by the religiously informed network of legal rights and universalistic solidarity that was Weber's focus in *The City*. The urban community, in fact, is now important only as the structurally autonomous staging ground for the instrumental bourgeoisie.

Just before he began *Economy and Society*, Weber wrote a long monograph, *The Agrarian Sociology of Ancient Civilizations*, in which this instrumental understanding of the preconditions for Western modernity is stated more clearly. Weber summarizes here much of his earlier work on ancient economic history, but he places these observations into a framework that moves away from the quasi-Marxist and Realpolitik propositions of the early writings, one which much more closely resembles his portrait of the system of traditional society in the later work. The problem that concerns Weber is why the modern style of capitalism failed to develop in these ancient societies which were in so many ways commercial and capitalistic. He includes here the familiar variables from his earlier work: the initial cheapness of slaves, the barrier that slavery later presented to rational economizing, the difficulties of relying upon military conquest for acquiring cheap labor power.[88] He now moves, however, to insert these factors into a slightly different empirical framework. In the ancient civilizations, he insists, the extensive centralization of political power made it impossible for private groups to accumulate capital and to create economic innovations in their own interest.[89] In the Roman Empire and in Egypt, this power assumed a patrimonial form, with liturgies imposed on the propertied class and "arbitrary domination exercised over conquered populations."[90] Although the form in the Greek city-states was different, the substance was much the same, for the city-states had "unrestrained and sovereign power . . . over the private property of their citizens."[91] Weber mentions the absence in ancient civilization of a sense of "vocation," yet he does so only once and in passing.[92] The reference is balanced, moreover, by an explanation for this absence in purely economic terms: work in general was discredited because so much of it was performed by foreign slave labor.[93] Weber's message about the traditionalism of ancient civilization, then, is almost exclusively instrumental and deterministic: "[The] process of control, monopoly, and bureaucratic regulation—often leading to the complete exclusion of private capital—developed inexorably in all the great monarchies of Antiquity."[94] The comparative method is external and observational, not internal and empathic. In antiquity, Weber writes, "bureaucracy stifled private enterprise."[95]

3. CONCLUSION: "KNOWING BETTER" AND THE IMPERATIVES OF THEORETICAL LOGIC

What is so troubling about Weber's political writings on traditional and charismatic authority is that he certainly knew better. The multidimensional strand of his other work is there for all to see, and Weber covered there many of the same empirical topics that are the subject of his political writings: the relationship between leader and disciples, the nature and process of premodern social order. What has happened in Weber's sociology of domination is that more instrumental presuppositions have produced different concepts and empirical propositions. In other parts of his work and thought, Weber understands these issues in a more complex way, but when confined by the presuppositions of his political sociology this understanding could not be articulated. Theoretical logic sets inexorable limitations. If action is not conceived as anything other than instrumental, and if the theorist is committed to a collective order, the analysis of empirical life will, inevitably, have a mechanistic and deterministic cast. The problem of order must be solved, and if it cannot be conceptualized as "interpenetrating" individuals from within, it will be conceived as coercing them from without, through sanctions and force. The voluntaristic quality of action drops out; motivation and culture no longer become compelling subjects for scientific analysis. Such was the fate of Weber's political sociology, a fate which few of his sympathetic interpreters have been willing to acknowledge.[96†]

This analysis of political authority, of course, was not confined to the most generalized level alone. It included a systematic and far-reaching empirical theory of the transition to modernity. More than forty years ago, Talcott Parsons ventured the opinion that Weber never developed the other, material side of the causal chain to match the essay on this transition in *The Protestant Ethic and the Spirit of Capitalism.*[97] We have seen that this is hardly the case; indeed, the theoretical "other side" of Weber's analysis burst the causal chain altogether. Yet Parsons' honest, though perhaps somewhat wistful, naïveté about Weber's historical theory continues to permeate Weberian thought today. Much more recently, for example, the often penetrating German interpreter Wolfgang Schluchter has attempted to "reconstruct Max Weber's analysis of modernity on the basis of his sociology of religion."[98] But if such a reconstruction is possible, it surely would not be "Max Weber's" theory of modernity, or at least not his only one. Yet Schluchter is certainly right to imply that every theory of modernity depends on the conception of the premodern society from which it is supposed to have emerged, and on the specific nature of this transition as well. Could it be that Weber's reductionist portrait of traditional life, and of the charismatic domination that periodically punctuates it, has set the stage for things to come?

Chapter Five

LEGAL-RATIONAL DOMINATION AND THE UTILITARIAN STRUCTURE OF MODERN LIFE

In contrast to traditionalist power, the legal-rational authority that characterizes modernity is, according to Weber, impersonal, legitimated not by custom but by law. Yet Weber also stresses that while custom is "received," law is "enacted," and if one considers Weber's comparative historical studies from a certain perspective, the concept of enactment implies that the impersonality of modernity is built upon individual responsibility and voluntarism: the demagogic activism of the Israeli prophets whose ethical commitment fired them to strengthen individual responsibility vis-à-vis political authority;[1†] the commitment to religiously informed legal "rights" that sustained the sequence of bourgeois urban rebellions in the Western city; the self-motivating qualities of Puritanism that allowed the Western bourgeoisie to overthrow the bonds of traditional economic authority; and the broad sense of individual rights that developed slowly through the course of Western civilization which combined with notions of "feudal right" to support the antitraditionalist forces of decentralization in the early modern period.[2] In all of these instances, men *enacted* their own rules in order to rise above the received exigencies established by the traditional authority of their time. Such enactment depended upon their reference to internal normative components, elements which, by definition, were differentiated from these external political exigencies and could, therefore, be related to a higher, transcendent authority.

I do not wish to gainsay in any way these elements in Weber's writing. Theoretically, they reflect the multidimensional strand in his work, the strand that constitutes his most important contribution to modern social thought. Ideologically and empirically, they present the optimistic side of his German liberalism, his sympathy for the Burckhardtian notion that individual emancipation is, indeed, the path of history, that material considerations need not necessarily deny spiritual ones, that men do have a certain freedom to determine the course of their existence. These are the commitments that the most important liberal interpreters of Weber have naturally wished to uphold—Parsons and Bendix in the Anglo-American scholarship, Tenbruck and Schluchter in the more recent German work[3†]—and there are, in fact, some indications in Weber's writing of continuity between the multidimensional history and the rational-legal tenor of modern times. The challenge of conserving individual responsibility certainly set the ideological framework for Weber's analyses of the value of individual leadership and parliamentary politics over bureaucracy; it was, similarly, the attempt to define the issue of moral responsibility—not the flight from it—that informed his distinction between fact and value in his methodology essays.[4†]

In some of his general sketches of modern societies, Weber indicates that social support for such continued critical activism may still exist. In his article on "Church and Sect in North America," for example, he argued that in the Anglo-Saxon world the "tradition of voluntary associations" continued, that it was wrong to see a society like America merely as a "human mass pulverized into atoms." Weber linked this continuing voluntarism, moreover, to the historical influence of Puritan religion: voluntary associations had an "inner character" that was "governed by the ancient 'sect spirit.' "[5†] By far the most famous argument, of course, for the continuity of active internal commitment in modern society is Weber's insistence on "vocation" in the speeches he first gave in 1917. Effective politicians, he argued in one speech, can have an "ethic of responsibility," where the "passionate devotion to a cause" is balanced by a sense of proportion about competing worldly interests, a perspective that makes the all-too-frequent self-serving vanity and fanaticism of political life less likely. The "lofty spirit of this vocation," Weber insists to his student audience, can give "inner strength" to political acts.[6] This continuity with the multidimensional history of religious rationalization is also clear in his famous speech on science. Science can be truly pursued, Weber argues, only if it becomes an "inward calling," a "passionate devotion" upon which the very "fate of his [the scientist's] soul" depends.[7] Only through such a strong internal commitment to the universalistic abstraction of science, Weber writes, can control over the objective world be attained, control in either a technological or a more political sense. The scientific, abstract way of thinking allows clarity about moral issues and provides a basis for critical skepticism toward the claims of worldly powers.[8] If it is a true vocation, therefore, science, like politics, can fulfill a "sense of responsibility," and a teacher who can communicate such an ethic to his students "stands in the service of 'moral' forces."[9] The vocational man in these public speeches, the *Berufsmensch*, is surely the secular representative of the active Puritan, the man who enacts law rather than the traditionalistic, passive recipient of fate.[10†] He weighs means and ends in a purposive and self-conscious fashion, but he never loses sight, all the while, of his overriding commitment to certain values. Such an actor performs in a *zweckrational* way, but this is *Zweckrationalität* in its pragmatic and still end-related rather than reductionist sense.

There are passages, even in his concrete institutional analyses, where Weber indicates that vocational rationality still exists. The most conspicuous instance occurs in the series of articles he wrote defending academic freedom in the German universities. Weber rooted such freedom, to the degree that it existed at all, in the professoriat's deeply felt sense of vocation, an internal commitment that he linked to patterns of normative order. The "proud tradition of academic solidarity," Weber wrote, gave to the faculties a "moral authority" that allowed them "independence vis-à-vis the higher [political] authorities."[11] In this struggle against institutional hierarchy, the faculty drew on the "moral credit" they had established with public opinion and with their students. They could continue to do so, however, only if they successfully maintained the "cultural consensus" within their ranks.[12] Even in Weber's more explicitly scientific work, there are implications that such a continuity can exist. In "Class, Status, and Party," for example, he insists that political parties can challenge economic interests in the name of the greater good, and that status ideals may create cross-cutting communities that discipline economic and political interests.[13] Even the formality of modern law can, on certain occasions, provide leverage for subordinate groups to gain substantive justice against their oppressors.[14†]

These are the most valuable kernels of Weber's analysis of contemporary society. They must be preserved, and their relevance to his multidimensional history of substantive rationality must be further elaborated.[15†] It is wrong, however, wishfully to proceed as if such fragments actually characterized the general scope of Weber's sociology of modern life. Those who do so, with even the best of intentions, are reading Weber in a particular polemical way, changing not only his presuppositional assumptions but his ideological evaluations and empirical observations as well. The truth is that we find in Weber's writing precious little continuity between the multidimensional history and the theory of modernity. Between the heroic voluntarism of Puritans and revolutionary citizens and the routine of contemporary life there is, for Weber, a radical disjuncture. In most of his broad characterizations of modern society, rationality has lost its normative and voluntary quality, order its internal reference to complexes of meaning. It is external not internal interest, Weber asserts, that determines the course of modern life. The passage which concludes *The Protestant Ethic and the Spirit of Capitalism* is famous, but few liberal interpreters have really been able to accept its meaning. "The Puritan wanted to work in a calling," Weber writes, while "we are forced to do so." There has been a historical movement from voluntarism to determinism. Voluntarism has been eliminated because "this order is now bound to the technical and economic conditions of machine production which today determine the lives of all the individuals who are born into this mechanism, not only those directly concerned with economic acquisition, with irresistible force."[16†]

Although Weber still rejects most of Marx's propositions, he has accepted Marx's understanding of the alienating, instrumental quality of action in the industrialized world.[17†] There is, he agrees, the "domination of things over men,"[18] and he prophesies that "we are involved in a development toward a world populated only by . . . order addicts [*Ordnungsmenchen*]."[19†] One difference from Marx is that this order comes from political, not just economic hierarchy. It is, for example, disciplined obedience that characterizes the operation of modern bureaucracy. "Rational *discipline*," Weber writes, is virtually "irresistible."[20] Rationalization, even if once a multidimensional process, is now a process of reification, not individuation. It strengthens the forces outside the actor, diminishing him in turn: "The content of discipline is nothing but the consistently rationalized, methodically prepared and exact execution of the received order, in which all [of one's own] criticism is unconditionally suspended and the actor is unswervingly and exclusively set for carrying out the command."[21] Order is received, not enacted; the actor is passive, not critical. Weber's model for this order is mechanical, rather than human. "The final consequences," he writes, "are drawn from the mechanization and discipline of the plant":

> The psycho-physical apparatus of man is completely adjusted to the demands of the outer world. . . . This whole process of rationalization, in the factory as elsewhere, and especially in the bureaucratic state machine, parallels the centralization of the material implements of organization in the hands of the master [*Herr*].[22†]

The logic of Weber's political sociology, focusing on the analysis of *Herrschaft*, or domination, carries directly into the sociology of contemporary economic and political life. For the most part, it is the simple struggle for coercive control, without ethical reference, that defines the contemporary political world. Power is merely "the chance of a man or of a number of men to realize their own will in a communal action even against the resistance of others."[23] The principal political vehicle of modern society, the political party, is presented as instrumental and quasi-military.

> Parties reside in a sphere of "power." Their action is oriented to-
> ward the acquisition of social power, that is to say, toward in-
> fluencing a social action no matter what its content may be.[24]

The cultural content of party action is unimportant, the "end" simply a "means" writ large. The leaders' ideas make no particular difference, for in any case they are without vocation. Because a party "always struggles for domination," its "leaders normally deal with conquest" alone.[25]

Status itself, though defined as an autonomous empirical sphere, is subject to the same presuppositional reduction. Consistently cut off from any reference to broader cultural meanings which would imply community, it is portrayed in an instrumentalized form as simply another means in the struggle for the appropriation of valued resources. Finally, Weber's discussion of the actual source of legal-rational legitimation— namely, rationally enacted law—is itself separated entirely from normative order and control. Whereas in the multidimensional description of precapitalist development Weber linked the development of law to qualities of self-activation, in his analysis of modern society law is dissociated from internal motivation and reduced to a technical means for ordering the calculation of group interest.

Why did Weber formulate modernity in such an abruptly discontinuous fashion? Weber himself, not surprisingly, has a purely empirical explanation for this rupture with his multidimensional account of Western history: although internal motivations were necessary for the initial break with tradition to occur, they were simply no longer needed once the imposing economic and political structures of modern capitalism had actually been constructed. After this point, Weber asserts, the pressures on the individual actor from these external sources were more than sufficient to motivate action. This is certainly his point in the final pages of *The Protestant Ethic and the Spirit of Capitalism*, and in a later essay he restates it even more directly. "On the whole," Weber insists, "the course of observable historical development does not clearly indicate a 'substitution' of consensual action by association so much as an ever wider-ranging instrumentally-rational [*zweckrational*] ordering of consensual action by means of statute and, especially, an increasing incidence of transformation of organizations into institutions organized on an instrumentally-rational [*zweckrational*] basis."[26]

The relative strength and weakness of this assertion in strictly empirical terms is not our concern here. As to the enormous instrumentalizing pressures in the transition to modernity and industrialization there can be no doubt, and if a theorist cannot systematically incorporate these pressures, as Durkheim could not, he has opened his empirical account to grave weakness. But to argue that instrumentalizing tendencies on an empirical and historical level must call out instrumentalist assumptions on the theoretical is to conflate levels of analysis which must be independent. In was, in fact, the major thrust of Weber's multidimensional work to demonstrate exactly this point, namely, that even instrumental rationality can have nothing other than a multidimensional base.

A long tradition of Weber interpretation—from Lukács and Löwith to Gerth, Mills, and Habermas—argues that Weber's instrumental modernity theory is justified on such empirical grounds. Yet there are polemical theoretical motives hidden beneath such claims, and each author, indeed, would argue that in most important respects the whole of Weber's contributions converge with Marx. Thus, while these instrumentalist readers may see Weber's modernity theory more clearly than his liberal readers, they just as drastically reduce Weberian theory to one of its parts. No matter what the empirical tendencies, therefore, I must insist that "facts" cannot supply the true reasons for the abrupt transition Weber describes. Beyond this purely theoretical argument, of course, the equivocation and ambivalence in Weber's own work stands as further evidence.

The seemingly empirical break in Weber's account of historical development conforms, in fact, to the presuppositional logic we have discovered in his accounts of earlier times. The shift toward instrumental action and external coercive order reflects the very same movement from multidimensionality to utilitarian reduction that underlies much of his historical and political sociology. Weber's vision of modern life can, indeed, amply be accounted for by viewing it as an application of the theoretical logic of his political sociology to the study of contemporary life. The normative aspects of modern rationality have been cast aside because that is precisely the fate of "legitimacy" in the political sociology. The coercive character of modern institutions has been stressed because, after all, the external focus of Weber's sociology of domination makes the issue of motivation unproblematic. If legitimacy functions merely to establish a particular framework for the exercise of *Herrschaft*, to designate the principal actors in different types of struggles for power, then it is perfectly appropriate that "rational-legal enactment" would be analyzed not as a belief motivating actors in the principled opposition to power but as a form of domination through which that power is exercised.

Of course, Weber still had a choice. We may assert that there is clear theoretical precedent for his instrumental turn, that he had clear and abundant theoretical resources upon which to draw, but this still does not explain why he necessarily applied these resources to his study of modern life. Instrumentalism could have been confined to premodern society; for his analysis of modernity Weber could have drawn, instead, on the multidimensional strand of his historical work. He did not choose to do so. Before we can further examine his reasons, we must explore much more thoroughly what this decision involved.

In Weber's view, the particular struggle for domination that marks the rational-legal structure of modern life has two sides. On the one side, there is the enforcement of rules by those legally empowered to establish them, which essentially comprises the domain of modern bureaucracy. On the other, there is the struggle over who will actually have such legal power to enact law, which Weber describes as the nonbureaucratic struggle for political control over the bureaucracy—the conflict over the "nonbureaucratic top"—that occurs in the contest for parliamentary office and in the conflict between parliament and governmental bureaucracy. After considering bureaucracy and politics, we will turn to the actual legal framework upon which both rely and to the stratification system that establishes the resources which limit their struggle.

1. BUREAUCRACY: THE IMPERSONAL FORM OF HIERARCHICAL CONTROL

It is possible, of course, to consider Weber's historic essay on bureaucracy from the perspective of the overall pattern of normative legitimation that such an organization of power demonstrates, the alternative to arbitrary collective control that it offers in contrast to the patrimonial system. Most contemporary Weber scholars have done so.[27†] But while such a reading certainly gives one important empirical reference of Weber's essay, it fails to come to grips with the real structure of theoretical argument that Weber presents. There are, indeed, occasional references in the opening pages to the "rights" of bureaucratic officials vis-à-vis hierarchical control,[28] an emphasis that would be an important part of any conceptualization of bureaucracy's normative legitimation and that would link it to the Puritan complex of "vocation" and the application of generalized, abstract rules. But after these first notations, Weber's famous essay on bureaucracy follows the same kind of "declension" as his writings on legitimacy. Rather than the motivational character and broad cultural moorings of this political structure, the central thrust of the essay concerns the issue of the *enforcement* of these rules through hierarchical control. Its first and most famous section, "Characteristics of Bureaucracy," is actually a detailed description of the particular objective arrangements through which this type of bureaucratic authority is able to exercise domination: through "channels of appeal," "jurisdictional 'competency,' " "a staff of subaltern officials and scribes," "segregation of official activity," and "thorough training in a field of specialization."[29] It is true that Weber considers generalized rules as an absolute prerequisite for such organizational arrangements to exist, but the focus of his attention is, quite clearly, on the structure of domination that is the result, not the nature of legitimation which facilitates it.[30†]

In fact, immediately after his elaboration of these details of hierarchical control, Weber explicitly defines the concept of "vocation" in a completely rational-intrinsic manner. He links it to the instrumental constraints of his political sociology of patrimonialism, not to the normative training of his multidimensional analysis. "The office is a 'vocation,' " he writes, first because it "is not considered a source of income property to be exploited for rents or emoluments,"[31] a situation which would, of course, be objectively impossible given modern conditions where political centralization has won the day and economic concentration has become a fact of life. "Nor," Weber continues, "is office holding considered a common exchange of services," but rather it is considered "an acceptance of a specific duty of fealty to the purpose of the office."[32]

Within a framework as instrumental as that of Marx, Weber is specifying his own, non-Marxist propositions about political life. Participation in bureaucracy is not compelled by economic interest: rather, it is responsive directly to political domination that is equally external and compelling. Finally, in what amounts to a direct confrontation with the notion that bureaucratic vocation is informed by the cultural definition of duty, Weber asserts that "modern loyalty" is purely a functional matter,[33] determined, that is, solely by the external exigencies of organization. Although he acknowledges that "these functional purposes, of course, frequently gain an ideological halo from cultural values," the reflected quality of this normative pattern is clearly emphasized; in any case, the "halo" is no more than a "surrogate" for a "personal master."[34] Marx, of course, rarely discussed the independence of bureaucracy; his model of capitalism was too monolithic to allow him to do so. Yet in terms of its general logic, Weber's discussion of this complicating form of hierarchy differs little from Marx. The normative referent of bureaucracy assumes for him an epiphenomenal form.[35†]

This Hobbesian structure is confirmed by the latter part of Weber's argument, the historical discussion of the origins of bureaucratic organization that constitutes, in terms of length, the greater part of the essay. While it was in the multidimensional aspects of his *Religion of China* that Weber effectively described the normative requirements for effective bureaucratic rationality, the historical analysis in the bureaucracy essay reproduces only the instrumental strand of that argument. As determinants of rational-bureaucratic domination Weber cites only the conditional developments which were at the center of his political history: the external situation must be structured so that bureaucratic rationality becomes the only efficient, and therefore the only probable, path.

Weber's first and most extensive discussion concerns the development of the money economy. Provision of official income either in kind or by sporadic taxation leads to a financial decentralization that undermines the possibility for direct hierarchical control over official action, for it throws the instrumental and self-interested actor back on the resources of local power: "All kinds of assignments of services and usufructs in kind as endowments for officials tend to loosen the bureaucratic mechanism, and especially to weaken hierarchic subordination."[36] Governments without a full money economy have, in fact, often been led to employ physical force or actual enslavement to approximate the unconditional obedience and passivity that Western bureaucracy has been able to achieve in a more individualistic and civil way. Still, Weber insists that in the West an official "subordinate[s] himself to his superior without any will of his own."[37] "A precision similar to . . . that of the contractually employed official of the modern Occident can only be attained—under very energetic leadership—where the subjection of the officials to the lord is personally absolute, i.e., where slaves or employees treated like slaves are used for administration. . . . Similar results have been sought by the prodigious use of the bamboo as a disciplinary instrument."[38] Bureaucracy is as enslaving as any violent force, but it works in Weber's view more like an efficient machine than a dictator, and it demands a similarly steady supply of material resources: "According to experience, the relative optimum for the success and maintenance of a rigorous mechanization of the bureaucratic apparatus is offered by an assured salary connected with the opportunity of a career that is not dependent upon mere accident and arbitrariness."[39]

Weber follows this analysis of economic underpinnings with a discussion of the causal influence of another factor in the bureaucratic actor's external environment, namely, the quantitative development of administrative tasks.[40] The most important of these, he asserts, are the demands for efficiency presented by the "capitalist market economy," which "demands that the official business of public administration be discharged precisely, unambiguously, continuously, and with as much speed as possible."[41] Weber refers also to qualitative changes of administrative tasks that created demands for increased efficiency, for example, the emergence of such national tasks as provision for a standing army, for public order, and for citizens' protection by police.[42] Appropriately, he concludes this historical analysis by constructing an empirical analogy that makes his presuppositional parallel to Marx eminently clear. To Marx's utilitarian proposition that power is based solely on the monopolization of the technical means of action, Weber adds the proposition that "technical" means can be extended to political as well as economic resources. "The bureaucratic structure goes hand in hand," he writes, "with the concentration of the material means of management in the hands of the master [Herr]."[43] Weber simply applies here his reductionist analysis of traditional domination—where the locus of military support was a major determinant—to the more specific case of modern bureaucracy.[44†]

The relatively few sociologists who have been sensitive to the debilitating instrumentalism and coercive thrust of Weber's bureaucracy theory have traced these problems to more specific levels of his argument: to an empirical misjudgment based on observation of the Prussian case alone, to an ideological commitment which made him partial to certain kinds of authoritarian controls, to a functionalist model that made him unable to understand informal relations and the "whole person."[45†] Each of these criticisms has some validity, but each ignores what seems to me the most general and ramifying source of the problem. Weber's presuppositions prevented him from articulating a more voluntaristic conception of bureaucracy even if he wanted to do so for ideological reasons (which, indeed, he wanted to do), even if he had observed other kinds of bureaucratic behavior (which, in fact, he had), and, finally, even if he did not have an equilibrium model of social life (which, indeed, he did not). Because Weber assumed instrumental motivation within the bureaucratic structure, action became unproblematic and of little theoretical concern. But without a focus on motivation, there is no possibility for rooting bureaucratic life in the voluntaristic acquiescence of its members, or for explaining resistance to bureaucracy at all.[46†]

2. DEMOCRACY: THE INCLUSION OF THE PERSONAL STRUGGLE FOR POWER

Weber's major discussion of democracy in the period of legal-rational legitimation occurs in the essay "Parliament and Government in a Reconstructed Germany," which follows the framework established in the analysis of bureaucratic life. The essay does, it is true, concern itself with the establishment of the ends of modern political action, that is, with the "nonbureaucratic top" of modern organization. Yet it relates these ends not to any normative elements, such as ethical systems and secular ideologies, but exclusively to the same kind of external conditional exigencies that were held to establish the bureaucratic "means." Such a reduction of ends to the status of means denies the very possibility for voluntarism that it was the purpose of this major essay on democracy to establish. This presuppositional failure explains the paradox that haunts Weber's democratic theory. Personally committed to democratic ends and the liberalization of the German state, Weber produced a political theory in which the value-oriented rationality of democratic behavior, its commitment to universalistic ethics and the rights of the individual, has very little empirical role.

The central point of Weber's essay is that parliamentary democracy introduces a voluntary element into the exercise of modern political authority. This position is indicated at the very outset by his description of Germany's plight without such democratic political forms; he castigates Germany as "a nation without any political will of its own," "a nation accustomed to fatalistic sufferance of all decisions" which had been led by a man, Bismarck, who never "suffered independent political minds."[47] We must understand, however, that the voluntarism Weber aspires to is directed merely to the achievement of more alacrity and efficiency in the struggles of political life: it is not voluntarism imbued by commitment to a normative, universalistic ideal. Weber's analysis of the democratic aspect of "enactment" emphasizes the role of legitimacy no more than does his analysis of the bureaucratic. Democracy, for him, is simply a different, more productive framework for the instrumental struggle for power, one that produces better results in the Darwinian "selection" process that he has previously defined as the substance of the struggle for political domination.

Weber's major concern is not substantive justice per se, but the quality of domination in modern rational-legal society. The problem is created by the omnipresence of bureaucratic leadership. "In view of the growing indispensability of the state bureaucracy and its corresponding increase in power," he asks, "how can there be any guarantee that powers will remain which can check and effectively control the tremendous influence of this stratum?"[48] The trouble with bureaucrats is that they are ineffective leaders, for bureaucracy does not offer the proper external conditions—the wide scope for individual initiative, the strong individual rewards—for "selecting out" the best qualified political leaders. "Why in the world," Weber asks, "should men with leadership qualities be attracted by a party which at best can change a few budget items in accordance with the voters' interests and provide a few minor benefices to the protégés of its bigshots? What opportunities can it offer to potential leaders?"[49]

For the individual politician, greater opportunities are matched by greater risks, and power, not money, is the true reward which makes such risks worthwhile. Only if the politician can calculate that risks may pay off will he invest his energy in opportunities: "For the modern politician the proper palaestra is the parliament and the party contests before the general public; neither competition for bureaucratic advancement nor anything else will provide an adequate substitute."[50] It is essential, therefore, to break away from the monopolization of politics by bureaucracy, for "only democracy can attract men of high caliber." But what, precisely, does Weber mean by "caliber"? He means the strength to pursue the Hobbesian struggle for power that is at the heart of modern politics. "For the tasks of national leadership," he writes, "only such men are prepared who have been selected in the course of the political struggle, since the essence of all politics is struggle."[51] Democratic competition for individual rewards is, quite simply, a more effective kind of selective device than bureaucracy. "It simply happens to be a fact that such preparation is, on the average, accomplished better by the much-maligned 'craft of demagoguery' than by the clerk's office."[52]

Even more important than the personal qualities of leaders, there is the relative responsibility produced by the institutional setting itself. Impersonal, bureaucratic leadership fails the nation because it does not provide a locus of responsibility for public decisions. Once again, it is absolutely essential to see that the "responsibility" about which Weber is writing is not the type of action produced by reference to a particular type of value system. He does not have in mind here the political responsibility of the Jewish prophets, which he discussed at such great length in *Ancient Judaism* as an internal commitment induced by prophetic invocation of the Israelis' transcendental religious belief in an ethical god.[53†] Nor does he envision here the secularization of this religious vocation that he described in his famous political speech as the "ethic of responsibility." As we will see shortly, the institutional basis for such an ethic is completely lacking from Weber's political theory. Rather, Weber's discussion of political responsibility in the present context has solely to do with the institutional locus of what is taken for granted as the typical and purely instrumental motivation of politicians. He is concerned, quite simply, with whether the "power to enact" is vested in the organization or in the individual. Only if the struggle for political power is a personal one, Weber believes, can the accountability of the leader to his followers be assured, because only in this case does the instrumental self-interest in office depend directly on meeting the needs of the public at large.

Once again, Weber has described a system of external sanctions and inducements that orders individual interest with predictable results. In this case, the results have an ethical value, but Weber's understanding of the system which produces this value is instrumental all the same. Only parliamentary democracy can institutionalize the personal struggle that makes governmental power responsive to the power of the masses. "This struggle for personal power and the resulting personal responsibility," Weber writes, "is the lifeblood of the politician."[54] It is for this reason that Weber spends a major section of his essay evaluating the details of the structural arrangements which, within the general parliamentary framework, best facilitate individual as opposed to bureaucratic control—the significance, for example, of mandating parliamentary review of the decisions made by the foreign policy bureaucracies.[55†]

Weber, then, maintains that modern political democracy operates successfully on purely utilitarian grounds. And it should be noted that this approach is not inconsistent with his better-known contention that parliamentary democracy reintroduces charismatic authority into mod-

ern life. As I have argued above, Weber's analysis of charismatic authority itself devolves not upon the relation between power, psyche, and
cultural values, but on the consequences of the very same kind of un-
structured personal power that is his focus in the parliamentary essay.
Power can be collectively or individually sought. The costs in terms of
systemic instability—given the self-interest of the leader's retinue—make
individual power difficult to sustain. This was the conclusion of Weber's
analysis of charismatic authority. Here, however, he argues that the cost
of the collective bureaucratization of leadership—the direction in which
the routinization of charisma inevitably leads—is equally intolerable.
For the personal interest of talented individuals, but more importantly
for the interests of the masses of people and the society itself, bureaucratic leadership must be limited by an efficient parliamentary order. In
the first—charismatic—instance, the instrumental analysis is conducted
purely in terms of likely empirical events. In the second—democratic—
case, Weber has postulated the instrumental requisites for democratiz-
ing processes which he concedes are less likely to happen, at least in the
German case. In either instance, however, the presuppositions of his political sociology are much the same.[56†]

Ironically, Weber himself sets up a contrast that serves to point up
the reductionist quality of this analysis of democratic process. Implicitly
on several occasions and on one occasion explicitly, he indicates in this
essay that the greater "responsibility" by which he has differentiated
democratic from bureaucratic authority must in fact be linked to an internal ethical conviction. Whereas "the civil servant must sacrifice his
convictions to the demands of obedience," activism is sustained because
"the politician must publicly reject the responsibility for political actions
that run counter to his convictions and must sacrifice his office to
them."[57] Yet nowhere in this entire essay does Weber discuss the complexes of meaning which might underlie such convictions and, thereby,
supply the foundations for such voluntary resistance, nor does he refer
in any way to such ethical convictions in his one explicit discussion of
parliamentary politics as a "vocation."[58†] To be sure, in the famous public speech "Politics as a Vocation" Weber insists that such ethical convictions are possible, and he demonstrates that he personally believes in
their necessity. Yet if his ideological commitment remains firm, it does
not necessarily inform his presuppositional or empirical work, contrary
to what most of his conscientious liberal interpreters would have us believe. An "ethic of responsibility" is ideal, but in practice Weber views it
as unlikely that the typical political actor would adopt it. Most political
action, he concedes even in that important public speech, occurs without
any sustained reference to normative concerns. If this empirical observation is partly in tension with his ideological evaluation of the good, his
presuppositional framework is even more so. Within the instrumentalist

framework of his political thought, Weber simply cannot explain the sociological structures that would produce modern ethical conviction.

It is ironic that Weber writes at different points in *Economy and Society* about the nation as a "community of sentiment" and about the "feeling of solidarity" that holds it together.[59] His informal political writings are, moreover, punctuated by references to the *Kultur* that every great nation-state must uphold.[60] In themselves, such understandings would certainly militate against any unequivocally instrumental reading of the politician's duty, for it would seem that the political leaders of such nations would be supported only if they referred to and articulated these subjective links. Yet these references are isolated ones. Indeed, if we are to understand Weber's political sociology of contemporary life correctly, we must see that he has supplied for his theory of instrumental responsibility a history of political development that reads subjective convictions like "honor" out of existence. In the early formation of nation-states, princely leaders and aristocrats of great individual wealth pursued politics honorifically, their financial independence allowing them to engage in politics for the sake of the cause itself.[61] Eventually, however, this form of independent political action either became bureaucratized—in which case the aristocrat joined with state officials to work against parliamentarism and the middle class—or democratized, in which case the institution of the political party gained sway over monarchical privilege.[62] In the latter, the more democratic alternative toward which every large nation was forced eventually to turn, a large and inclusive "public" was formed. Yet this new electoral mass, Weber maintains, was actually itself dominated by organizational exigencies: by the political party. For how else, he asks, could it be made politically effective? This political organization, in turn, became constantly preoccupied with the need for operating funds. As functionaries of large-scale political organizations rather than men of independent wealth, political actors now could only live "off" politics, not "for" it.

As late as the nineteenth century, however, democratic politics, at least in England, remained largely aristocratic. The democratic clubs continued to be led by men of independent wealth, local notables for whom political life remained an honorific avocation rather than a business.[63] In the course of the nineteenth century, though, the underlying exigencies of modern political life eventually triumphed. Honorary notables gave way to political managers. The pressures were objective, and the motives for reform efficient and instrumental.

> The occasion for this development was the democratization of the franchise. In order to win the masses it became necessary to call into being a tremendous apparatus of apparently democratic associations. An electoral association had to be formed in

> every city district to help keep the organization incessantly in
> motion and to bureaucratize everything rigidly.[64]

From a dedication to the cause itself, politics turns into a governance by
"machines," political organs led by professionals outside parliaments
who, because of the "necessity to woo and organize the masses," develop
"the utmost unity of direction and the strictest discipline."[65] The leaders
of the machine live "off" politics in an instrumental way. "The boss has
no firm political 'principles,'" Weber asserts; "he is completely unprincipled in attitude and asks merely: What will capture votes?"[66] His followers usually are motivated by similarly instrumental reasons.

> The party following, above all the party official and party en-
> trepreneur, naturally expect personal compensation from the
> victory of their leader—that is, offices or other advantages. They
> expect that the demogogic effect of the leader's *personality* dur-
> ing the election fight of the party will increase votes and man-
> dates and thereby power, and, thereby, as far as possible, will
> extend opportunities to their followers to find the compensation
> for which they hope.[67]

Although Weber does mention charisma in a less instrumental way, the
general thrust of this more rationalized treatment is unmistakable.[68]
Even the most divergent political parties are similarly "unprincipled,"
their mutual opposition stimulated simply by the scarce supply of material rewards: "They are purely organizations of job hunters drafting
their changing platforms according to the chances of vote-grabbing."[69]
This last statement refers to the United States, but the observations are
intended to be universal. Like Marx in *The Communist Manifesto*, Weber
has supplied an empirical history of Western development that justifies
his theoretical commitments to an antinormative position.

The upshot of Weber's speech on politics, then, is hardly that a normative order exists from which political actors formulate guiding ethics,
ethics of either "conviction" or "responsibility." The choice he portrays,
rather, is between a leaderless nation, governed by bureaucrats or misled
by fanatics, and a machine-dominated democracy led by demagogues
who nonetheless are more responsible leaders in an objective sense. The
focus of his essay "Parliament and Democracy in a Reconstructed Germany" is precisely on the conditions that can produce this latter, more
responsible situation. The explicit and self-conscious focus of this systematic analysis of democracy, in other words, lies exclusively with the
issue of its external integuments. Though formally free, mass democracy
for Weber is really the dictatorship of the masses by the leaders of the
machine, a "plebiscitarian" situation in which irresponsible ambition
and purely personal will hide "behind a legitimacy that is *formally* de-

rived from the will of the governed."[70] In part this was an empirical judgment. As Weber wrote to his friend and student Robert Michels, "Such concepts as 'will of the people,' genuine will of the people, have long since ceased to exist for me; they are fictitious."[71] In part, it was ideological. Weber, motivated by a residue of mandarin unease with popular action, might have agreed with Meinecke's conservative assertion that effective leadership could be obtained only by the "temporary dictatorship of trust."[72] Yet Weber had certainly observed empirical cases to the contrary, and even if he suffered a mandarin unease this can in no way be taken as ideological approval.[73†] Weber was enormously contemptuous of the passivity and instrumentalism of the plebiscitarian democracy he described as inevitable. Given his presuppositional commitments, however, he could articulate no alternative. The instrumentality of his modern political actors makes them passive vis-à-vis external power and purely expedient in their response to the advantages for exploitation it presents.[74†] Even democratic politics, it seems, is fit only to deal with the means of human action, not the ends. Weber's analysis of democracy has sustained the utilitarian framework of his political sociology.

3. LAW: THE EXTERNAL REFERENCE OF FORMALIZED NORMS

Weber has described modern legal-rational society as a clash of interested individuals and groups, defining "rational interest" in the purely utilitarian sense of that term. Once again, his political sociology has emphasized domination, not legitimation, in the operation of political power. The fact remains, however, that Weber did write extensively on at least one normative element in political life—the law—and he claimed for this element a range of influence in the same modern period which I have described in sections 1 and 2 as a model of instrumental action. It is for this reason crucial to understand the particular structure of Weber's historical sociology of law. For although the normative character of modern law is formally maintained, its social function is considered by Weber to be perfectly consistent with a Hobbesian perspective on the structure of modern life.

The transformation of this normative element is effected in the following manner. In the course of Weber's monograph on law, which is basically chronological,[75] the meaning of "enactment" actually shifts from a multidimensional to a more instrumental understanding. The voluntary aspect of the legal structure evolved gradually in the pores of traditional society, and it was reflected in two facets of legal development. First, on the individual level, Weber emphasizes legal "rights" as providing a certain degree of freedom vis-à-vis externally binding conditions.

"Every right," he argues, "is thus a source of power of which even a hitherto entirely powerless person may become possessed." Such rights allow "an individual autonomy to regulate his relations with others by his own transactions."[76] In historical terms, Weber links this internal voluntary element to the impact of religious values, particularly to the kind of religious abstraction in Christian formulations: "The true concept of endowment [i.e., the creation of rights] both in its substantive and technical aspects was almost everywhere developed under religious influences."[77] Second, on the institutional level, the early voluntaristic implications of law were reflected, according to Weber, in the flexibility of lawmakers vis-à-vis received legal, or quasi-legal, formulations. Weber similarly associated this element of flexibility with the influence that normative cultural complexes could bring to bear on the law. He describes "charismatic revelation," for example, as "the parent of all types of legal enactment."[78] Charisma is here a specification of religious inspiration, and it allows an internal reference that differentiates legal actors from deterministic objective constraint.

> The new norms found their source in the inspiration or impulses, either actual or apparent, of the charismatically qualified person and without being in any way required by new external conditions.... The men who normally used these primitive methods of adapting old rules to new situations were the magicians, the prophets, or the priests of an oracular deity.[79]

Weber contends, however, that in the course of the historical development that brought modern capitalism to the Western world, the voluntaristic character of these two prototypical legal phenomena was reversed.[80†] Once again, theoretical logic is presented as echoing historical rupture. In Weber's view, modern capitalism has reduced rights from an end to a means, and the modern legal order is simply one more instrument manipulated in the pursuit of interest. Contract, the prototypical expression of individual right, is reduced to a vehicle for exchange in a utilitarian sense, and becomes merely one more contribution to the formal order of domination that structures modern life. "The result of contractual freedom, then," Weber writes, "is in the first place the opening of the opportunity to use, by the clever utilization of property ownership in the market, these resources without legal restraints as a means for the achievement of power over others." In fact, the link between legal and economic interest, another form of *zweckrational* order, is quite direct: "The Parties interested in power in the market thus are also interested in such a legal order."[81]

Although the normative status of legal rights cannot itself be altered, Weber insists that these are norms which no longer function as independent mediation vis-à-vis external power. "They are accessible only to the owners of property," Weber writes, "and thus in effect support their very autonomy and power positions."[82] In fact, for all practical purposes, the contribution of this normative legal element is to increase the role of the external coercive element in action. "A legal order which offers and guarantees . . . ever so many 'freedoms' and 'empowerments,' " Weber writes, "can nonetheless in its practical effects facilitate quantitative and qualitative increase not only of coercion in general but quite specifically of authoritarian coercion."[83] True, these last quotations refer to the rights of actors in the economic marketplace, but that is precisely the point: Weber's analysis of rights in modern society has virtually no other referent. With certain exceptions to be noted below, law functions either as means or as condition vis-à-vis economic demands. In neither case does it provide the basis for "enactment" in a voluntary, critical manner.

The same kind of inversion from early normative to contemporary instrumental occurs, according to Weber, on the institutional level of legal action. Lawmakers no longer have any freedom vis-à-vis received formulations, for such voluntarism would create an element of chance for the very economic and political groups whose interest has converted modern legal action into instrumental calculation. Weber's emphasis on the lack of autonomy in the modern legal apparatus is so great, in fact, that he acknowledges certain crucial similarities between the modern judge and a nonhuman cog in a machine. "The conception of the modern judge as an automaton into which legal documents and fees are stuffed at the top in order that it may spill forth the verdict at the bottom along with the reasons, read mechanically from codified paragraphs"—this conception, Weber writes, while "angrily rejected" by those who "glorify the 'creative' discretion of the official," is not an unfair "approximation" of the "type [that] is implied by a consistent bureaucratization of justice."[84†] In society as a whole, the modern judge is reduced to the status of a "means." The implication of such a formulation is that although the judge's rulings still introduce order among competing interests, it is an ordering in which rational orientations to conditions can be assumed and from which, therefore, objective predictions can be made. Though normative in an ontological sense, such legal rules function in an epistemologically instrumental and material way, as a purely external form of collective order. The law's normative impact is achieved more through its enforceability than through any belief in the legitimacy of its normative meaning.[85†]

These two prototypical examples illustrate Weber's belief that under modern conditions the law does not create a normative reference for the society as a whole. According to the imperatives of theoretical logic, this status of means could be achieved only by separating the normative element from any relationship to subjective systems of meaning, for in this way it is open to the exclusive determination of the conditional elements of the situation. This is, indeed, precisely the theoretical function of Weber's conceptualization of modern law as "formally rational," that is, as radically separated from the contrasting type of "substantively rational" law that invokes nonlegal values for its legitimation.[86†] Certainly there is an important empirical difference between these legal orders, for law does seem to become more specialized and autonomous—i.e., more formal in Weber's sense—with historical development. Yet the distinction is also motivated by a vital theoretical interest as well. The independence of modern legal rationality could be accepted, but this abstraction could still be observed as relying for its ultimate vitality on the abstraction and universalism of the cultural order itself. Weber, however, insists this is not the case. Although rational legal thought formally retains normative status, it produces reasoning that approximates the instrumentally *zweckrational* motivation by which Weber has characterized modern political and economic behavior. Thus Weber writes that whereas substantively rational law considers the intentions of actors and relates them to motives and values, formally rational law proceeds only from what is externally observable; it can, in other words, be explained without reference to empathic understanding. More importantly, whereas substantively rational law justifies itself, at least in part, by reference to generalized ethical beliefs, formally rational law is legitimated purely in terms of logical deduction from established precedent.

Weber makes this crucial distinction as sharp as possible by associating substantive rationality exclusively with the natural-law theory of the 18th-century Enlightenment and the 19th-century socialist movement. With the conclusion of these particular historical periods, Weber argues, the law lost its vital connection to meaning and belief. The resulting formalization allowed it to become a mere tool for interest.

> Legal positivism [i.e., purely formal rationality] has, at least for the time being, advanced irresistibly. The disappearance of the old natural law conceptions had destroyed all possibility of providing the law with a metaphysical dignity by virtue of its immanent qualities. In the great majority of its most important provisions, it has been unmasked all too visibly, indeed, as the product or the technical means of a compromise between conflicting interests.[87]

Whereas the connection of natural law to broader cultural beliefs allowed it to maintain an emphasis on the voluntaristic aspect of "rights" and, therefore, on the critical question of the legitimation of power, the formalization of modern legal thought has eliminated this voluntarism and shifted the focus to political domination. "This extinction of the metajuristic anchorings of the law," Weber writes, "also extraordinarily promoted on the whole the actual obedience to the power, now viewed solely from an utilitarian standpoint, of the authorities who claim legitimacy at the moment."[88†]

Weber does not assert the exclusivity of legal formal rationality in a completely unequivocal manner. Just as in his discussion of other spheres of modern life, he presents in the interstices of his argument the ambiguous shadow of a counter analysis. In the final pages of his discussion of modern law, Weber notes the existence of more voluntaristic law-making and more substantively rational legal thought outside of continental Europe, most notably in England and America. He predicts, moreover, that the intrusion of natural law will occur everywhere in modern society during periods in which oppressed groups and classes struggle to assert their economic rights.[89] Yet, as in the other segments of his contemporary analysis, these suggestions stand outside the main thrust of Weber's argument. To be systematically integrated, they would demand the continuous relation of law to broader normative order and would, necessarily, produce a very different understanding of legal relations themselves.

Weber's legal sociology, like each of the other sections of his work, usually has been read with polemical intent, in terms of the presuppositional wishes and orientations of the interpreters themselves. It has been read as fully informed by cultural reference, as totally lacking in references to religion and culture, and, somewhat ambiguously, as in between. These understandings have been rationalized, moreover, by reference to virtually every level of Weber's argument.[90†] There are, indeed, instances in Weber's writings of each of these kinds of sociological reasoning, yet we can understand the source of this ambiguity only if we comprehend the strains in the most general presuppositions that inform Weber's thought. For in Weber's sociology of law we find recapitulated the entirety of his theoretical development. In the historical discussions there are strands of truly multidimensional reasoning and, side by side, passages of dichotomizing logic. In the discussion of contemporary law, this awkward concreteness gives way to full-blown, though still non-Marxist, instrumentalism. The legal relations that set the limits for bureaucratic and political conflict cannot very well depart from the theoretical logic that informs that fateful struggle—nor, in fact, can the stratification that supplies this conflict with its fundamental resources and rewards.

4. STRATIFICATION: THE INSTRUMENTAL COMPETITION FOR GENERALIZED MEANS

In the history of sociological debate over Weber's stratification scheme, important arguments have been made for both its instrumental and its normative focus. The complexity and durability of this debate can be understood only if we see that Weber's theoretical ambivalence has, in fact, allowed both readings to find textual evidence for their a priori positions. When we read this work closely, however, we observe much the same theoretical declension as we have found elsewhere in Weber's works. True, this theoretical movement against nonrational order remains very different from Marx's in any empirical sense. Weber has a more complex model of the social system, and pays more attention to the growth of the middle classes and the fragmentation of the proletariat; he sees the state as an independent arena for contest, and appreciates the role of institutions like education as mediations for mobility.[91] Yet for all of this critical empirical difference, the presuppositions of Weber's theory move back toward Marx's instrumentalism; they depart from the sensitivity to sacred attachments that Durkheim exhibited and from the multidimensionality of other important segments of Weber's work.

In the course of his most important essay in stratification, "Class, Status, Party," Weber identifies three different kinds of ends which individual or collective actors can differentially pursue and which can be distributed unequally in society. These are material goods and the opportunity to earn income,[92] a particular life style or social honor more generally,[93] and political power over the staff that directs the state.[94] On the basis of Weber's own multidimensional treatment of each of these ends in other segments of his work, we can imagine a very rich and complex analysis: economic goods would be related to class groupings and hence to culturally mediated ideologies; honor would be informed by contrasting economic ethics; political power would be mediated by the impact of citizenship and by the norms of the legal order generally; finally, emotional solidarity, exclusive or inclusive, would be a continuous mediating force. On the basis of Weber's differentiation of ends, in other words, we would certainly expect that at every point the struggle for these unequal "goods" would be mediated by an overarching symbolic order.

There are, indeed, certain examples of exactly this approach in Weber's treatment of stratification. In one aside in his major essay, for example, he insists that it is the different attitudes toward authority rooted in American Puritanism and German Lutheranism that inform the different status orders of the two countries. "The 'equality' of status among the American 'gentlemen,' " Weber writes, "is expressed by the fact that outside the subordination determined by the different functions of business, it would be considered strictly repugnant—wherever the old tradition still prevails—if even the richest boss, while playing billiards or cards in his club in the evening, would not treat his clerk as in every sense fully his equal in birth right . . . but would bestow upon his clerk the condescending 'benevolence' marking a distinction of 'position,' which the German boss can never dissever from his attitude."[95] The same understanding of the subjectively mediating force of status informs, in another essay, Weber's conceptualization of the impact of racial groups on society. Race, he insists, "creates a 'group' only when it is subjectively perceived as a common trait: this happens only when . . . some common experiences of members of the same race are linked to some antagonism against members of an *obviously* different group."[96]

But if this were to be the principal theme of Weber's treatment, the differential ends he has identified would have to be conceptualized as subjectively felt goals influencing every choice of means—goals that were, in part, the specification of a broader cultural order. This, however, is not the case. Instead, we see a powerful movement toward rationalizing the action upon which stratification is based. The differential ends become "means" to one another, or else they become "conditions." They are reduced to means, as Weber writes at the very beginning of his major essay, because they are all "phenomena of the distribution of power."[97] Each kind of good is used by self-interested actors to gain their will over others: "We understand by 'power' the chance of a man or of a number of men to realize their own will in a communal action even against the resistance of others.[98] What are means to one actor, of course, are limitations to another, and each kind of good may present an external condition vis-à-vis the striving for another. Thus, Weber writes:

> "Economically conditioned" power is not . . . identical with 'power' as such. . . . Man does not strive for power only in order to enrich himself economically. Power, including economic power, may be valued "for its own sake." Very frequently the striving for power is also conditioned by the social "honor" it entails.[99]

In the initial stages of his treatment of class or economic stratification, Weber indicates a tentative movement away from this reductionistic path. He defines class in an extremely narrow way, limiting it to chances for success in the market itself. Such a narrow economic orientation, he argues, can constitute only one of the analytical dimensions of "class" if that concept is more broadly understood as a group of similarly situated economic actors engaging in socially or politically relevant action. "The direction in which the individual worker . . . is likely to pursue his interests," Weber writes, depends on his subjective perception, which is determined either by affective "communal" ties or by a more purposeful decision about his wider needs. These ties, according to Weber, depend on certain aspects of the normative order: on general cultural conditions, on the state of intellectual development, on the contrasts between the worker's situation and those of other groups, and on the "transparency" of the connection between the causes of his situation and objective economic conditions.[100] These early observations, if pursued,

could have brought Weber's stratification theory into a consistent relationship with his multidimensional writing on class and class ideologies.
Such initial possibilities, however, are not, in fact, followed through: in
the rest of his essay Weber treats class as if it indicated a concrete group
activated by purely economic means, a group that conditions other dimensions of stratification without any reference to the cultural framework outlined here.

If any other dimension of stratification were to contribute to a more
multidimensional approach to class, it would be the status order. Weber
acknowledges that "status groups are normally communities,"[101] and it
is communities that are the important alternative to instrumental grouping in his earlier view of class action. According to this understanding,
then, classes could act outside a narrow market situation only insofar as
they also constituted status groups. Status, after all, is determined by
negative or positive attributions of social honor, and classes could be
linked to such estimations in diverse ways depending on their normative
order and material contexts. Weber does acknowledge that the life style
of status groups can, in fact, be linked to the consumption of goods
which classes can be conceived as producing.[102]

When we look for such a multidimensional approach to status, however, we are disappointed. Weber launches a fundamentally reductionistic explanation of status, on two different fronts. He insists, first, that
status is not actually independent of productive property. "Property as
such is not always recognized as a status qualification," he acknowledges, "but in the long run it is, and with extraordinary regularity."[103]
Thus, Weber writes that in the relatively pure democracy of the United
States only individuals from the same tax bracket dance with one another. In these terms, status is a means for the further organization of
class interests, with neither status nor class being mediated by broader
cultural considerations. Instead of showing how status operationalizes
and specifies broader normative factors, or utilizing status to demonstrate how classes move from merely economically defined abstract
entities to active communities, Weber has reduced status group to class.
Not only does he assume that classes act on purely economic motives, but
actually that these motives are stronger and more important than the
status group's independent processes of honor formation. What translates the class's economic motives into a social form is now unanswered
and forgotten, for status itself is a residual category.

But even when Weber does not consider status a mere reflection of
class and productive property, he still treats it as a material condition,
one pursued, moreover, with instrumental motive. Status position is the
result of "usurpation,"[104] and it provides a position of power that allows
an actor to monopolize goods. Material and nonmaterial things, though
not economic in themselves, become vital as objects with which to so
usurp monopolistic control: Weber lists special costumes, special foods,

arms, artistic practices, and marriageable daughters.[105] Weber can now conceptualize the possibility for conflict between honorific groups that monopolize status and class groups defined purely by property. Each is a self-interested entity trying to protect its "means." For example, if status honor is equalized between two competing groups, any acquisition of economic property would present opportunities for honor that would tilt the balance of power. Weber's actors, in this situation, are purely instrumental; they make and act upon a utilitarian calculus of interest.

> Given equality of status honor, property *per se* represents an addition even if it is not overtly acknowledged to be such. Yet if such economic acquisition and power gave the agent any honor at all, his wealth would result in his attaining more honor than those who successfully claim honor by virtue of style of life. Therefore all groups having interests in the status order react with special sharpness precisely against the pretensions of purely economic acquisition. In most cases they react the more vigorously the more they feel themselves threatened.[106]

Economic acquisition is viewed as a threat not because of internal repugnance but because of the calculation of external position.[107]

The empirical divisions between hierarchies of stratification, then, introduce complexity into Weber's analysis, but it is a complexity unmatched in more general theoretical terms. The same violence to his multidimensional theory pervades his analysis of the third hierarchy, that of power. Parties, Weber writes, "residue in a sphere of 'power,'" and they desire to gain leverage over the action of others "no matter what its content may be."[108] "Party leaders are concerned with the conquest" of power alone, and their struggle is determined not by normatively mediated ends but by conditions, the "structure of domination" within which they operate.[109] Though parties are not necessarily identified with classes, their instrumental orientations often make them congruent with particular economic groups. Weber predicts, in fact, that commonality of instrumental orientation leads, mechanically, to a process of equilibrium between political, economic, and honorific rank. Stable status groups, in his view, eventually develop commensurate economic rewards and even legal privileges. This abstract analysis of the rationalizing movement from status to money and power matches the historical analysis, earlier described, of the movement of the nouveau riche from mere wealth to the acquisition of high status, a development Weber apparently regards as equally inevitable. In both discussions, motives are taken to be instrumental and other dimensions of stratification are taken as completely external conditions.[110]

In a legal-rational society, then, there is a pluralization of contexts and resources for individual and group struggle, for the framework of domination is more impersonal and less likely to be controlled by any single group than in premodern life. Despite ambiguous gestures to the contrary, however, Weber generally defines these stratification hierarchies as three different kinds of external order, and he describes the struggles that they produce as proceeding along *zweckrational*, instrumental lines. The contradictory tendencies in contemporary stratification literature can now be understood: their roots lie in Weber's own work.[111]†

5. A LIBERAL IN DESPAIR: THE IDEOLOGICAL MOMENT IN WEBER'S INSTRUMENTAL REDUCTION OF MODERNITY

The particular quality of Weber's conceptualization of modern society can be understood only if we see that its presuppositional framework emerges from the instrumental reduction of his political sociology. At every point, Weber's portrayal of modern industrial society follows the lead of the dichotomous and instrumental logic we discovered earlier in his historical accounts of political life. We can now return to the question posed at the beginning of this chapter: Why in these sections of Weber's work which concern the modern period should the instrumental line of his reasoning stand so starkly alone? For each of his evaluations of other historical periods, there exists a parallel analysis of the influence of normative structures. Why, in the modern analyses, are there instead only residual categories and ad hoc references? Why is there no multidimensional sociology, no matter how isolated, of the modern period? The answer to this question, I would suggest, shifts the focus of attention away from the presuppositional to the ideological level.

Anglo-American students of Weber's writing on modern industrial society have had a difficult time understanding the nature of his ideological orientation because they associate a liberal political position with optimism about the future. Anglo-American Marxists, therefore, have looked at the instrumentalism and resigned passivity of Weber's construction of modernity and have labeled him as a conservative who painted a picture rationalizing the industrial status quo.[112] Yet, although this empirical perception of his modernity theory is basically correct, such an evaluation conflates Weber's empirical description with his ideological judgment. The fact is that Weber, like Marx, was critical of what he observed in modern life. Liberal theorists in the Anglo-American tradition, in contrast, have been more aware of this moderately critical tone, and have read Weber as an ideological moderate of the welfare-state variety. They have seen Weber's commitment to self-discipline and freedom, his rejection of the millennial hopes of revolutionary socialism and reaction alike, and have made him a "realistic" and "pragmatic" political theorist.[113]† This judgment, however, is based on a perception of

Weber's sociology of modern life which, I have tried to show in this chapter, is essentially misleading, for it suggests that Weber placed ethics, vocation, and solidarity at the center of his vision of modern society.

The fact is that Weber did not see hopeful and progressive signs in the empirical development of Western society either in the short or in the long run, and in this he decisively differed from Durkheim and Marx. Yet he remained a "liberal" all the same, though a liberal of the specifically German type. Weber had a tragic view of history. He committed himself, nonetheless, to struggling for the preservation of the individual rights and group equality he valued as important. Weber, then, was not simply a pessimistic German mandarin opposed to modernity and industrialization, to *Gesellschaft* in a reactionary way, even if he did share much of the mandarin distrust for modern rationalization. Not simply a pessimist, he was a heroic pessimist; not simply a moderate liberal, he was more truly a "liberal in despair."[114†]

The historical roots of this tragic sensibility in German ideology have been briefly discussed in the first chapter. Rather than further elaborate this ideological position—which is not in itself of primary concern—I will investigate more deeply the historical process by which this ideological pessimism was spelled out in Weber's thought, the vision of historical decline that informed his vivid sense of the impoverished instrumentalism of modern life. Every vision of decline, of course, postulates a golden age that there has been decline from. In Weber's personal view, there seems little doubt, the high point of civilizational development was inspired by Puritanism. "It is to the radical individualism of the sects," he wrote in a personal letter in 1906, "that the world owes freedom of conscience and the elementary 'rights of man'—things that none of us today could do without."[115†] On the one hand, the Puritan lived in a world that was integrated by an all-embracing *Weltanschauung*, a religious view that was accepted as having ultimate validity and which could not be questioned. These ultimate values connected the emotional, moral, intellectual, and even aesthetic elements of the Puritan's experience, and such cultural integration allowed his life to become "meaningful." On the other hand, however, the Puritan pushed against the irrational and merely taken-for-granted aspects of nature and society, placing as much strain on his ultimate commitments as they would bear. Dedicated to science and this-worldly calculation, to steely self-discipline and individual productivity, the Puritan gained more freedom vis-à-vis the conditions of this world than any before him, without giving up the taken-for-granted assumptions that made such control meaningful.

Puritanism, then, was for Weber the perfect expression of *Wertrationalität*, the "value rationality" that emphasizes rational calculation but makes these calculations only in close relation to a system of ultimate and unquestioned commitments. Puritan *Wertrationalität* is transitional between traditional and modern culture, for it has strong elements of universalism and individuality yet remains tied to an other-worldly source. The problem, for Weber, is how the full transition to modernity can be accomplished, for this is a movement of secularization that involves the abandonment of *Wertrationalität* for *Zweckrationalität*, for a rationality which can evaluate ultimate values themselves, judging one against another in terms of purely this-worldly standards of abstract rationality. This transition from *Wertrationalität* to *Zweckrationalität* as the prototypical form of action marks the transition from a religious to a nonreligious world, a process Weber calls "disenchantment" or, more literally, "de-magicification" (*Entzauberung*). This transition is difficult for Weber to conceptualize clearly, because his personal commitment to the tightly integrated, culturally undifferentiated world of Puritan religion makes him suspect that any nonreligious life will lose its "meaning." Weber is committed to secular rationalism, but he is ambivalent about its consequences for cultural life. Since it undermines *Wertrationalität* and religious integration, there seems a good chance that it will sever the relation to values and meaning as such, though in principle it simply secularizes ultimate values and submits them to universalism of a higher order of abstraction. The problem that Weber faces, in other words, is whether the *Wertrationalität* which was inspired by a religiously integrated culture is equivalent to meaning and value reference as such. This problem is perfectly articulated by the ambiguity in his definition of *Zweckrationalität* discussed at an earlier point (ch. 2, sec. 1), for this "purposive rationality" can be read either as a pragmatic and substantively rational form of action that is still ethically committed or as rationality of an instrumental type that has eliminated normative reference altogether.

This tension that exists in Weber's ideological evaluation translates itself, therefore, into ambiguities in his empirical sociology, and ultimately influences his most general presuppositions as well. Corresponding to this tension, indeed, we can find in Weber's work both "weak" and "strong" theories of disenchantment or secularization. On one side, we can locate an image of modern life as a dualistic world, a world where the clear differentiation between abstract, universal ethics and this-worldly demands has replaced the monistic fusion of these demands within religious society. Puritanism, in this view, is seen not as a golden age but rather as the penultimate step before it, as an incipiently dualistic world-view still camouflaged by monistic commitments. Disenchantment, then, is here equated simply with increasing intellectualization and rationalization, not with instrumentalism as such. Rather than rendering man passive, it makes him the master, for with man's new reference to abstract universalism there are "no mysterious incalculable forces that come into play."[116] Life is still meaningful, although the achievement of meaning is more difficult because it is immanent. Instead of monism, there is now "polytheism," for the more rational and autonomous individual must choose among competing standards of ultimate value.[117] Yet action still involves a value reference, and an individual can still "give himself an *account of the ultimate meaning of his own conduct.*"[118] It is this strand of ideological acceptance of modernity that informs the multidimensional fragments of Weber's theory of contemporary life, for this substantively rational actor is the man of a chosen "vocation."

In his "strong" theory of disenchantment, Weber expresses the other side of his ambivalence about modernity, contradicting this more hopeful portrayal of secularized society with a pessimistic evaluation of modern life as a declension from the Puritan heights. In this version, science becomes for Weber the prototype of modern action, the basic form in which rationality is pursued. This science, however, is portrayed as *Zweckrationalität* in its merely calculating and technical form.[119]† Weber now draws a strict line between modern action and its religious counterpart. "The tension between the value-spheres of 'science' and the sphere of 'the holy,' " he insists, "is unbridgeable."[120] This statement, of course, can imply either the antagonism of scientific thought to ultimate values in the religious sense of unquestionability or the rejection of value-reference per se, a reference for which the "holy" is prototypical. In his strong theory of disenchantment, Weber takes the second path. With the triumph of science, he argues, nothing can "simply be accepted."[121] If nothing is simply accepted, however, action is consigned to instrumentality, for no matter how subject to reason, values always involve an element of just such an ultimate acceptance: they refer to a normative order whose roots transcend any individual actor. Every value critique must be made with reference to some other taken-for-granted value, and the process continues in an unending chain.

Weber appears, therefore, to be postulating the gulf between religious and nonreligious thought in an epistemological way, and in doing so he is expressing his deep pessimism about the possibility for meaning in modern life. In a crucial and much neglected essay, entitled "Religious Rejections of the World and Their Directions," he argues just that. In a disenchanted culture where scientific instrumentalism is the dominant mode of thought, no cultural integration or meaning is really possible. The different dimensions of cultural life have been severed from any interconnection. Science and rational calculation have been cut off from ethical considerations, art has been dissociated from morality and intellect, and emotional life can be pursued only by the individual alone.[122] Ultimate values, Weber argues, "have retreated from public life;" they have gone "into the transcendental realm of mystic life or into the brotherliness of direct and personal human relations."[123] In these terms, of course, intellectualism is hardly the progressive liberator of a more rational humanity. We know, in fact, that despite his fervent public commitment to the values of Puritan asceticism and rationality, in his *personal* life Weber became increasingly interested in, and perhaps drawn to, the mystical and directly personal aspects of human affairs.[124†]

Can modern man be satisfied with the bleak instrumentalism of modernity that Weber has described? If social action is instrumental, that is one thing, but has human nature itself so changed in the course of disenchantment that cultural meaning is no longer needed? Drawing, perhaps, on his own personal experience, Weber denies that this historical process could have such an effect. The need for salvation remains; there is still an existential and psychological desire for "living in a union [*Gemeinschaft*] with the divine."[125] Weber describes a number of ways this need can be met—all of them outside the realm of public, institutional life. The path taken by most modern men, in Weber's view, is withdrawal from the demands for rationality and continuous judgment toward a pseudo-reconstruction of religious life. There are, for example, the "petty prophets" of the lecture room, who generate a faithful student following by providing *ersatz* salvation, an illusion which hides from the follower "the fundamental fact that he is destined to live in a godless and prophetless time."[126] There are various forms of bohemian estheticism, where "art takes over the function of a this-worldly salvation . . . from the routines of everyday life, and especially from the increasing pressures of theoretical and practical rationalism."[127] There is also the escape into eroticism, where "the erotic relation seems to offer the unsurpassable peak of the fulfillment of the request for love in the direct fusion of the souls of one to the other." Eroticism, Weber writes, "rests upon the possibility of a communion [*Gemeinschaft*] which is felt as a complete unification" and which "is so overpowering that it is interpreted 'symbolically': as a sacrament."[128]

Weber has described modern social life as a period in which the synthesis of idealism and materialism has been torn asunder. Weber sees himself, and modern man, as surrounded by institutions which are purely material in their substance, "iron cages" from which all value has been drained. At the same time, the people who inhabit these dwellings are enveloped from within by spontaneous impulses like the very ones Idealist philosophers eulogized as freedom.

These "empirical observations," I would contend, result, in part, from the tremendous pessimism with which Weber was inclined to view the emergence of a nonreligious world. These very empirical observations, nonetheless, gave him "scientific" support for the instrumentalism of his presuppositional stance. For if institutions are unvalued, if people are guided either by calculation or by impulses uncanalized by ethical belief, then the theoretical framework of the political sociology would certainly apply.

Yet despite this presuppositional and empirical acceptance, Weber has not withdrawn his earlier critical stance toward unreconstructed idealism and materialism in the ideological realm. His tragic pessimism has induced him to paint a grim portrait of the possibilities for conviction, but his heroism motivates him, at the same time, to reject the easy escapes from modernity that he has foreseen. Weber is harsh in his judgment of "the escape from the necessity of taking a stand on rational, ethical grounds"; he condemns "the refusal of modern men to assume responsibility for moral judgments."[129] The only acceptable way of life, for him, is "to measure up to workaday experience," to immerse oneself in the lifeless world and to form a personal ethic which will allow continued responsibility. For the extraordinary person, the person who can refuse the blandishments and resist the resignation of contemporary life, an ethic of responsibility is still possible. But certainly this is the ethic of the "virtuoso." Weber has not given up his commitment to the notion of free will, even if he has given up the idea that voluntarism can be institutionalized in the collective social order. Even in the completely rationalized world, the individual has freedom to carve out a meaningful course, but he can do so only *as* an individual, without any connection to institutional life.[130†] In a paradoxical way, therefore, the continuity of Weber's faith in individual freedom serves to underscore the instrumental and mechanistic quality of his general sociology of modern life.[131†]

Chapter Six

WEBER INTERPRETATION AND WEBERIAN SOCIOLOGY

"Paradigm Revision" and Presuppositional Strain

Even in Weber's earliest writings, we can now see, his theoretical intentions were fraught with ambiguity. On one side, he clearly devoted himself to combining into a broader whole the instrumental and idealist traditions he had inherited from the German intellectual tradition. On the other side, however, he produced explanations in those early writings in which each tradition was held to explain historical development without reference to the other. If there was a bias in that early work, it was toward the materialist side. Weber was determined to avoid the idealism of his conservative forefathers; he was inspired by the revival of historical materialism, and he further elaborated the tradition of Realpolitik. The idealist dimension existed in his early work, but it played a more isolated and hesitant role.

In the mature sociology that began after the breakdown period, Weber articulated a theoretical synthesis never before achieved, indeed, never even attempted by the other founders of classical sociology. He converted the idealist and materialist traditions into analytic strands of a more inclusive multidimensional order, so that instead of choosing between them he could devote his sociology to establishing the nature of their interrelation. Weber specified this presuppositional breakthrough in empirical propositions of enormous comparative and historical breadth, studies that were mediated by a complex and differentiated model of social life, by a method that integrated "understanding" with observation, and by an ideological commitment to the liberation of the individual from debilitating internal and external constraint. Yet despite this theoretical breakthrough, Weber's later sociology remained flawed by serious ambiguity. The unsureness was expressed most directly by the dichotomous logic that informs, or deforms, much of the later work, a theoretical strategy whereby Weber gives up any attempt to interrelate the very traditions he had tried elsewhere to synthesize. And this later writing also continues to reflect the earlier presuppositional tilt toward instrumental thought. No idealist strand shadows Weber's later multidimensional thinking, but a mass of instrumentalist theorizing does. Influenced by this general inclination, Weber's commitment to the methodology of *Verstehen* falls by the wayside, and though his model remains complex, its autonomous segments are now all informed by a similar logic. The tragic pessimism that colors Weber's ideological hope for human freedom makes an independent contribution to this theoretical declension, for it adds an evaluative legitimacy to instrumental observations established on other, more analytic grounds.

If an interpretation of a great thinker's work is to have distinctively theoretical significance, it must not only provide insight into the more difficult areas of his thought but should also provide an overarching explanation that links the disparate parts of his work into some meaningful whole. As in the readings of Durkheim and Marx, I have tried to supply this kind of interpretation for Weber's work. Yet an interpretive, theoretically self-conscious reading should do still more. An interpretation is powerful, I would suggest, to the extent that it can provide an explanation not only for the thinker's own writings but for the interpretations of that work as well. Interpretation, I have insisted throughout this book, always has a polemical interest of its own, yet this polemical interest must substantiate itself in the original text. For an interpretation is as two-directional as any more "scientific" work: it has a priori interests, but it is also informed by the structure of the empirical world—that is, by the textual reference. It is because of this empirical referent that interpretation usually proceeds along the fault lines of the original work. It responds to strains at every level of the scientific continuum, but the most general and ramifying problems, those which set the most serious agenda for interpretation, occur on the presuppositional level itself.

As we have seen at every point in our discussion, no interpretive literature is more contradictory than the Weberian one. There are claims for the perfectly multidimensional Weber whose political writing is fundamentally informed by the comparative sociology of religion—this is the Parsonian tradition, shared also by the more recent German criticism of Tenbruck and Schluchter. There are assertions for a similar multidimensionality which place the religious sociology under the rubric of a normatively sensitive political analysis—the interpretation of Bendix and Roth. There are "tough-minded" interpreters who read Weber as a pure instrumentalist but who place this orientation within a framework that grants an autonomy to political life—Dahrendorf, Wrong, Aron, and Collins. Finally, there are those who agree about this instrumentalism but regard it as more "socially" rooted and, in this way, place Weber under the guiding rubric of Marx—the tradition formed by Löwith, Mills, Rex, and Habermas, and more recently maintained by Beetham and Zeitlin. None of these interpretive strands is simply "wrong" in the narrow empirical sense of that term. We have seen that each, indeed, can draw sustenance from certain strands in the original work. Still, none is correct as a true estimation of the theoretical whole.[1†]

No reading, I have argued, is launched in a casual way, for merely "academic" reasons. Each is an attempt to legitimate a certain form of sociology, or, as is often the case, an attempt to discover commitments that will convince the scholarly reader to embark on some future sociological path. "Weberian sociology" virtually converges with sociology itself; its divisions parallel the subfields of every sociology text. Readings of Weber's work, therefore, have inspired or legitimated virtually every major conflict in the specialized sociologies. In the notes to the different segments of my discussion, I have discussed some of these specialized debates. Our concern here, however, is with "Weberian sociology" in its more generalized form, not as it has provided exemplars for specific empirical work but as it has inspired and legitimated entire sociological traditions. Weber never created a school in the same sense as Durkheim or Marx; he had few direct students, and the upheavals of the 1920s and 1930s created a historical hiatus between his work and its scholarly effects. Yet in the postwar period there did emerge distinctly Weberian traditions. Like the Durkheimian and Marxist traditions before them, these strands of Weberian sociology implicitly derived from the strains in the work of their founding father. The sociologies that bear Weber's name have championed one part of his work as the true whole, and the strands of interpretation have been directed toward rationalizing such choice. At the same time, however, despite explicit disclaimers, each Weberian tradition is at some level aware that a selective choice has actually been made, even that Weber's work manifests unresolved inconsistencies. Each Weberian tradition, then, is not just a reading but also a revision, an attempt to "straighten out" Weber's thinking by making it consistently informed by a single theme.

In the "functionalist" sociology of the Parsonian tradition, Weber's comparative religious studies provide the umbrella for a multidimensional exploration of social life. Sensing Weber's dilemma without ever stating it in a generalized form, Parsons argued that cultural patterns were an analytic part of every concrete social institution, thus formalizing Weber's critique of materialism, and that internalized culture also canalized every psychological impulse, thus "completing" his critique of idealism.[2†] On the level of the social system itself, Parsons used Weber's work to trace intricate interchanges between every subsystem, so that political exigencies affected institutionalized values and the latter affected political power in turn. In his later work Parsons concentrated on the integrative subsystem he called the societal community, and he argued that his empirical insight derived in important ways from Weber's *The City*.[3] With this latter strategy, Parsons could not only draw legitimacy for a multidimensional theory from the most political of Weber's synthetic works, but under its authoritative camouflage he could also suggest an analytical framework that promised to resolve the bifurcating strains in the original work. It is revealing of the strains that Parsons implicity sought to revise that even within his own tradition of Weberian sociology his followers divided along the fault lines of Weber's original work. Students like Bellah, Geertz, and Little have given primary emphasis, within the Parsonian synthesis, to religious and normative pressures, and Parsons himself evidenced an even stronger strain toward making the differential impact of religion primary.[4†] Such students as Smelser and Eisenstadt, by contrast, while taking into account Weber's comparative religious scheme, particularly emphasized independent political and economic developments.[5†]

Though not a "tradition" in the same sense as Parsonianism, the reading explicated in Bendix's magisterial intellectual biography of Weber has represented and inspired a Weberian sociology that placed Weber's multidimensional history into a more political mode. It is surely not coincidental that the work which keyed Bendix's sociology was also *The City*, for this is the place where political and religious strands of Weber's thought come together with such strong implications for contemporary analysis. Yet where Parsons took *The City* as specifying the integrative solidarity that is implied by universalistic monotheism, Bendix read it as an investigation of the legal ties of citizenship that Western states, influenced by the Western cultural tradition, would require and enforce. These specifically legal definitions of universalism are paramount in Bendix's histories, limiting the coercion of the state, on the one hand, and the effects of industrialization, on the other.[6] Bendix, then, places *The City* in the context of Weber's political rather than his religious history, and in his earlier work Lipset does much the same. For Lipset, who worked closely with Bendix, the crucial variable is the timing of state formation vis-à-vis industrialization. The earlier the state formation, the more likely will the state be inclusive enough to extend citizenship rights to the lower classes. Only an independent state, one that so institutionalizes legal citizenship, can ameliorate class conflict so that working-class interest becomes channeled into support for nonrevolutionary struggle.[7] In his later writings, when he came to be more influenced by Parsons' work, Lipset's sociology reveals a consistent attempt to combine this politically-directed synthetic theory with variable religious effects.[8] Roth, Bendix's student and younger colleague, stayed more firmly within the political revision of the multidimensional theory.

Roth formulated the concept of "negative integration" to describe the excluded condition of the German working classes in the imperial period, and he made this rebellious solidarity an independent variable; yet he described this condition as the result of authoritarian state-formation and aristocratic control, making no reference to the long-term effects of German religion.[9]

Other versions of Weberian sociology have implictly revised Weber's work in a more one-sidedly instrumental way. Dahrendorf formulated the purest form of this Weberianism in his early paradigm for "conflict sociology," defining hierarchical domination as the determinant of all collective order and denying that institutional differences between types of domination—let alone normative variations—had to be taken into account.[10] Dahrendorf's later work moved back toward a more multidimensional Weberianism, but it was the early model that became formulated as a general theory of "conflict sociology" by Collins, a student of Bendix who turned toward a more one-dimensional path. Rooting itself entirely in Weber's political history, Collins' theory elaborated a hypertrophied instrumentalism in a series of wide-ranging empirical propositions.[11]† Horowitz and Huntington applied the same kind of anti-normative theory of domination to Third World nations and the problems of development, Huntington insisting in particular that the normative aspects of legitimation were of no concern and that an effective leader supported by disciplined staff and party could impose coercive order on a passive nation.[12]

The other strand of instrumental sociology inspired and legitimated by Weber took a distinctively more Marxian path. Its practitioners shared the instrumental assumptions of the more purely Weberian instrumental theory, but they argued for the state's strong—if not complete—dependence on economic society. Weber became important, therefore, not as an alternative to Marx but as a theoretical means of supplying Marxist sociology with a more complex and interdependent model. Mills' writing presented the paradigmatic argument along these lines; Mills treated stratification as conflict over different commodities, elites as oriented purely to usurpation, charisma as instrumental to manipulated consent, and the superficially autonomous state as primarily related to economic imperatives.[13] Rex tried to convert "conflict sociology" into a neo-Marxist form by reading Weber's analysis of domination as a struggle between ruling and subordinate classes rather than one between political groupings as such.[14] Lockwood pushed Weberian sociology even further in this direction, citing Weber mainly to support Marx's materialist injunctions against "normative functionalism."[15]

Contemporary Marxist theory presents the apotheosis of this movement. Many contemporary Marxists, indeed, now read Marx—consciously or unconsciously—through Weberian eyes. This movement was initiated by Lukács, who used Weber's (and Simmel's) analysis of the instrumentalizing effects of *zweckrational* institutions to make an argument for the centrality of commodity fetishism in *Capital*.[16] Habermas offers this Weberianized Marxism in its most extreme form. Focusing on conflicts between different rationalities, he locates the tension between formal and substantive rationality in the tension between the capitalist system's demands for efficiency and the individual's need for emotional succor, for aesthetic expression, for moral commitment, and for truth. The empirical center of Habermas' social system, moreover, is a relatively autonomous state whose interchanges with economy and culture expose it to the destructive threat of illegitimacy.[17] Instrumental Weberianism has also spread to Marxism in less disciplined ways. It is, for example, difficult to understand the now widely spread institutional emphasis in Marxist writing on the (even temporally) autonomous state without appreciating the long-range impact of Weber's work.[18†]

In the background to these revisionist applications of Weberian sociology, we can see, if we look closely enough, the shadows of the other two figures who defined the classical tradition: Durkheim and Marx. These thinkers, after all, sketched the alternative pathways of sociological idealism and materialism, and as Weber's later followers tried to make him more consistent they usually pushed him more in one of these directions than the other. We have seen at various points in this discussion the crucial relevance of Marx for Weber interpretation, a relevance which is especially clear because of the tilt toward materialism that exists in Weber's own work. If Marxists have used Weber as a means to complicate their model of society, Weberians of an instrumental bent have pushed Weber toward Marx in an effort to add further empirical substance to Weber's sociology of domination—to transform it into a more complete theory of society. That Marx was a primary inspiration for sociologists like Mills and Rex is clearly the case, yet the same can also be said for conflict theorists like Dahrendorf and Collins. Huntington is even more precise, acknowledging the formative impact on his Weberian postulates of Lenin himself. Significant reference to Marx, despite strong empirical and ideological disagreement, can even be discerned in the political emphasis of the multidimensional Weberianism of Bendix, Roth, and Lipset.[19†]

There has been much less frequent reference in these chapters to the possible influence of Durkheim on Weberian theory, but the impact is inevitable if there is a strong push to read his work as consistently including the normative dimension of order. In the preceding volume of this study, I showed that Durkheim's contemporary followers, in the effort to revise his idealism, often drew directly from Weber's work (vol. 2, ch. 9).

The reverse is also the case. Where are the promoters of a voluntaristic Weberianism to turn, in their analyses of modernity, if not to the brilliant descriptions of normative modernism that Durkheim made in his later work?

Parsons is the principal figure in this cross-fertilization. As the major mediator between English-speaking students and the works of both of these classical figures, Parsons argued from the outset for the "convergence" of their theories. In fundamental respects this claim was false. We can now see, in fact, that far from presenting an objective reading of these two classical figures, Parsons was actually attempting a far-reaching revision of the weaknesses he implicitly sensed in each. By claiming for the concepts of "legitimacy" and "charisma" in Weber's political sociology the same theoretical and empirical status as "the sacred" in Durkheim's religious writing, Parsons opened the way for a fully multidimensional "Weberian" sociology of modernity.[20†] Extrapolating from Weber's multidimensional history, the Parsonians tried, in an unacknowledged way, to present the theoretical framework for modernity that Weber "would have presented" if he had continued in the multidimensional vein.[21†] This is not to say, of course, that these Parsonians closely shared Weber's ideological or empirical commitments. As quintessentially "American" theorists, they were closer to Durkheim's relative optimism than to the tragic sensibility of Weber. Yet they pressed their case for extrapolation nonetheless, and they extended the multidimensional history to contemporary life in a way that none had done before them. Such an effort could not have been attempted without the incorporation of significant parts of Durkheim's thought. Of course, while Bendix and Roth have resolutely refused such cross-breeding, they have resisted instrumentalism all the same.[22†] Still, by not drawing upon Durkheimian theory, they have severely limited their access to the normative and subjective aspects of modern life.

It was because of Weber's inability to follow the kind of insight Durkheim achieved into the normative elements of modernity that the debilitating antinomies of the classical tradition were maintained. Durkheim himself, of course, established a one-sided approach to modern order. It was Weber who created the connection between ideal orders and instrumental ones, who found a way to relate the understanding of voluntary and normative pressures to the instrumentalism of Marx. Weber understood the manipulative potential and resistant hardness of institutions; Durkheim, with rare exception, did not. Yet Weber's extraordinary synthesis foundered. His reduction to instrumental order has roots in his sociology of traditional and charismatic domination, and it involves theoretical difficulties of a purely analytic sort. But these problems can best be described empirically in terms of the difficulty Weber had in conceptualizing the transition to modernity.

Weber could not understand how religion, or religious-like phenomena, could continue to inform the collective order of a secular society. Durkheim could, and this understanding is what allowed him to describe with such great sensitivity the subjective processes of modern life. For Weber, if cognitive rationality was to be sustained, it had to be sharply separated from "simply accepted" values (see ch. 5, sec. 5); for Durkheim, the opposite was the case. Without the support of nonrational and symbolic elements, Durkheim knew, the distinctiveness of modernity would be caricatured and misunderstood. Where Durkheim spoke of moral education, Weber could find only technical training; where Durkheim described the modern state as involved in a continual process of value definition in reciprocity with the will of the masses, Weber interpreted this government as simply another manifestation of impersonal domination and manipulation; where Durkheim knew that even modern law was redolent with subjectively imputed authority, Weber saw only formal and external control; and where Durkheim perceived rationality as the most sacred belief of modern life, Weber perceived only the debasing reduction of rationality in the service of coercive control.[23†] Durkheim's conceptualization of contemporary normative order allowed him to elaborate *zweckrational* action in a substantive direction, to describe a social rationality that was neither instrumental nor absolutist. It is ironic that only by incorporating such normative understanding could Weber have successfully transcended the theory upon which it was based. To go beyond Marx and Durkheim, Weber's revolutionary theory would have had to incorporate the theorizing represented by both.

In the final volume of this work, I will examine the modern theorist who tried to take up where Weber left off. Weber's work represented the classical attempt at synthesis; Talcott Parsons' represents the principal contemporary effort to reconstruct the tensions that Weber left at least partly unresolved. Parsons could learn from Weber's mistakes, and from the mistakes of Marx and Durkheim as well; that he was not, in the end, any more successful than Weber at presenting a consistently synthetic theory testifies to the obdurate strength of the antinomies of theoretical thought.

Notes

CHAPTER ONE

1. Merton, "On Sociological Theories of the Middle Range," in his *On Theoretical Sociology* (New York, 1967), pp. 39–72, quoting p. 63. Arthur Stinchcombe adopts much the same position in *Constructing Social Theories* (Baltimore, 1968). This view of Weber, which sees his work as focusing on the most empirically specific forms of propositional relationships, is shared by Julien Freund, who has written the major introduction to Weber's thought in the French language (I except the more sophisticated work of Raymond Aron). Freund writes:

> "Weber was the first in practice to place sociology on a strictly scientific basis. Indeed, what strikes us in Weber's work is the total absence of preconceived doctrines or a priori syntheses. He was a pure analyst, whose sole concern was to gain a sound knowledge of historical data and to interpret them within verifiable limits. . . . Weber systematically resisted synthesis [although] he attached a definite value to it as an intellectual procedure in formulating the circumscribed significance of a given phenomenon. . . . Errors and inadequacies undoubtedly occur in Weber's work, but they are the errors of a scientist. They are due, for example, to lacunae in information or to weaknesses in critical interpretation stemming from failure to make the necessary comparisons." (*The Sociology of Max Weber* [New York, 1969], pp. 13–14.)

This assertion conflates a presuppositionless science with caution about systematic conceptualization. The two, however, have nothing in common, and while Weber did exhibit the latter caution, he could not have achieved the former even if he had wanted to. Freund's perspective on the sources of the limitations of Weber's science could not be more different from mine.

137

2. Rex, *Key Problems in Sociological Theory* (London, 1961), p. 125.

3. Lockwood, "Some Remarks on 'The Social System,' " *British Journal of Sociology* 5 (1956):134–145; Dahrendorf, *Class and Class Conflict in Industrial Society* (Stanford, Calif., 1959), pp. 166–167. Dahrendorf's subsequent opinions seem to give to Weber a more normative reading, however.

4. In "A Comparative Approach to Political Sociology" (pp. 42–67 in Reinhard Bendix et al., *State and Society* [Berkeley and Los Angeles, 1968]), Randall Collins claims that Weber was concerned only with instrumental, self-interested actors engaged in conflict, that he reduced religion to the imposition of beliefs on others without their voluntary consent, and that his work generally should be viewed as an extension of Marx's. In his more recent "Weber's Last Theory of Capitalism: A Schematization" (*American Sociological Review* 45 [1980]:925–942), he takes the same perspective: "Weber diverges from the Marxian [theory of the state] by being [even] a more thoroughgoing conflict theorist" (p. 941).

5. Zetterberg, *Theory and Verification in Sociology*, 3d ed. (Totowa, N.Y., 1965), pp. 67–68.

6. Bendix, "Two Sociological Traditions," pp. 282–298 in his and Guenther Roth's *Scholarship and Partisanship: Essays on Max Weber* (Berkeley and Los Angeles, 1971). The attack on functional models in favor of institutional models is one of the underlying themes of Bendix's *Max Weber* (Berkeley and Los Angeles, 1961). It is also a major premise in Martindale, *The Nature and Types of Sociological Theory* (Cambridge, Mass., 1960), pp. 377–393.

7. Mommsen, *The Age of Bureaucracy* (New York, 1974), p. 25; Aron, "Max Weber and Power Politics," pp. 83–100 in Otto Stammer, ed., *Max Weber and Sociology Today* (New York, 1971).

8. Marcuse, "Industrialization and Capitalism in the Work of Max Weber," pp. 201–226 in his *Negations* (Boston, 1968), p. 202.

9. Aron, *Main Currents in Sociological Thought* (New York, 1970), 2:219–317; for similar arguments, see Bendix, "Max Weber's Interpretation of Conduct and History," *American Journal of Sociology* 51 (1946):518–526, esp. 518, and Martindale (n. 6 above).

10. Ashcraft, "Marx and Weber on Liberalism as Bourgeois Ideology," *Comparative Studies in Society and History* 14 (1972):130–168, esp. 157.

11. Kolko, "A Critique of Max Weber's Philosophy of History," *Ethics* 70 (1959): 21–36, esp. 25; Landshut, *Kritik der Soziologie* (Munich and Leipzig, 1927), p. 79.

12. Parsons, *The Structure of Social Action* (New York, [1937] 1968), pp. 500–578, 640–686. (I discuss this interpretive issue in more detail below, and particularly in vol. 4.) Jere Cohen, Lawrence E. Hazelrigg, and Whitney Pope note this problem in a strong way in their "De-Parsonsiz-

ing Weber: A Critique of Parsons's Interpretation of Weber's Sociology,"
American Sociological Review 40 (1975):229–241, esp. 236–240, yet they
view this tendency in Parsons' interpretation as consistent, which it is
not, and they also view Weber's original, preinterpreted work as satisfactory in itself, another claim which I will dispute below.

13. Salomon, "Max Weber," *Die Gesellschaft* 3 (1920):131–153, quoted
in Wolfgang J. Mommsen, "Max Weber as a Critic of Marxism," *Canadian
Journal of Sociology* 2 (1977):374; Schumpeter, *Capitalism, Socialism, and
Democracy* (New York, 1947), p. 11.

14. Lichtheim, *Europe in the Twentieth Century* (New York, 1972), pp.
56–61; cf. his *Marxism* (New York, 1965), p. 385, n. 3, where he echoes
Schumpeter's statement.

15. Zeitlin, *Ideology and the Development of Sociological Theory*
(Englewood Cliffs, N.J., 1968), pp. 111–158; Gerth and Mills, eds., *From
Max Weber: Essays in Sociology* (New York, [1946] 1958), p. 63.

16. Bendix, *Max Weber* (n. 6 above), passim; Parsons, *Structure* (n. 12
above), passim.

17. *Max Weber*, p. xix.

18. Ibid.

19. For an excellent intellectual history of the period, see Fritz K.
Ringer, *The Decline of the German Mandarins: The German Academic
Community, 1890–1933* (Cambridge, Mass., 1969), particularly ch. 3, "Politics and Social Theory, 1890–1918," pp. 128–199. For more general background on some of the more extreme forms of this disdain for industrial
society, see Fritz Stern, *The Politics of Cultural Despair* (Berkeley and Los
Angeles, 1961).

20. Wilhelm Windelband, *Präludien*, quoted in Ringer, p. 103.

21. Ernst Troeltsch, "Natur-recht und Humanität in der Weltpolitik"
(1923), quoted in Ringer, pp. 100–101.

22. For a discussion of the Verein in historical context and its relationship to Weber, see Ringer, esp. pp. 143–162; Joseph Schumpeter, *History of Economic Analysis* (New York, 1954), pp. 800–820, 843–855; James
J. Sheehan, *The Career of Lujo Brentano* (Chicago, 1966); and Marianne
Weber, *Max Weber: A Biography* (New York, [1926] 1974), pp. 126 ff. For a
discussion of the growing statism and militarism of the German middle
classes, see Gerhard Ritter, "The Militarization of the German Middle
Class," in his *The Sword and the Scepter* (Coral Gables, Fla., 1970), pp.
93–104.

23. See Ringer (n. 19 above), p. 170 and passim.

24. Max Weber, "Capitalism and Rural Society in Germany," in Gerth
and Mills (n. 15 above), pp. 363–385; see pp. 370–372 for the reference to
the well-being of the working classes and passim for the negative references to the Junkers. For Weber's clear political sympathies with many
of the goals of the German Social Democratic party, see Mommsen, "Max

Weber as a Critic of Marxism," *Canadian Journal of Sociology* 2 (1977):396, n. 29 (translation altered). Mommsen writes, on the basis of Weber's personal correspondence:

> Already in 1909 Weber devoted thought to the possibility of joining the Social Democratic Party, but he considered this a mere theoretical possibility. He maintained that ultimately effective support of the interests of the proletariat would be only possible by a declaration in favor of Social Democracy. This, however, he was not prepared to do. He wrote to Tönnies, "The only thing I could not honestly do is subscribe to the *Credo* of the Social Democracy [since] I do serve other gods also—although it is after all just the same as paying lip service to the Apostles' creed."

In another personal letter, in 1920, Weber wrote: "I cannot become '*Mehrheitssozialist*,' for this party has to make the same compromises in the direction of the socialization [of key industries as the Independent Socialists] (against the convictions of their scientifically trained members)" [ibid.]. Mommsen adds: "Otherwise he [Weber] might have joined the Social Democratic Party." This last suggestion carries the point too far. Weber also described himself, in a letter to Robert Michels, as a "class conscious bourgeois" (1906; quoted, ibid., p.374; translation altered). His sympathies with the conditions and plight of the working class must be separated from support for the ideological aspirations of organized socialism.

25. In many important ways, in fact, Weber's liberalism resembles that of his older colleague, Brentano (see Sheehan, n. 22 above). Brentano had very strong disagreements with Schmoller, his cofounder of the Verein, over the latter's faith in authoritarian bureaucracy; Brentano was a strong Anglophile, with a belief that Germany must follow the English style of trade unionism; Brentano was also, like Weber, a close friend of the Protestant reformer Friedrich Naumann. Brentano, Weber, and Naumann all agreed in the early 1890s that the only way to salvage German liberalism would be to form an alliance between workers and progressive capitalists under the leadership of the educated members of the middle class and at the expense, primarily, of the Junker aristocracy. For this end, they probably would have preferred a split in the German Social Democratic party in order to work more closely with the moderate socialist revisionists like Bernstein, whom all of them knew and worked with on various occasions. It might be noted, in this context, how much this implicit strategy resembled that of the Durkheimians in France at about the same time, particularly that of Durkheim's student Bouglé. In Germany, however, this liberal intention was couched in a more pessimistic, even tragic perspective on the possibilities for reform, a difference which had important implications for German sociology. For more on this issue, see Arthur Mitzman's interesting contrast between Durkheim

and Tönnies as representatives of their respective middle classes and intellectual generations (*Sociology and Estrangement* [New York, 1973], pp. 108–112).

26. Marianne Weber (n. 22 above), p. 86, from a letter Weber wrote to his mother in 1884.

27. Ibid., pp. 88–89, italics in original.

28. My discussion of the intellectual influences on Weber and the tensions in his early writings, therefore, is entirely analytical. In contrast to the discussion of Durkheim (vol. 2), I do not intend to make any argument for chronological development within the early period.

29. Wilhelm Dilthey, "An Introduction to the Human Studies," in his *Selected Writings*, ed. H. P. Rickman (Cambridge and London, 1976), pp. 157–167; cf. H. Hodges, *The Philosophy of Wilhelm Dilthey* (London, 1952), and H. Tuttle, *Wilhelm Dilthey's Philosophy of Historical Understanding* (Leiden, 1969).

30. These statements are quoted by Carl Hinrichs in his "Introduction" to Meinecke, *Historicism* (London, [1936] 1972), pp. xl–xli.

31. "Leben ist Wirken, und Wirken ist Kampf"—quoted in R. I. Frank's "Introduction" to Max Weber, *The Agrarian Sociology of Ancient Civilizations* (London, 1976), p. 24.

32. Quoted in G. P. Gooch, *History and Historians in the Nineteenth Century* (London, [1913] 1954), p. 460. As Gooch clearly indicates, the experience of the defeat of the German liberals in the 1848 revolution was crucial for Mommsen's later intellectual development.

33. For the translation of a significant part of this address, see "Economic Policy and the National Interest in Imperial Germany," in W. G. Runciman, ed., *Weber: Selections in Translation* (Cambridge, 1978), pp. 263–268, esp. p. 267. It should be noted, in this connection, that the heightened social conscience manifested by some leading intellectuals in Weber's generation was also reinforced by the revival of neo-Kantianism in late nineteenth-century Germany, a revival that gave to the compromised inheritance of liberal idealism a more critical twist. Although some leaders of this movement, e.g., Heinrich Rickert, had a strong impact on Weber's specific formulations of methodological issues, more important, I believe, is the fact that neo-Kantianism provided him with a resource for distancing himself from the revival of materialist analysis even while he significantly incorporated it. These liberal intellectuals gave to Kant's categorical imperative a social importance that mandated critical attitudes toward dominant, conservative authority, and for many democrats of the period it provided the moral and philosophical underpinnings for their identification with the socialist and working-class movement. See Thomas E. Wiley, *Back to Kant* (Detroit, 1978), esp. chs. 6–7.

34. For these historical issues, see Guenther Roth, "The Historical Relationship to Marxism," in Bendix and Roth (n. 6 above), pp. 227–252, esp. pp. 232–235 and notes. According to a study by Sombart which Roth cites, before 1883 there were only 20 publications on Marx, between 1884 and 1894, when the third volume of *Capital* was published, there were 58, and between 1895 and 1904 there were 214.

35. Quoted in Dieter Lindenlaub, *Richtungskämpfe im Verein für Sozialpolitik* (Wiesbaden, 1967), 2:277; cf. Colin T. Loader, "German Historicism and Its Critics," *Journal of Modern History* 48, no. 3 (1976):85–199, esp. 101. Loader's article provides a good intellectual background to the social-science debates of the time.

36. This historian is Lindenlaub, in *Richtungskämpfe*, p. 291.

37. Ibid., p. 274.

38. Quoted, ibid., p. 281; cf. Arthur Mitzman, *The Iron Cage* (New York, 1970), pp. 130–131.

39. Gooch (n. 32 above), pp. 336–342, and Frank (n. 31 above), pp. 26–27. For a good discussion of the materialist current that emerged in Germany in the latter part of the nineteenth century, see Michael Ermarth, *Wilhelm Dilthey: The Critique of Historical Reason* (Chicago, 1978), "Materialism and Positivism, 1850–1875," pp. 62–79.

40. Thus Goldschmidt, in his *Universal History of Commercial Law,* dedicated to Mommsen, had written of the "epoch of the greatest moral degeneration of the Roman state, when the ruling strata, profiting from the most barefaced exploitation of the provinces, indulged in the wildest speculation and most ruthless capitalism; when the owners of the latifundia had become big industrialists, and the demand for luxuries by the old and new aristocracy, which had amassed fantastic wealth through war, plunder, and extortion, could be satisfied only by the most extended world trade" (1891, completely revised from the first edition in 1864; quoted in Roth [n. 34 above], p. 236). For Weber's reference to Meitzen, see Weber, *Die römische Agrargeschichte in ihrer Bedeutung für das Staats- und Privatrecht* (1891; Amsterdam, 1962), pp. 5, 6.

41. Lindenlaub (n. 35 above), p. 276; Roth, p. 237. Schmoller apparently also attacked Rodbertus, putting him in the same boat with the socialist leader and sometime follower of Marx, Lassalle.

42. Troeltsch writes further:

Weber has everywhere used the ideas of the Marxist questioning after the link of base and superstructure and precisely in this regard has his research yielded the most interesting and significant results. Thus, in his *Roman Agrarian History,* he has illuminated the history of landed property or, as Marx says, the secret history of Rome; in addition, this study has clarified the economic basis of the decline of antiquity and the transition to the middle ages. (*Der Historismus und seine Probleme,* in *Gesammelte Schriften* [Tübingen, 1922], 3:367.)

Karl Löwith has written in a similar vein:

> It is remarkable that neither Marxist nor bourgeois sociology notices that Weber's sociology is the counterpart to Marx's *Capital.* The essay on the social basis of the decline of ancient civilization presupposes the method of historical materialism; in this essay, Weber's point of departure is the contradiction between the relations of production and the forces of production. ("Entzauberung der Welt durch Wissenschaft," *Merkur* 196 [June 1964]:504.)

The Baumgarten quotation is from Roth, p. 235. In this interesting historiographic article, upon which I have drawn for some of the important facts mentioned here, Roth's conclusion is that the impact of Marxism on Weber was very limited or, more likely, nonexistent. Roth cites, e.g., the fact that there is no evidence that Weber had read Marx at the time he was doing his early work. In arguing for some distinctive influence, I have sought to demonstrate that whether Weber had read Marx is not crucial for the question of whether he was affected by Marxism or by materialist thinking more generally. In my view, Roth treats the question too much as a historical and not enough as a theoretical point.

43. Weber, "The Stock Exchange," in Runciman, *Selections* (n. 33 above), pp. 374–377, quoting p. 377. This selection is from "Die Börse II" (1896), reprinted as "Ergebnisse der deutschen Borsenenquete" in Weber, *Gesammelte Aufsätze zur Soziologie und Sozialpolitik* (Tübingen, 1924), pp. 318–322.

44. See Bendix, *Max Weber*, p. 28, from "Borsenenquete," *Zeitschrift für gesamte Handelsrecht* 45 (1896):114–116.

45. Quoted in Mommsen (n. 7 above), pp. 29–30. The statements are from the section of Weber's 1895 inaugural speech that Runciman (n. 33 above) did not translate. For more on Weber's Realpolitik attitude and his understanding of national imperialism, see Mommsen, pp. 41–42.

46. Quoted in David Beetham, *Max Weber and the Theory of Modern Politics* (London, 1974), p. 219. Weber made these statements in 1894 in a speech to Naumann's Protestant Social Congress.

47. Ibid.

48. Weber, *Die römische Agrargeschichte* (n. 40 above), p. 6. This was not, however, Weber's first major study. In 1889 he completed his first dissertation on trading companies in the Middle Ages, which I do not deal with here.

49. Ibid.

50. Ibid.

51. Ibid., p. 7.

52. Weber, "The Social Causes of the Decline of Ancient Civilization," *The Agrarian Sociology of Ancient Civilizations* (n. 31 above), pp. 387–411. The "Social Causes" essay, published in 1896, should be read with the 1891 dissertation (n. 40 above), rather than with the monograph *Agrarian*

Conditions in Antiquity, with which it is now published. Although earlier versions of the latter date to the late 1890s, the final version was published in 1908 and bears a much closer resemblance to the writing of Weber's later period than the 1896 essay.

53. Weber, "Social Causes," p. 399.

54. Ibid., p. 410. It should be noted that the 1891 dissertation was not only a study of political and economic conflict. It also discussed legal structures at great length, yet these, too, generally reflect an instrumental bent.

55. Weber, "Die Verhältnisse der Landarbeiter im ostelbischen Deutschland," *Schriften des Vereins für Sozialpolitik* (Leipzig, 1892), vol. 55; "Privatenqueten über die Lage der Landarbeiter," *Mitteilungen des ev.-soz. Kongresses,* vol. 3 (April–July 1892); "Die ländliche Arbeitsverfassung," *Schriften des Vereins für Sozialpolitik* (Leipzig, 1893), vol. 58; "Entwicklungstendenzen in der Lage der ostelbischen Landarbeiter," *Archiv für soziale Gesetzgebung* (1894), vol. 7. In the following discussion, I draw mostly from the last article, published in 1894, which is the only one translated into English (see n. 56). There are some empirical and ideological differences among the four pieces, but for our theoretical purposes the 1894 piece is certainly representative.

56. Weber, "Developmental Tendencies in the Situation of East Elbian Labourers," *Economy and Society* 8 (1979):177–205, quoting 177. (This is a translation of the "Entwicklungstendenzen" of 1894.) In "Social Science and Political Commitments in the Young Max Weber," Vernon K. Dibble has shown that in these early writings on agricultural conditions in Prussia Weber's colleagues on the Verein project presented much more individualistic analyses of the situation. Where they emphasized contractual agreements, Weber emphasized organization; where they emphasized personality, he emphasized characteristics of capitalism as an economic system. (*Archives des sociologie européenes* 9 [1968]:92–110). I would disagree with Dibble, however, in his presentation of the early Weber principally as a materialist, let alone one in the tradition of Marx.

57. Weber, "Developmental Tendencies," p. 178.

58. Ibid.

59. Ibid., p. 179.

60. Ibid., pp. 181–183.

61. Ibid., p. 183.

62. Ibid., p. 180. He expands these conditions, still in an instrumental way, on p. 184.

63. Ibid., pp. 184–193.

64. Ibid., p. 193.

65. Ibid., pp. 187, 199.

66. "Die Verhältnisse," pp. 9–10; "Developmental Tendencies," pp.

179–180. For *Klassenherrschaft*, see "Entwicklungstendenzen," pp. 4–9, 20. This term ("class domination") is frequently used by Marx. I will comment on the translation controversy over *Herrschaft* in my discussion of Weber's political sociology.

67. "Developmental Tendencies," p. 191.

68. Ibid., 190.

69. Ibid., p. 180, italics in original.

70. Weber, "The Stock Exchange" (n. 43 above), p. 375.

71. Discussed by Bendix (n. 6 above), p. 27, referring to Weber, "Börsenenquete" (n. 43 above).

72. "The Stock Exchange," p. 376–377.

73. "Die Verhältnisse," p. 796.

74. *Die römische Agrargeschichte* (n. 40 above), p. 1.

75. This quotation is from the 1893 "Die ländliche Arbeitsverfassung," in Mitzman (n. 45 above), p. 105.

76. Weber, "Economic Policy and the National Interest in Imperial Germany" (n. 33 above), p. 267.

77. Ibid., p. 263; cf. pp. 266–267 and "Developmental Tendencies," p. 201.

78. "Developmental Tendencies," pp. 178–179.

79. Ibid., p. 178.

80. Ibid., p. 180.

81. Ibid., p. 202.

82. Weber made this statement in his 1895 inaugural address, reprinted in *Gesammelte politische Schriften* (Munich, 1911), pp. 7–30, quoting p. 13. Runciman (n. 13 above) did not translate this segment.

83. Ibid.

84. "Die Verhältnisse," pp. 797–798.

85. "Developmental Tendencies," p. 191.

86. Ibid.

87. "Die Verhältnisse," pp. 796–798.

88. Ibid., p. 202. The impact of the neo-Kantian twist to liberal idealism is, perhaps, particularly evident in this quotation (see n. 33 above).

At approximately the same time, Weber wrote in a similar vein, in a Christian magazine, *Die christliche Welt*, defending the right of working class to education.

> Modern workingmen want more than forbearance, compassionate understanding, and charity; they demand the recognition of their right to reflect about the same things, and in the same way, as the so-called educated people. . . . Their intellect has emancipated itself from bondage to tradition, and we should not only understand this and view it with indulgence, but take it into account and recognize it as something justified. (Quoted in Marianne Weber [n. 22 above], p. 133.)

89. "The Social Causes of the Decline of Ancient Civilization" (n. 52 above), p. 398.

90. Ibid., p. 400.

91. Ibid., p. 410.

92. Need I add that I am not speaking of actual influence or concrete reference? Weber and Durkheim were contemporaries, but no one has been able to establish any references by either to the other's work. I am using "Durkheim," then, to indicate the theoretical position which I attributed to him in vol. 2.

93. Bendix (n. 6 above), pp. 42, 29, italics added.

94. Mommsen (n. 7 above), ch. 2, "The Champion of Nationalist Power Politics and Imperialism," pp. 22–46.

95. Dibble (n. 56 above), passim.

96. See n. 42 above.

97. Parsons (n. 12 above), p. 503. Carl Mayer makes the same point: "In the first phase of [his] scientific work . . before 1900, what Weber did was to utilize the categories in Marx's system in a unique manner for his own investigations" ("Max Weber's Interpretation of Karl Marx," *Social Research* 42[1975]:700–728, quoting 701). Anthony Giddens argues, similarly, that Marx's studies of capitalism in Rome converged with Weber's subsequent investigations ("Marx, Weber, and the Development of Capitalism," in Giddens, *Studies in Social and Political Theory* [New York, 1977], pp. 183–207, see pp. 197–198).

98. Mitzman (n. 38 above), p. 79. Alone among these interpreters of Weber's early works, Mitzman recognizes at one point that Weber offers a competing explanation to the one he himself has highlighted. Yet in the very process of recognizing that Weber has also suggested material along with psychological factors, Mitzman tries to explain this ambiguity in a way that eliminates its theoretical independence. Instead of an analytic problem, it must be a psychological and, ultimately, a "social" one.

> Ockham's razor or any other rule of intellectual parsimony would suggest that the material factor of a declining living standard had destroyed the *Instmann*'s [land worker's] "extraordinarily secure economic position" and thus might alone be sufficient to explain [his] flight from the Junker estates. But Weber does not even make the connection. When the fuses of logical connection blow in the mind of a man of genius, one can only assume an emotional overload. Certainly, on the basis of what we already know about Weber, it is reasonable to assume that he was himself obsessed by the same "psychological factors of overwhelming force" that he attributed (projected?) to the land workers. (P. 101.)

I am not, of course, in any manner ruling out the possibility that a relationship could be drawn between the ambiguities and inconsistencies of Weber's theoretical logic and his psychological and social situation. I would simply argue, first, that before any connection can be correctly established the true theoretical situation must be pursued independently and, second, that the cognitive level has some independent status vis-à-vis the psychological, so that any psychological predisposition would have to be mediated by intellectual concerns.

CHAPTER TWO

1. Siegfried Landshut, *Kritik der Soziologie* (Munich and Leipzig, 1927), p. 38.

2. Hans Freyer, *Soziologie als Wirklichkeitswissenschaft* (Leipzig and Berlin, 1930), p. 147.

3. Talcott Parsons, *The Structure of Social Action* (New York, [1937] 1968), vol. 2.

4. Reinhard Bendix, *Max Weber: An Intellectual Portrait* (Berkeley and Los Angeles, [1960] 1978), pp. xxiii–xxiv, and p. 285.

5. Although Bendix states at one point merely that "in conception and scope [Weber's] political analysis stands on a par with his sociology of religion" (ibid., p. xxiv), the implicit object of his book is to organize the sociology of religion within the more political categories and in the more political context of the sociology of domination. "Since the original remained incomplete," he writes, "Weber's attempt to integrate his work demands an interpretation." Bendix provides this by placing the work in a new context: "My purpose in writing this book has been to make Weber's sociological work . . . more thematically coherent than it is either in the original or in translation" (p. xix).

> I have, therefore, organized the materials of Weber's sociological studies in line with what I take to be the systematic core of his posthumous work, *Wirtschaft und Gesellschaft* [*Economy and Society*] (p. xxiv).
>
> Weber's earliest work as a social scientist was devoted to the study of status groups and the influence of ideas on behavior. These interests set the stage for his three-volume work on the sociology of religion, which dealt among other things with the *power* of individual leaders or of status groups like priests in their relations with the masses. In his later studies this subordinate interest in the phenomenon of power became the dominant theme, and one may ask what Weber conceived to be the relation between these two major parts of his work. Unfortunately he died before he could integrate his various substantive studies in an explicit manner. It is possible, however, to find clues for such an integration in his work, especially in the framework of definitions that he wrote toward the end of his life. (P. 285, italics in original.)

Roth takes much the same position in his reconstruction of the relative importance of different dimensions of Weber's work—although he tilts

toward the political sociology even more strongly. See "Introduction,"
pp. xxxiii–cx in Max Weber, *Economy and Society*, ed. Guenther Roth and
Claus Wittich (Berkeley and Los Angeles, 1978), hereafter cited as *ES* (cf.
ch. 4, n. 28, below).

Most of the segments of *Economy and Society* were first published in
English as independent works, and many students of Weber may still
rely on these rather than the 1,500-page edition prepared by Roth and
Wittich. I have, therefore, cited the independent works, followed by the
corresponding location in *ES*. I cite the original German only when it differs in some significant way from the English translation(s) cited, or
when I have inserted some word or phrase from the original or reference
to the literal meaning.

6. Günter Abramowski, *Das Geschichtsbild Max Webers* (Stuttgart,
1966), p. 12.

7. F. H. Tenbruck discussed these bibliographic issues in "Das Werk
Max Webers," *Kölner Zeitschrift für Soziologie and Sozialpsychologie* 27
(1975): 663–702 (published in translation as "The Problem of Thematic
Unity in the Work of Max Weber," *British Journal of Psychology* 31[1980]:
316–351). Schluchter's research has yielded much the same result; see
his "Excursus: The Selection and Dating of the Works Used," in Guenther
Roth and Wolfgang Schluchter, *Max Weber's Vision of History: Ethics and
Methods* (Berkeley and Los Angeles, 1979), pp. 59–64. For some of these
recent developments in the German literature on Weber, see Stephen
Kalberg, "The Search for Thematic Orientations in a Fragmented Oeuvre:
The Discussion of Max Weber in Recent German Sociological Literature," *Sociology* 13 (1979): 127–139. Tenbruck's researches were stirred
in part by the "revisionist" bibliographical work of Benjamin Nelson;
see, e.g., Nelson, "Max Weber's 'Author's Introduction' (1920): A Master
Clue to His Main Aims," *Sociological Inquiry* 44 (1974): 269–278. None of
these bibliographic claims are definitive, however; their most important
effect, in my view, is to throw doubt on any analytic argument that rests
on such historical-bibliographic foundations.

8. Tenbruck, "The Problem of Thematic Unity," p. 344; for Schluchter
and Nelson, see n. 7 above. In fact, what appears as Weber's "Introduction" to *The Protestant Ethic and the Spirit of Capitalism* (1904–1905) in
the English edition (New York, [1930] 1958) was probably the last piece
he wrote, finished in 1920.

9. Tenbruck, p. 327.

In speaking of Weber's comparative studies of religion, I am primarily referring to the monographs on China, India, and ancient Israel,
although the essays "Religious Rejections of the World and Their Directions" (n. 30 below), "The Social Psychology of World Religions" (n. 133
below), and the "Author's Introduction" to *The Protestant Ethic and the
Spirit of Capitalism* would also be included in this category of later re-

ligious writings. With the exception of the last essay noted, all these works were published by Weber between 1915 and 1919 in the *Archiv für Sozialwissenschaft und Sozialpolitik*. Afterward, Weber revised some of these pieces, added the "Author's Introduction," and prepared them for republication as his collected essays in the sociology of religion (*Gesammelte Aufsätze zur Religionssoziologie*), which also included his revised *The Protestant Ethic and the Spirit of Capitalism* and "The Protestant Sects and the Spirit of Capitalism" (1906). The collection was published posthumously in three volumes in 1920–1921 in Tübingen.

10. I have drawn this chronology from the work of Tenbruck, Nelson, and Schluchter, cited above, and from Eduard Baumgarten, *Max Weber: Werk und Person* (Tübingen, 1964); Paul Honigsheim, *On Max Weber* (New York, 1968); and Marianne Weber, *Max Weber: A Biography* (New York, [1926] 1974). I am grateful to Professor Steven Seidman for his help on this issue. Without further research, however, this chronology remains an approximation.

11. Weber, "Die Wirtschaftsethik der Weltreligionen: Religionssoziologische Skizzen," *Archiv für Sozialwissenschaft und Sozialpolitik* 41 (1915): 1, quoted in Schluchter (n. 7 above), pp. 63–64.

12. The focus here is on the development of a more consistently voluntaristic, multidimensional theory on the most general level, that of Weber's presuppositions. In his ideological evaluation of modern life, a less voluntaristic understanding of modernity may have emerged. It seems likely, as Mitzman emphasizes, that for psychological reasons associated with the failure to resolve fully the emotional problems which produced his breakdown, Weber entered the period of his mature writings with a significantly more pessimistic view of the possibility for freedom in his own time—though in making this transition he was also motivated by the strong antimodernist and conservative strains in German ideology, as well as, of course, by real shifts in the German situation. Before the breakdown, Weber was more positive and confident about the possibility of replacing the Junker class, about the future of progressive historical change, about the successful application of aggressive national power. In the later period, there is a pronounced note of despair in his understanding of developments. (Arthur Mitzman, *The Iron Cage* [New York, 1970], passim.) Once again, I must stress that such ideological considerations can, in their turn, be articulated only in conjunction with the independent development of presuppositions. Before these later ideological evaluations are considered, the nature of Weber's independent theoretical commitments should be fully understood.

In making this argument for the further development of Weber's theoretical orientation, I am not arguing that his empirical understanding drastically changed. As Guenther Roth notes, Weber had already begun to lecture on the relationship between Protestantism and capitalism in Heidelberg in 1897 (Roth, "The Historical Relationship to Marxism," in Reinhard Bendix and Guenther Roth, *Scholarship and Partisanship: Essays on Max Weber* [Berkeley and Los Angeles, 1971], pp. 227–252, see p. 244). Indeed, many of the empirical emphases in the early writings are continued in the later work, as will become evident. Here I argue only that the presuppositional position Weber brought to his empirical interests underwent a significant shift.

13. Cited in Guy Oakes, "Introduction," in Max Weber, *Roscher and Knies: The Logical Problems of Historical Economics* (New York, 1975), p. 15, from Weber, *Gesammelte Aufsätze zur Wissenschaftslehre*, 3d ed. (Tübingen, 1968), p. 218, hereafter cited as *GAW.*

14. Weber, *Roscher and Knies*, p. 191 (*GAW,* p. 132). Because of the controversy over the meaning of *Zweckrationalität* in Weber's formal conceptual scheme—which will be discussed shortly—I will alert the reader to the appearance of *Zweck* wherever it occurs in these crucial early formulations.

15. Ibid., pp. 120–121.

16. Ibid., p. 191.

17. Ibid., p. 192 (*GAW,* p. 132).

18. Ibid., p. 121, italics in original (*GAW,* p. 64).

19. Ibid., p. 192; cf. pp. 192–193.

20. Ibid., p. 191.

21. Ibid., p. 192. This position undoubtedly reflects the impact of the neo-Kantian refraction of German Idealism which I refer to in ch. 1.

22. Ibid., p. 61.

23. Max Weber, " 'Objectivity' in Social Science and Social Policy," pp. 50–112 in his *The Methodology of the Social Sciences* (New York, 1949), p. 64. This essay is among the earliest writings after Weber's recovery; it was published in 1904.

24. Ibid., p. 65 (*GAW,* p. 163).

25. Ibid., pp. 68–69.

26. Ibid., pp. 64–65.

27. Ibid., p. 70.

28. Ibid., p. 81, italics in original.

29. Ibid., p. 70.

30. Weber, "Religious Rejections of the World and Their Directions," pp. 323–359 in Hans Gerth and C. Wright Mills, eds., *From Max Weber* (New York, 1958), p. 328.

31. " 'Objectivity' " (n. 23 above), p. 81, italics in original.

Critics of "functionalist sociology," in either its Durkheimian or its Parsonian form, have often portrayed Weber as an "individualistic" rather than a "collectivist" thinker. (See, e.g., Reinhard Bendix, "Max Weber's Interpretation of Conduct and History," *American Journal of So-*

ciology 51 [1946]:518–526, and his later *Max Weber* [n. 4 above], pp. 288–291; Don Martindale, *The Nature and Types of Sociological Theory* [Boston, 1960], pp. 377–393; and Steven J. Lukes, *Emile Durkheim* [New York, 1972], pp. 19–20.) Perceiving Weber's emphasis on concrete groups and individual phenomena like leadership, these critics have mistakenly identified such emphases with philosophical nominalism. There certainly are important distinguishing qualities about such an emphasis, but they are not located on the generalized level that identifies a theorist's orientation to social order as I have defined that problem. In these presuppositional terms, Weber was certainly a collectivist: he sought to analyze the arrangements that structured individual action. Thus, as I have indicated above, he was concerned with "values," "culture," "institutions," and "orders," and with the sui generis principles around which they were organized. That this perspective informed his actual empirical work will be demonstrated throughout the analysis which follows. I indicate it further in the conceptual discussion that immediately follows in the text. Weber was concerned with the "uniformities of action," and he believed that it is with these *"typical modes of action"* that sociology is concerned.

The documentation for the assertion of Weber's nominalism rests mainly with the opening sections of his *Economy and Society*. Here Weber directly criticizes functional and organismic reasoning in sociology. What is important to understand, however, is that in these passages he is not criticizing the notion that collective order exists but rather specific ways of framing this existence. He objects, on the one hand, to those forms of idealist theorizing in which spirit (*Geist*) is given the qualities of an active historical agent. Against this notion he argues that "there is no such thing as a collective personality which 'acts' " (p. 14) and that "collectivities must be treated as *solely* the resultants and modes of organization of the particular acts of individual persons" (p. 13, italics in original). On the other hand, Weber's criticism is directed against "structuralist" functional theories that exclude subjectivity. He juxtaposes a focus on "functional relationships" with an analysis of "the subjective understanding of the action of the [society's] component individuals" (p. 15). In terms of the understanding of order that I have offered, of course, a collective emphasis excludes neither a focus on individuals as active agents nor, certainly, the subjective understanding of the sources of action.

It is revealing, in these terms, to compare Weber with Durkheim. Durkheim also criticized the organicism of German (and French) thought. He insisted that concrete actors are the only sources of "social order," and he made this commitment, much as Weber did, because of his sympathy with the individualistic liberal tradition. Durkheim focused on the uniformities of social life, but, again, like Weber, he tried to connect these uniformities to processes of individual interaction. The difference between the two thinkers, then, was not over their self-conscious intentions but in their respective abilities to realize them. Durkheim's understanding of the "social" sometimes appeared to be similar to the organicism criticized by Weber—in part because, particularly in the early phases of his career, he was so affected by utilitarian individualism that he could portray the social only as acting "coercively" against the free individual. This problem was reinforced by the full-blown positivism which often led Durkheim, despite his more general theoretical intention, to describe the force of collective arrangements in a mechanical way. Thus, while Durkheim readily agreed with Weber's strictures against mechanical functionalism and reified organicism, he was not always able to make this agreement clear. Weber, by contrast, suffered from neither of these limitations. Better versed than Durkheim in cultural history and symbolic philosophy, he more easily could articulate the relation of individuals to cultural tradition. He understood from the beginning that human motivation was intrinsically informed by cultural life. Equally important, and this also can be attributed to the German intellectual milieu, Weber never shared the slightest whiff of Durkheim's positivism. Since symbolic interpretation was part of his scientific method, he had no difficulty in understanding it to be part of the actor's relationship to the social world.

I am not asserting that differences between Weber and Durkheim do not exist. My point is simply that the differences do not revolve around the presuppositional question of individualistic versus collectivistic order. In addition to the contrasts which I have cited as explanations for their *apparent* divergence, there also is an important distinction to be made in their respective understandings of the appropriate model for analyzing collective life. Durkheim did employ a functional model; Weber eschewed systemic models for more institutional ones. Still, on the presuppositional question of individual versus collective order both theorists substantially agreed. And if Weber was in a better position than Durkheim to present an alternative to organicist thinking, this does not imply that he always made use of this relative clarity, as the discussion in the chapters following will amply show.

32. Weber, *Theory of Social and Economic Organization* (New York, [1947] 1964), pp. 115–118, hereafter cited as *TSEO*; *ES*, pp. 24–26.

33. Ibid., p. 123; *ES*, p. 30.

34. Ibid., p. 116; *ES*, p. 25.

35. Ibid.

36. In terms of this presuppositional reference, "traditional" action is a residual category. Its presuppositional components break down into either "affective" or "*wertrational.*"

37. Ibid., p. 117; *ES*, p. 26.
38. Ibid.
39. Ibid.
40. Ibid.
41. Ibid.
42. *TSEO*, p. 120; *ES*, p. 29.
43. *TSEO*, p. 121; *ES*, p. 29.
44. *TSEO*, p. 122; *ES*, p. 30.
45. Ibid.
46. Ibid.
47. *TSEO*, pp. 107–108; *ES*, p. 18, italics in original.
48. *TSEO*, pp. 107–108; *ES*, p. 18, italics in original. In Weber's formal discussion of the different types of social groups that occurs later in this first chapter a similar, though more latent tension can be found. In sec. 9 of the chapter, Weber suggests that there are two basic types of social relationships which are the basis of collective action: communal and associative. He explicitly derives these from Tönnies' dichotomy, naming them *Vergemeinschaftung* and *Vergesellschaftung*. In terms of his formal discussion, Weber allows that the latter, associative relationship could include both *zweckrational* and value-related kinds of action, yet his identification with Tönnies indicates in a more implicit way the problems I have just pointed out, i.e., his partial tendency to understand the collective order associated with *zweckrationalität* as only instrumental. Tönnies postulated two kinds of will or action, *Wesenwill* ("natural will") and *Kürwille* ("rational will," or *Willkür*). The former indicates primitive, unreflective emotional action, the latter refers to action that is rational, calculated, artificial, and technical, unrelated to deeply held values. These wills correspond to different orders, *Wesenwill* to community or *Gemeinschaft*, and *Willkür* to association or *Gesellschaft*—the latter characterizing the predominant order of modern times. Tönnies' *Gesellschaft* expressed his deep alienation from modern industrial society, for it identified the relationship of pure instrumentality of exchange, the soullessness of capitalist economic life. The term, in fact, was based at least in part on the kind of action that Tönnies had discovered in the social theory of Hobbes (pt. 2, sec. 14 of *Gemeinschaft und Gesellschaft*), whose work he translated into German. A socialist, Tönnies identified *Gesellschaft* with the impersonal, commodity-dominated capitalist world described by Marx (sec. 40, pt. 1). (For a good discussion of these issues in Tönnies' work, see Arthur Mitzman, *Sociology and Estrangement* [New York, 1973], pp. 63–100.)

Despite Weber's formal denial, then, it is not entirely fortuitous that he has offered a definition of group life in terms of Tönnies' concept, for his own discussion of order earlier in this work rested partly upon a similarly instrumental understanding of *Zweckrationalität*. Tönnies' "rational will," in fact, reveals the same ambiguities as Weber's "purposefully rational action." Tönnies formally identifies it with self-conscious thinking about an end, but as he develops the concept further it comes increasingly to resemble more purely instrumental antivoluntary acts.

> In the ideal case [of rational action], the end itself—i.e., the thought of it—dominates all other thoughts and considerations and, therefore, all deliberate actions. They must serve the end or purpose, conduce toward it, or at least not impede it. Therefore, many ends or purposes become subservient to one single end, and many thoughts are amalgamated into one leading idea, the realization of which seems to serve their own ends. These secondary ends are thus themselves degraded to mere means, viz., in regard to the ulterior purpose. The perfect domination of thinking over volition [i.e., natural will] would establish a hierarchy.... [Thus,] in defining his rational will as disposal of means man transforms a piece of his imaginary freedom into its very opposite, which at first is itself only imaginary but becomes real in the process. His own master otherwise, man becomes, in thus pledging himself, his own debtor and servant. (Pp. 120, 126 in Charles Loomis' translation, *Community and Society* [New York, 1963].)

Cf. Fritz Ringer's statement that "Tönnies associated *Kürwille* with what Max Weber later called *zweckrational* behavior" (*The Decline of the German Mandarins*, [Cambridge, Mass., 1969], p. 165).

The analytical problems in Weber's typology of action have rarely received the examination they deserve because most analysts have focused on their empirical or ideological reference alone. Bendix, e.g., speaks of the categorizations simply as "common sense" empirical generalizations (*Max Weber* [n. 4 above], p. 288, n. 8, and p. 477), and pays them no further attention. Virtually alone among Weber's interpreters, Parsons recognizes the serious nature of the problem—he orients himself directly to the presuppositional level—despite the fact that in considering Weber's work as a whole he treats the problem as anomalous. Thus, Parsons notices the tension between normative and instrumental usages of *Zweckrationalität* (*TSEO*, p. 115, n. 38 [ed.'s note]), and provides an excellent account of how a concept that denotes such exclusive rationality is incompatible with a more fully developed conception of the "unit act," his technical term for the category of social action. "The criteria by which rational types are distinguished [by Weber]," he writes, "are not adequate to describe . . . a total unit [because] a 'purely rational' act or system is a contradiction in terms—it is not 'objectively possible'" ("Introduction," in *TSEO*, p. 17). Parsons also comes closer than any other commentator to considering the possible consequences of this generalized reduction. Because "Weber falls into . . . thinking in terms of a certain kind of abstract dichotomy," the normative, or nonrational, value element may come to be considered as outside the boundary of *concretely* rational activity: "Elements which may well in some empirical cases be integrated with the rational elements in a system, are pushed into conflict with it" (ibid., p. 16). The penetrating quality of this observation will be apparent in subsequent chapters. My present analysis, however, seriously departs from Parsons' in that he actually considers the source of this dichotomizing error to be Weber's meta-methodological commitment to "theory building" on the basis of the empirical generalizations Weber calls ideal types. Parsons' criticism of the ideal typical method is clearly related to his evaluation of the action problem:

> The ideal type contains no particular statements of fact. But it does, logically, involve a fixed relation between the values of various variable elements involved. If analysis is confined to its use, certain possibilities of variation on other levels are arbitrarily excluded from consideration. . . .
> The use of the ideal type concentrates attention on extreme or polar types [and] leads to a kind of "type atomism," one aspect of which is to minimize the elements which link the type in question with other elements of the structure of the same system. (Ibid., pp. 13, 15.)

Since the weaknesses in Weber's action discussion are not, in Parsons' view, actually related to Weber's theorizing itself, Parsons can sustain his interpretation that Weber's work is consistently multidimensional. It is because of this bracketing of his crucial objections to Weber that Parsons' analysis of Weber's understanding of action converges with Bendix's.

Because of the fundamental ambiguities in Weber's understanding of *zweckrational*, I have generally refrained from offering an English translation when the term occurs in Weber's text. The English phrase "purposefully rational," e.g., implies a normative reference, whereas the phrase "instrumental action" implies a purely materialist orientation. Since it is precisely the impossibility of both connotations that Weber's ambiguous usage of *zweckrational* allows, it seems best to avoid a translation that commits the term to one connotation rather than the other.

49. For a recent methodological discussion, see Thomas Burger, *Max Weber's Theory of Concept Formation: History, Laws, and Ideal Types* (Durham, N.C., 1976).

50. This sentence is from Weber, *Roscher and Knies* (n. 13 above), p. 149; the preceding sentence is from the same, pp. 64–65, italics added.

51. *TSEO,* p. 88; *ES,* p. 4.

52. *Roscher and Knies,* p. 125.

53. Ibid., italics in original; cf. pp. 128–129.

54. Ibid., p. 142 (*GAW,* p. 83). While in the German Weber speaks of this cultural context as an "influencer" of behavior, the distinction between "influence" and "determination" is not automatically apparent,

since "determination" itself can be meant in a hard or soft sense. This is the same point I made in the discussion of Engels' famous "Letter to Bloch" (vol. 2, ch. 10). So much has been made of the linguistic categories Engels employed—"influencing," "determining," "corresponding to"—that his actual theoretical logic has been ignored. These words can have different meanings depending on their context, and this context must be comprehended in terms of the theoretical architecture within which they are deployed.

55. *TSEO*, pp. 90–92; *ES*, p. 5.

56. Ibid., p. 91; *ES*, p. 5, italics added.

57. Ibid.

58. Ibid., pp. 107–108; *ES*, p, 18, italics added.

59. Ibid., p. 108; *ES*, p. 18 (Weber, *Wirtschaft und Gesellschaft* [1922; Tübingen, 1956], p. 13, hereafter cited as *WG*).

60. Ibid.

61. Ibid.; *ES*, pp. 18–19.

62. Ibid., p. 97; *ES*, p. 11.

63. Ibid.

64. *Roscher and Knies*, p. 177 (*GAW*, p. 118).

65. Ibid., p. 183.

66. Ibid.

67. *TSEO*, p. 97; *ES*, p. 10.

68. Ibid.

69. Ibid.

70. As Weber himself often remarked, in Western society the concept of "rationalization" is multivocal: the world can be rationalized in a number of different ways and, in fact, has been. See. e.g., Weber, *The Protestant Ethic* (n. 8 above), pp. 13–31; "Religious Rejections," (n. 30 above), p. 293; "The Meaning of 'Ethical Neutrality' in Sociology and Economics" (1971), pp. 1–49 in *Methodology* (n. 23 above), pp. 34ff. The principal types of empirical processes or instances Weber evoked with this term were: (1) purely pragmatic and calculating action; (2) systematized action in the sense of consistent and methodical—formally rational—action; (3) universalistically regulated action—as regulated, e.g., by science; (4) substantively rational action, where universalistic reference is used to gain ends that the actor values above others. All four of these types can be subsumed, of course, under *zweckrational* and *wertrational* types of actions, a typology which, I have suggested earlier, has purposes other than simple empirical generalization. The historical process referred to above as "religious rationalization" involves aspects of the second, third, and fourth types of rationalization. The economic rationalization that this normative rationalization produces also involves aspects of these types—although, as I insist in the text, it is not rationalization of the first type. My intent in this section is not to illuminate this

empirically arresting diversity of societal rationalizations but rather to demonstrate that in producing them Weber also had a general theoretical point in mind—the requisites of a multidimensional presuppositional position—and that he complicated his empirical picture in order, at least in part, to amplify and specify this point. For discussions of rationalization from a more empirical perspective, see Ann Swidler, "The Concept of Rationality in the Work of Max Weber," *Sociological Inquiry* 43 (1973): 35–42; Wolfgang Schluchter, "The Paradox of Rationalization: On the Relation of Ethics and the World," in Roth and Schluchter, *Max Weber's Vision of History* (n. 7 above), pp. 11–64; Stephen Kalberg, "Max Weber's Types of Rationality: Cornerstones for the Analysis of Rationalization Processes in History," *American Journal of Sociology* 85 (1980):1145–1179; and Donald N. Levine, "Rationality and Freedom: Weber and Beyond," *Sociological Inquiry* 51 (1981): 5–26. Among all these discussions, Levine's is the most careful to interrelate presuppositional, empirical, and ideological levels of Weber's analysis, and his discussion of the philosophical roots of Weber's multidimensional perspective on rationality is an exceptionally searching one. I believe, nonetheless, that Levine "reads into "Weber's work more consistency on this issue than actually exists (see below, particularly chs. 4–5 and ch. 6, n. 21).

71. Weber, *Protestant Ethic*, p. 53.

72. Ibid., pp. 102–103.

73. Ibid., p. 108.

74. Weber, *The Sociology of Religion* (Boston, 1963), p. 166; *ES*, p. 542.

75. *Sociology of Religion*, p. 166.

76. *Protestant Ethic*, p. 117. Cf. Weber, *Gesammelte Aufsätze zur Religionssoziologie*, 3 vols. (Tübingen, 1920–21), 1: 14–15, hereafter cited as *RS*.

77. *Protestant Ethic*, p. 117, italics added.

78. *Sociology of Religion*, p. 168; *ES*, p. 544 (*RS*, 1:14–15).

79. Ibid., pp. 167–168; *ES*, p. 543 (*WG*, p. 423).

80. *Protestant Ethic*, p. 101 (*RS*, 1:91).

81. *Sociology of Religion*, pp. 172–173; *ES*, pp. 547–548 (*WG*, pp. 426–427).

82. *Protestant Ethic*, pp. 101–102.

83. Ibid., p. 103 (*RS*, 1:93).

84. Ibid., p. 224 (*RS*, 1:99n.). More literally translated, "into the field" reads "onto the track," a phrase which relates directly to Weber's more general discussion of the role of ideas in history, as will be seen in sec. 5 below.

85. *The Sociology of Religion*, pp. 207, 220–222.

86. Weber, *The Religion of China: Confucianism and Taoism* (Glencoe, Ill., 1951), p. 241.

87. Ibid., p. 228.

88. Ibid., p. 242.

89. Ibid., italics added.

90. Ibid., p. 144.

91. Ibid., pp. 144–146.

92. Ibid., p. 145.

93. Ibid., p. 235.

94. Ibid.

95. Ibid.

96. Ibid., p. 241.

97. Ibid., p. 236.

98. Ibid., p. 241.

99. Ibid.

100. Ibid., pp. 236–237. *"Sachlich"* can also be translated as "objective," as it has been in some earlier quoted passages.

101. Ibid., p. 236.

102. Ibid., pp. 236–237.

103. Ibid., p. 246.

104. Ibid.

105. Ibid., p. 241 (*RS*, 1:528). *"Versachlichung"* can also be translated as "reification." Since it is Lukács and other twentieth-century Marxists who have emphasized the "reified" character of modern capitalism, this usage points to the kind of similarities between Weber's and Marx's views of modern capitalism that I will emphasize in later chapters.

106. "Crucial experiment" is the way Talcott Parsons designated Durkheim's method (*The Structure of Social Action* [New York, [1937] 1968], p. 501).

107. *Sociology of Religion* (n. 74 above), p. 117; *ES*, p. 499. The present discussion refers to chs. 1–5 of *The Sociology of Religion*. Chs. 9–16 were important for the discussion of normative rationalization in the preceding section. Chs. 6–7 constitute the subject of the consideration of social class I will make below.

108. Ibid., p. 3; *ES*, p. 401.

109. Ibid.

110. Ibid., p. 10; *ES*, p. 407.

111. Ibid.

112. Ibid., p. 13; *ES*, p. 409 (*WG*, p. 325).

113. Ibid., p. 14; *ES*, 410 (*WG*, p. 326). Weber uses *"sachlich"* (here translated as "functional") and *"objectiv"* (here translated as "objective") interchangeably.

114. Ibid., p. 14; *ES*, p. 411.

115. Ibid., pp. 14–15; *ES*, p. 411.

116. Ibid., p. 15; *ES*, pp. 411–412 (*WG*, pp. 326–327).

117. Ibid.

118. Ibid., pp, 15–16; *ES*, p. 412.

119. Ibid., p. 16; *ES*, p. 412.

120. Ibid.

121. Ibid., pp. 22–23; *ES*, pp. 417–418 (*WG*, pp. 330–331). Weber's Latin *ratio*, which Roth and Wittich translate as "reason," is rendered by Parsons, with perhaps more thematic justification, as "the process of rationalization."

122. Ibid., pp. 22–23; *ES*, pp. 417–418.

123. Ibid., pp. 35–36; *ES*, p. 430.

124. Ibid., pp. 35–36; *ES*, p. 430.

125. Weber, *Ancient Judaism* (New York, 1952), p. 268.

126. Ibid.

127. Ibid., p. 275, italics added.

128. Ibid., italics added.

129. Ibid., p. 281.

130. Ibid.

131. These propositional arguments are the main focus, e.g., of most of the essays in Seymour Martin Lipset's and Reinhard Bendix's classic reader, *Class, Status, and Power* (New York, 1953). In the most sophisticated recent attempt to resolve this Marx-Weber debate, Anthony Giddens' *The Class Structure of Advanced Societies* (New York, 1973), the problem remains much the same. Although Giddens uses Weber to bring a greater variety of system elements into our understanding of how economic class relationships become structured, he still takes the concept of class as epistemologically satisfactory.

> The major problems in the theory of class ... do not so much concern the nature and application of the class concept itself, as what, for want of a better word, I shall call the *structuration* of class relationships. ... It is useful to follow and develop certain of Weber's insights in this respect. ... The most important blank spots in the theory of class concern the processes whereby "economic classes" become "social classes," and whereby in turn the latter are related to other social forms. ... [I wish] to focus upon *the modes in which* "economic" relationships become translated into "non-economic" social structures. (P. 105, italics in original.)

Giddens, in other words, has disconnected Weber's propositional innovations about pluralized stratification processes (the "translation" and "structuration" processes) from any reference to Weber's more generalized critique about the very presuppositions within which a "class" must be theoretically perceived. In terms of this more general revision, even the "pre-structurated" economic relationships must themselves be related to normative order, for their impact on consciousness cannot be conceived without it. Aside from problems in general theoretical logic, this problem occurs because of the influence of Marx's original formulation of the issue, where the "consciousness" of a class is usually equated with "class consciousness" in Marx's sense of a cohesive anticapitalist ideology which unites members of a similar structural position. In the Weberian terms I am suggesting here, however, it is clear that classes have "consciousness" at every point and, in fact, that the very existence of class is inseparable from the normative order (itself a multidimensional product) which, when internalized, defines for its members the meaning of their material environment.

132. Reinhard Bendix is perhaps the Weber scholar who has been most influential in bringing out the role of normative order in Weber's approach to class and its relationship to his sociology of religion (see e.g., "Status Groups and Classes," pp. 85–87 and passim in Bendix, *Max Weber* [New York, 1962]. One problem in Bendix's analysis, however, is his insistence that Weber employed the term "status group" rather than "class." Bendix justifies this usage textually by arguing that in the discourse of imperial Germany *Stand* usually implied social rank and status rather than simply objective position and power. This is certainly true, but we must also recall that Weber was in self-conscious rebellion against the status obsessions, and pretensions, of this German ideology. In fact, throughout Weber's work we can find *Stand* used in a neutral and purely conceptual way to indicate quite simply hierarchical ranking. We also find, indeed, numerous references to "class" in a purely economic sense, and to purely political groups, usages which will be investigated in the following chapters. For now, I wish simply to point out that in his effort to make Weber's work consistently multidimensional, Bendix too easily forecloses the question by equating every reference to *Stand* with "status group." (Although Bendix's treatment has been by far the most influential account, the most brilliant single essay on the interaction of Weber's theory of religion and his theory of class is, perhaps surprisingly, Talcott Parsons' "Introduction" to *The Sociology of Religion* [n. 74 above], pp. xix–lxvii, esp. pp. xxxvii–xlv.)

133. Weber, "The Social Psychology of World Religions," in Gerth and Mills, *From Max Weber* (n. 30 above), pp. 267–301, quoting p. 268, italics added.

134. Carlo Antoni, e.g., argues that this instrumental reference makes Weber's position virtually identical with Marx's analysis of ideology. "The various ethical systems," he writes, "here appear only as projections of class interest—they are indelibly stamped with designations such as 'bureaucratic,' 'warlike,' 'bourgeois,' and petty 'bourgeois' " (p. 138 in Carlo Antoni, "Religious Outlooks and Social Classes," pp. 135–140 in Dennis Wrong, ed., *Max Weber* [Englewood Cliffs, N.J., 1970]). Thus, Antoni forces Weber into a form of one-dimensional thought: "The real problem in these studies [of comparative economic ethics] is not the way in which the economic ethic determines a given socio-economic order but the way in which the socio-economic order determines the ethic" (ibid.).

135. "The Social Psychology of World Religions," p. 270.

136. Ibid., p. 286.

137. For the cultural heritage, see ibid., passim, and below in the text. For the upper-class prophet, see ibid., p. 277; *The Sociology of Religion*, pp. 101–102; *Ancient Judaism*, pp. 277–279.

138. "The Social Psychology of World Religions," p. 280. Weber uses the same phraseology about ideas as "tracks" in *The Protestant Ethic*, though this is not translated in the English version (see n. 84 above).

139. *Sociology of Religion*, p. 80; "Social Psychology," p. 283.

140. *Sociology of Religion*, p. 85; "Social Psychology," p. 283.

141. *Sociology of Religion*, pp. 89–90; "Social Psychology," p. 28–281.

142. *Sociology of Religion*, p. 97; *ES*, pp. 482–483 (*WG*, pp. 378–379).

143. "Social Psychology of World Religions," pp. 284–285, italics added.

144. *Sociology of Religion*, p. 97; *ES*, p. 483, italics added.

145. "Social Psychology," p. 284.

146. *Sociology of Religion*, p. 99; *ES*, p. 484.

147. Ibid., p. 96; *ES*, p. 482 (*WG*, p. 378).

148. Ibid., pp. 96–97; *ES*, p. 482.

149. "Social Psychology," p. 290. As if to underscore the independent importance of this prophetic promise, Weber follows his two chapters on class and religion in the *Sociology of Religion* segment of *ES* with seven chapters on comparative discussion of religious ethics.

150. For Weber's formulations on the structural position of the proletariat as an influence on its ideology, see *Sociology of Religion*, p. 100; for a general parallel between the asceticism of proletarian ideology and that of Puritanism, see *Protestant Ethic*, p. 162. For a discussion of proletarian ideology as a variant of the natural law tradition—itself partly the secularization of the transcendent Christian God—see Weber, *Law in Economy and Society* (New York, 1954), pp. 284–300. A good discussion of these issues in Weber's work is in Guenther Roth, "Religion and Revolutionary Beliefs: Sociological and Historical Dimensions in Weber's Work—In Memory of Ivan Vallier (1927–1974)," *Social Forces* 55 (1976): 257–272.

151. For a detailed discussion of the high degree of rationalization of this material component, see Weber's *General Economic History* (Glencoe, Ill., [1927] 1950), pp. 275–314 (reprinted with an introduction by Ira J. Cohen [New Brunswick, N.J., 1981]).

152. *Protestant Ethic*, p. 24. These considerations indicate the error of those materialist critics who treat the *Protestant Ethic* as an exercise in, or even the prototype of, idealist history. Gabriel Kolko argues, e.g., that the book is purely about "*Geist*" and that it makes no reference to material facts ("A Critique of Max Weber's Philosophy of History," *Ethics* 70 [1959]: 21–26, esp. 25). Richard Ashcraft suggests, similarly, that the *Protestant Ethic* "contained Weber's 'historical explanation' of the rise of

capitalism" and that it "relied upon the exaggeration of one factor of social life" ("Marx and Weber on Liberalism as Bourgeois Ideology," *Comparative Studies in Society and History* 14[1972]:130–168, quoting 160).
The class context of Weber's explanation shows that the second part of
this contention is incorrect, and the subsequent chapters of my discussion will demonstrate that this monograph on Protestantism hardly presents Weber's historical explanation of Western capitalism as such. The
multidimensional portrait I am presenting also disagrees fundamentally
with the recent attempt by Jere Cohen, Lawrence E. Hazelrigg, and
Whitney Pope to argue that Weber's treatment of traditionalism is only
instrumental, that it contains no reference to normative considerations
("De-Parsonsizing Weber: A Critique of Parsons' Interpretation of
Weber's Sociology," *American Sociology Review* 40 [1975]:229–241, esp.
231). While we will see later that there are, in fact, strong elements of
such treatment, to suggest this analysis as interpreting the totality of
Weber's work is to eliminate completely its most important achievement.

The interpretation presented here is much closer to that of some recent German criticism. Friedrich Tenbruck argues in "Das Werk Webers"
(n. 7 above) that Weber presented a multidimensional scheme of historical process where religious rationalization as an imminent development
played a vital role, but where material interests also played a significant
part. Tenbruck insists, as I have done here, that "interests" for Weber are
blind, that the specific content is imprinted by religious process ("The
Problem of Thematic Unity" [n. 7 above], pp. 334–342). Wolfgang
Schluchter has advanced much the same position in "The Paradox of Rationalization: On the Relation of Ethics and World," pp. 11–64 in Roth
and Schluchter, *Max Weber's Vision of History* (n. 7 above). I would disagree with these interpreters only in the weight I give to this multidimensional sociology in the totality of Weber's development—a point to which
we will return in subsequent chapters.

153. *Protestant Ethic*, p. 200, n. 23 (*RS*, 1:50).

154. Ibid., pp. 67–68.

155. Ibid., pp. 67–68.

156. Weber, *The City* (New York, 1962), pp. 127–129; *ES*, pp. 1260–
1262.

157. Ibid., p. 102; *ES*, p. 1242, italics added.

158. Ibid., p. 89; *ES*, p. 1227.

159. Ibid., pp. 90–91; *ES*, pp. 1228–1229.

160. Ibid., p. 89; *ES*, p. 1227.

161. Ibid., p. 91; *ES*, p. 1229.

162. Ibid., p. 109; *ES*, p. 1246. In the German text, Weber uses the
term *Bürger* for citizen, and Roth and Wittich often translate it simply as
"burgher." *Bürger* can denote a townsman, or middle-class person, but it
is also the principal word for citizen. *Bürgerkunde* is "civics," and *Bur-
gerrecht* usually means "civic law" or "civil freedom." This last usage

gets to the important substantive point, for it is clear from the general context of Weber's essay that when he uses *Bürger* he means much more than simply the reference to the physical location of the tradesman within the town walls. The issue is never put so clearly as in Weber's lecture on "citizenship" in his *General Economic History:*

> In the concept of citizenship [*Bürgertum*] as it is used in social history are bound up three distinct significations. First, citizenship may include certain social categories or classes which have some specific communal or economic interest. As thus defined the class citizen is not unitary; there are greater citizens and lesser citizens; entrepreneurs and hand workers belong to the class. Second, in the political sense, citizenship signifies membership in the state, with its connotation as the holder of certain political rights. Finally, by citizens in the class sense, we understand those strata which are drawn together, in contrast with bureaucracy or the proletariat and others outside their circle, as "persons of property and culture," entrepreneurs, recipients of funded incomes, and in general all persons of academic culture, a certain class standard of living, and a certain social prestige. The first of these concepts is economic in character and is peculiar to western civilization. There are and have been everywhere hand laborers and entrepreneurs, but never and nowhere were they included in a unitary social class. The notion of the citizen of the state has its forerunners in antiquity and in the medieval city. Here there were citizens as holders of political rights, while outside of the occident only traces of this relation were met with, as in the Babylonian patriciate and the Josherim, the inhabitants of a city with full legal rights, in the old Testament. The farther east we go the fewer are these traces; the notion of citizens of the state is unknown to the world of Islam, and to India and China. Finally, the social class signification of citizen as the man of property and culture, or of one or the other, in contrast to the nobility, on the one hand, and the proletariat, on the other, is likewise a specifically modern and western concept, like that of the bourgeoisie. . . . The citizen in the quality of membership in a class is always a citizen of a particular city, and the city in this sense, has existed only in the western world. (*General Economic History* [n. 152 above], pp. 315–316.)

This passage well communicates the fact that when Weber employs *Bürger* he denotes very much the English concept of "citizenship" rather than just town dweller, if not precisely the same thing.

The phrasing of this passage, however, is not actually Weber's own, for *General Economic History* was sewn together from the notes his students made from the last lecture course he gave before his death. All that Weber himself left, in the editors' words, was "a bundle of sheets with notes little more than catchwords set down in a handwriting hardly legible even to those accustomed to it. . . . No manuscript or even coherent outlines by Weber himself were available." (S. Hellmann and M. Palyi, "Preface to the German Edition," ibid., pp. xviii.) For this reason, the

General Economic History is one of the least reliable texts in Weber's corpus. For the most part, it merely brings together findings that Weber had set forth in works that he prepared for publication. Weber gave this course because of pressing solicitation by his students, who found his preceding lectures too dry and abstract. As the editors remark, "Even if Weber had lived longer he would not have given his *Economic History* to the public, at least not in the form in which we have it here. Utterances of his prove that he regarded the work as an improvisation with a thousand defects, which had been forced upon him." (P. xvii.) In contrast, Durkheim's posthumously published lectures were taken from notes he had written out in full sentences and in great detail.

163. *The City* (n. 156 above), p. 90; *ES*, p. 1228, italics in original (*WG*, p. 936).

164. Ibid., p. 105; *ES*, p. 1243.

165. As my notes indicate, I am drawing in this and the following paragraph from Weber's *The Religion of India* (New York, 1958). For more on this monograph, see ch. 3, n. 73.

166. *Religion of India*, pp. 6, 22.

167. Ibid., p. 144.

168. Ibid.

169. Ibid., p. 145.

170. Ibid., pp. 37–38.

171. *The City*, pp. 109–110; *ES*, p. 1247. *The City*, and particularly this emphasis on the longevity of certain patterns of Western normative order, demonstrates the fallacy of Eugene Fleischmann's contention that "the relations conceived by Marx between infrastructure (economic) and superstructure . . . are correct in Weber's eyes in the sense that economic relations demonstrate a much greater degree of stability and durability than the creations of the spirit" ("De Weber à Nietzsche," *Archives européenes de sociologie* 5 [1964]:190–238, quoting 195). Weber actually argues quite the opposite. It is on the basis of such faulty reasoning that Fleischmann argues for the "Marxist" character of Weber's theorizing—"Most of the great works of Weber were conceived from the perspective of 'verifying' the truth of the Marxian theory about the relations between infrastructure and superstructure" (p. 194), a thesis that is profoundly incorrect.

172. *The City*, pp. 109–110; *ES*, p. 1247.

173. Ibid., pp. 111–176; *ES*, pp. 1244–1304.

174. Ibid., p. 115; *ES.*, p. 1250.

175. Ibid., p. 114; *ES*, p. 1249.

176. Ibid. Weber adds here that the independent military power of the Western city was also a basic factor.

177. Ibid., p. 100; *ES*, p. 1239.

178. Ibid., p. 144; *ES*, p. 1278.

179. Ibid., p. 175, italics added.
180. Ibid., p. 148; *ES*, p. 1281.
181. Ibid.
182. Ibid., p. 148; *ES*, pp. 1281–1282.
183. Ibid., p. 169; *ES*, p. 1302, italics in original.

CHAPTER THREE

1. Max Weber, *The Religion of China: Confucianism and Taoism* (Glencoe, Ill., 1951), p. 25.
2. Ibid.
3. Ibid., p. 42.
4. Ibid.
5. Ibid., p. 61.
6. Ibid., pp. 61–62. Cf. Weber, *Gesammelte Aufsätze zur Religionssoziologie*, 3 vols. (Tübingen, 1920–1921), 1:348–349, hereafter cited as *RS*. As before, I indicate the German original only when it differs in some significant way from the translation, or when I have added some phrase from the original or reference to the literal meaning.
7. Ibid., p. 47.
8. Ibid., pp. 47–48 (*RS*, 1:330–332).
9. Ibid., p. 56.
10. Ibid., p. 60.
11. Ibid., p. 95.
12. Ibid., p. 60.
13. Ibid., p. 41.
14. Ibid.
15. Ibid., p. 45.
16. Ibid., p. 60; see also p. 78.
17. Ibid., p. 114.
18. Ibid., pp. 100–101 (*RS*, 1:391–392). The German *"Willkür"* is, we recall (ch. 2, n. 48), the term Ferdinand Tönnies employed to indicate the peculiarly antinormative character of modern rational action. This term was related, in the thought of both Tönnies and Weber, to Weber's understanding of *Zweckrationalität* (ibid.).
19. Weber, *Religion of China*, p. 20, italics added; see also p. 14.
20. Ibid.
21. Ibid., pp. 248–249 (*RS*, 1:535).
22. Ibid., p. 249.
23. Ibid. (*RS*, 1:536).
24. Ibid., p. 104, italics added (*RS*, 1:394–395).
25. Ibid. In German, this sentence has an even more startlingly discontinuous impact: "To talk about this ethos is our proper theme, which we have now finally reached" (*RS*, 1:395). In terms of actual chronology,

Weber apparently composed the second part of the China monograph before the first. In terms of the theoretical concerns dealt with here, however, this biographical fact makes no difference.

26. Ibid., p. 122.

27. Ibid. The examination system, it should be noted, is itself ascribed by Weber to the influence of instrumental, purely rational factors: to the struggle between patrimonial princes and the literati. Ibid., pp. 50, 116.

28. Ibid., p. 123 (*RS*, 1:412).

29. Ibid.

30. Ibid., p. 125.

31. Ibid., pp. 142–146.

32. Ibid., p. 142.

33. Ibid.

34. Ibid., p. 132.

35. Ibid., pp. 126–127 (*RS*, 1:415).

36. Ibid., p. 130 (*RS*, 1:418).

37. Ibid., p. 131.

38. Ibid., p. 160.

39. Ibid., pp. 164.

40. Ibid., pp. 146–147.

41. Ibid., p. 147 (*RS*, 1:435).

42. It should be noted that both law and science were emphatically linked to religious conceptualization in the works that were the subject of the multidimensional analysis in ch. 2 above, particularly in *The Sociology of Religion* and *The Protestant Ethic and the Spirit of Capitalism*. They are also so linked in the typological discussion, "Puritanism and Confucianism," that concludes *The Religion of China* (ch. 7).

43. *Religion of China*, pp. 147, 151.

44. Ibid., p. 158.

45. This "theoretical break" in the writings on religion has not been noted by the major interpreters of Weber's work. His materialist interpreters, like Carlo Antoni (see ch. 2, n. 134), naturally read the work through its materialist strand alone, and make it consistently instrumental. But those interpreters committed to multidimensionality view the studies of religion as equally consistent, even though this consistency, in their minds, is in the service of a very different theory. The most influential of these have been Reinhard Bendix and Talcott Parsons.

Bendix's "intellectual portrait" quite rightly identifies an intention in Weber's studies of religion to transcend the dichotomizing of rational and nonrational elements (see the general statement in *Max Weber* [New York, 1962], pp. 257–260). Nonetheless, Bendix's penetrating presentation of the details of Weber's argument on China (pp. 98–141) is marred by his failure to observe the vagaries in the manner in which Weber carries out this intention—or, more accurately, the way this synthetic intention is cross-cut by another, less multidimensional one. Consequently, Bendix simply reproduces the contradictory elements in Weber's argument instead of criticizing them. E.g., in presenting Weber's views on the education of the literati (pp. 122–123) he combines references to power interests and commitment to ethical maxims without noting—any more than Weber himself—anything problematic about the juxtaposition. And in his discussion of the bureaucratic suppression of attempts at reform, Bendix mentions only the instrumental motivation to preserve prebendary power (pp. 132–134), ignoring, as Weber frequently does, the voluntaristic, ideal elements involved. At the most general level, Bendix's attempt to create consistency where none exists can be observed in the manner in which he paraphrases Weber's crucial transitionary statement at the end of pt. 1 of *The Religion of China*. Whereas Weber's own statement actually represents an abrupt shift in emphasis to the leading role of religious rather than structural factors, Bendix's presentation, which is intended as a paraphrase, reads as follows: "These obstacles [the state and family structure] were strongly reinforced by a particular mentality, the Chinese 'ethos' " (p. 116). But this subtly alters Weber: the abrupt contrast introduced by raising the issue of religion as an independent factor is here viewed simply as "reinforcement" of the initial position.

There are a number of reasons for these weaknesses in Bendix's otherwise impressive presentation. Bendix is intent on reading Weber as utterly consistent, for he hopes that in this way the Weberian corpus will provide an alternative not only to functionalism but to Marxism, and not only on empirical and theoretical grounds but on ideological ones as well. In addition, Bendix devotes his main effort to ferreting out the overall organization of Weber's historical-empirical propositions, paying insufficient attention to the presuppositional framework of argument. Finally, aside from that aspect of his effort which is intended to function simply as a conduit for Weber's thought, Bendix's thinking manifests certain theoretical ambiguities of its own. Presumably in contrast to approaches to Weber which he considers overly idealist, Bendix asserts that Weber's central focus in his religious sociology is not ideas per se, nor interests in themselves, but the process of "group formation" as it represents the nexus of these two forces. The disadvantage of focusing on such a specific and concrete concept, however, is that Weber himself continually uses the "group" concept in differing presuppositional contexts. His accounts of the relation between interests and ideas in the formation of the Chinese literati, e.g., assumed antithetical forms *despite* the fact that the focus throughout remained the "group."

As for the brief treatment of the China monograph in Parsons' *The Structure of Social Action* (New York [1937] 1968), which is much less ambitious in scope than Bendix's discussion, it is sufficient to note that

Parsons also makes no reference to any conflict in Weber's discussion. He describes it simply as an instance in which "Weber deals with both sides of the causal chain" (p. 539). This treatment provides the best possible illustration of how Parsons fails to recognize in the substance of Weber's work the problems he noted in Weber's conceptual discussion, problems which he rightly perceived could lead Weber to treat rational and nonrational factors in a dichotomous way (see my discussion in ch. 2, n. 48).

46. Weber, *Ancient Judaism* (New York, 1952), p. 370.

47. Ibid., p. 33, italics added.

48. Ibid., p. 36.

49. Ibid., p. 39.

50. Ibid., p. 68. Weber notes that such debt remission was not always honored in fact, testifying, once again, to the continuous multidimensional logic at work.

51. Ibid., pp. 75–76.

52. Ibid., p. 79.

53. Ibid., p. 33.

54. Ibid., p. 83.

55. Ibid., p. 75.

56. Ibid., italics added.

57. Ibid., p. 79.

58. Ibid.

59. Ibid. Weber noted this increased stability particularly in the Rechabites. At an earlier point, he contrasted the Rechabites and the Bedouins in a manner that emphasized the crucial differentiating quality of the normative variable:

> [The Rechabites] were small stock breeders. Like the Bedouins, they disdained houses and fixed settlements, shunned fixed agriculture and drank no wine (Jer. 35). [Unlike the Bedouins, they viewed their way of life] . . . as a heavenly commandment laid upon them by the founder of the organization, the prophet of Yahwe, Jonadeb ben Rechag. (Ibid., p. 38.)

60. Ibid., p. 80, italics added (*RS*, 3:88).

61. Ibid., pp. 118–139, 219–234.

62. Ibid., p. 39 and, more generally, pp. 24, 42, 51, 56, 68, 100.

63. The point here is not that the postulate about the conflict between Israel's ideology and its political developments was the inevitable result of Weber's employment of a multidimensional approach to explanation, for I do not intend to reduce empirical facts completely to presuppositions, or events to models. My point, rather, is that the conflict which actually did exist between covenant ideas and political bureaucracy could not have been accurately portrayed outside of this multidimensional

context: there would have been no possibility of making reference to an independent religious tradition with which political developments had to interact. By the same reasoning, a more multidimensional explanation of Confucianism would not have altered Weber's insight into its pro-bureaucratic, authoritarian thrust. It is the particular empirical situation which decides the relative complementarity or antagonism of ideal and conditional phenomena; whether or not this empirical relationship can actually be expressed, however, is a theoretical issue.

64. Ibid., pp. 100–101.

65. Ibid., p. 101.

66. Ibid., p. 112.

67. Ibid., p. 111.

68. Ibid., p. 164.

69. Ibid., p. 167; see also p. 120.

70. Ibid., pp. 277–279, 281.

71. Ibid., pp. 288–291, 297–300, 312–314.

72. Weber himself made this connection between the Old Testament prophecy and plebeian protests against patrician urban sibs in the Western city (ibid., p. 117).

73. This chapter has concentrated on the monographs on China and Israel because of their extremely clear parallels and antipathies not only to one another but to dominant themes in Weber's political and contemporary writings as well. This is not to say that *The Religion of India* (New York, 1958) is in any sense a monograph of lesser importance; indeed, in purely empirical terms it is the most striking *religious* contrast that Weber ever drew to the this-worldly asceticism of Western religion. For the light it throws on the theoretical strains in Weber's work more generally, I should like to comment briefly on the theoretical relationship of this third volume of Weber's comparative sociology of religion to the other two.

The Religion of India does not decline as far as the China monograph to theoretical dichotomization and instrumental logic, but it comes far short of achieving the synthetic understanding of *Ancient Israel*. As in *The Religion of China*, there is a chronological sequence to the analysis. Weber's focus is first on material and then on ideal factors: Pt. 1 is entitled "The Hindu Social System," and pt. 2, "Orthodox and Heterodox Holy Teaching of the Indian Intellectuals." Weber's major empirical reference is the irrational barriers to economic and political rationalization presented by Indian society, and for this he offers two different kinds of explanations. He concentrates first on the inability of Indian groups to "fraternize" in the kind of egalitarian or at least formally universalistic way which Weber identified as so crucial for revolutionary conflict to develop in the Western city (see the discussion earlier in this chapter). This inability to fraternize made the efficient division of labor impossible. To explain the source of such a barrier to fraternization, Weber points to the centrality of caste and the dominate power position of the Brahmins. He describes the latter as a particularistic, self-interested, and Machiavellian status group. The source of the Brahmin caste's power, and of the caste system in general, Weber finds in group conflict of an instrumental if not exclusively economic sort. India was structured along the lines of feudal-patrimonial interest conflict, yet this systemic conflict was cross-cut by the armed invasion and conquest by a strikingly different ethnic and racial group. In this way, instrumental contest for ethnic privilege became superimposed over political and economic struggle. The result was that ethnically homogeneous family groups assumed political and economic power through the usurpation of "clan charisma," and they wielded this power through a monopoly of ritual technique (pp. 1–64, and passim). The victory of the Brahmins promoted a fiercely hierarchical status order, one in which legal rights and privileges were the result of struggle by materially unequal groups (see, e.g., pp. 16–18).

In the midst of this fundamentally instrumental analysis (for the similar ambiguities in Weber's formal "status" theory, see ch. 5, sec. 4, below), Weber acknowledges that "perhaps, too, in the past, religious hopes were frequently an important factor in the Hinduization of . . . pariah peoples" (p. 17), and toward the end of this initial discussion he describes the close fit between the cyclical theology of karma, which allows status change only through rebirth in the next life, and the material demands of the social system itself. Then, near the end of pt. 1, strangely echoing the sequence of the China monograph, we encounter this abrupt admonishment: "We repeat . . . that this well-integrated, unique social system could not have originated or at least could not have conquered and lasted without the pervasive and all powerful influence of . . . the specific Brahmanical theodicy." Weber describes the latter as "in its way a stroke of genius" and he insists that it "plainly is the construction of rational ethical thought and not the product of any economic 'conditions.'" He concludes that "only the wedding of this thought product with the empirical social order through the promise of rebirth gave this order its irresistible power" (p. 131).

The first part of the India monograph presented little evidence for this multidimensional declaration, and when Weber begins pt. 2 he seems to reiterate his earlier position: "The fact that the Brahmanical priestly stratum was a distinguished and cultivated nobility" was what "determined its religiosity" (p. 137). Yet the last two-thirds of the book treats the "other side," focusing almost exclusively on the normative patterns of the religious promise of Indian belief. Weber's empirical focus shifts away from fraternization and caste power to the other-worldly direction of the Brahmins' subjective concern, a focus that made them uncommitted to intense and dynamic economic and political rationalization. This new focus is still directed, of course, to the problem of India's lack of normative rationalization, for the absence of a systematic and abstract monotheism meant there was no cultural reference point against which all earthly beings must distance themselves and must, perforce, be equal in their radical inferiority. But over and above any empirical shift, Weber's theoretical focus is now almost completely on normative order and internal constraint. Patrimonial power position is still a fact, but the withdrawal from worldly struggle, Weber now believes, "was determined by the world image of Indian religious philosophy which in its consistency left no choice other than yearning for salvation" (p. 167). In fact, in the final pages of his essay Weber seems to attribute the Brahmins' exclusivity and worldly passivity—the factors he had earlier linked to economic, material, and status conflict—directly to the consequences of theology itself: "That such religious wisdom, in the nature of the case, remained mystical in character had two important consequences. First was the formation by the soteriology of a redemption aristocracy, for the capacity for mystical gnosis is a charisma not accessible to all. Then, however, and correlated therewith it acquired an asocial and apolitical character. Mystical knowledge is not, at least not adequately and rationally, communicable. Thus Asiatic soteriology always leads those seeking the highest holy objectives to an other-worldly realm of the rationally unformed" (p. 331).

Weber has certainly demonstrated that both normative and instrumental developments were vital to the facts of Indian development and the lack thereof. He has not shown, however, how these can be analytically intertwined.

CHAPTER FOUR

1. Max Weber, *The Theory of Social and Economic Organization* (New York, 1947), p. 102; *ES* (see ch. 2, n. 5), p. 14.

2. Ibid.

3. Ibid.

4. Ibid.

5. Ibid., p. 124; *ES*, p. 31.

6. Ibid., pp. 124–125; *ES*, p. 31, italics added.

7. Ibid., p. 124; *ES*, p. 31, italics in original.

8. Ibid., p. 121; *ES*, p. 29 (Weber, *Wirtschaft und Gesellschaft* [1922; Tübingen, 1956], p. 21; hereafter cited as *WG*).

9. Ibid., p. 122; *ES*, p. 30 (*WG*, p. 21).

10. Ibid., p. 124; *ES*, p. 31.

11. Ibid. (*WG*, p. 22).

12. Ibid., italics added.

13. Ibid.

14. Weber may also be referring here to the distinction, to be discussed below, between order as maintained through "interest" as against that maintained through "power." Still, this does not alter the problem of his discussion in the slightest. If he is doing so, he is stressing, from the present perspective, the presuppositional similarities of the modes.

15. Ibid., p. 133; *ES*, pp. 39–40, italics added.

16. Ibid.; *ES*, p. 38, italics added.

17. Ibid.

18. Ibid., p. 146; *ES*, pp. 48–49.

19. Ibid., italics in original.

20. Ibid.

21. Reinhard Bendix seems to me absolutely correct in his translation of *Herrschaft* as "domination," and in his equation of Weber's concept of "domination" with "authority" (*Max Weber* [Berkeley and Los Angeles, [1960] 1978], pp. 291–292). In contrast, Parsons' translation of *Herrschaft* as "imperative authority" obscures the instrumental and coercive implications that, I believe, more closely correspond to Weber's intention in choosing this word. *Herrschaft* is based on *Herrscher* ("ruler"). Its historical association with feudal lordship reinforces its clearly authoritarian implications. The English "domination" comes from the Latin *dominus*, a good equivalent for *Herrscher.* The best discussion of these etymological issues can be found in Wolfgang J. Mommsen, *The Age of Bureaucracy* (New York, 1974), p. 72. (Cf. Guenther Roth's "Introduction" in *ES*, pp. xciv–xcvii.)

22. This important "model" distinction has already been noted in my discussion of Weber's early writings (ch. 1) and analysis of his theory of revolution in *The City* (ch. 2). For other instances when Weber insists on this distinction, see Max Rheinstein, ed., *Max Weber on Law in Economy and Society* (New York, 1954), pp. 322–328, and, of course, the famous essay "Class, Status, and Party," which I will discuss at some length below.

23. Weber, *Theory of Social and Economic Organization* (n. 1 above), p. 152; *ES*, p. 53.

24. Ibid., p. 327; *ES*, p. 215, italics added (*WG*, p. 159). This quotation is from the opening to ch. 3 of *ES*, which is an elaboration of the conclusion to ch. 1. A similar passage from much later in the same work underlines even more explicitly the reductionist quality of this authority definition by phrasing individual acquiescence merely as an "as if" proposition:

> The manifested will (command) of the ruler or rulers is meant to influence the conduct of one or more others (the ruled) and actually does influence it in such a way that their conduct to a socially relevant degree occurs *as if* the ruled had made the content of the command the maxim of their conduct for its very own sake. Looked upon from the other end

this situation will be called obedience. (*Max Weber on Law in Economy and Society* [n. 22 above], p. 328; *ES*, p. 946, italics added.)

25. Thus, while Bendix's discussion of the authority-interest distinction clearly brings out the empirical and conceptual issues involved, it does not correctly consider Weber's more general purpose: Bendix believes the importance Weber gives to "command" is perfectly consistent with a subjective view of legitimacy (*Max Weber*, pp. 290–297).

Following Bendix, the German interpreter Günter Abramowski insists on the same multidimensionality in the conceptualization of the political sociology. "Every authority," he writes about Weber's definition, "must above all attempt to arouse and sustain the belief in its legitimacy" (*Das Geschichtsbild Max Webers* [Stuttgart, 1966], p. 121). Yet Abramowski's substantive discussion of the political sociology in *Economy and Society* actually gives little evidence of the role of belief in Weber's work (pp. 121–136). Similarly, following Parsons, David Little asserts that in Weber's work "authority is invariably treated" in connection with religion (*Religion, Order, and Law* [New York, 1969], p. 9). But to assert this invariable connection, Little must reach outside the formal conceptual discussion itself: he combines Weber's formal definition of legitimacy with religious references in *The Protestant Ethic and the Spirit of Capitalism* and "The Social Psychology of World Religions" (p. 6, n. 1; p. 7, n. 3).

26. In *Class and Class Conflict in Industrial Society*, Ralf Dahrendorf treats subjective legitimacy as epiphenomenal (Stanford, Calif., 1959, pp. 168–169), and "authority" simply becomes a matter of institutionalized versus personal power (p. 166).

This demand for consistency, in other words, occurs in the tradition of instrumental Weberian interpretation as much as in the tradition which views Weber as having achieved multidimensionality. Mommsen, e.g., rightly emphasizes this instrumental strand in Weber's work, arguing that with it Weber "deliberately cut out all references to the possible case that the legitimacy of the system is derived from certain fundamental value-oriented attitudes of the 'governed', as is the case with the traditional doctrine of democracy" (*The Age of Bureaucracy* [n. 21 above], p. 81; this latter, political implication of the instrumental definition of legitimacy is considered in the next chapter). Yet Mommsen wrongly equates this instrumental strand with the entirety of Weber's treatment of political order. In much the same way, Arthur Mitzman is only partly correct in his contention that Weber's political sociology is the simple "transposition of Marx's monistic explanation from economics to politics" (*The Iron Cage* [New York, 1970], p. 184; cf., Hans Gerth and C. Wright Mills, "Introduction," in Gerth and Mills, eds., *From Max Weber: Essays in Sociology* [New York, 1946], pp. 3–74, see pp. 46–51).

27. For example, Peter M. Blau observes in Weber's definitions the "paradox" that "authority denotes imperative control, from which there is no easy escape, yet a major criterion of it is voluntary compliance" ("Critical Remarks on Max Weber's Theory of Authority," in Dennis Wrong, ed., *Max Weber* [Englewood Cliffs, N.J., 1970], pp. 147–165, see p. 148). Blau asserts that Weber's theory "has not resolved" the question posed by authority as voluntary control, asking, "How can compliance be imperative if it is voluntary?" (p. 156). But Blau attributes this confusion to an empirical difficulty in Weber's studies, namely, that he considered only the operation of already established power rather than the question of power's origin (p. 149); he takes for granted that on the more general level Weber had a multidimensional intention.

28. Thus, Guenther Roth writes in his "Introduction" to *ES*:

> The Sociology of Domination is the core of *Economy and Society*. The major purpose of the work was the construction of a typology of associations, with most prominence given to the types of domination and their relation to want-satisfaction through appropriation. To be sure, religion and law were constituent parts of the work, irrespective of whether Weber planned the chapters to be as comprehensive as they finally came to be, but the 1914 outline and the proportions of the manuscript show the Sociology of Domination to be the central theme. In the reception of the piecemeal translation of *Economy and Society* [i.e., the translations up until the edition Roth is introducing], the Sociology of Domination has been obscured as a whole. Until now, nearly half of it was untranslated; the other half was divided among three different translations. (P. lxxxviii.)

The importance of this weighting can be seen from the fact that not only does Roth place the sociology of domination, particularly the historical chapters, at the center of *Economy and Society*, but he makes the claim, in the very first sentence of his Introduction, that the latter work is "the sum of Max Weber's scholarly vision of society" (p. xxxiii). Until Roth's and Wittich's edition, to be sure, the historical chapters (particularly chs. 12–15) which are the substance of the present discussion had remained mostly untranslated, and this contributed to the misunderstanding of Weber's political sociology.

29. *Max Weber on Law in Economy and Society* [n. 22 above], p. 335; *ES*, p. 953.

30. Ibid., p. 336; *ES*, p. 954, italics added.

31. Ibid., pp. 336–337; *ES*, p. 954, italics in original. I have maintained Rheinstein's translation [n. 22 above] because it is more literal and in this case more evocative of Weber's theoretical intentions.

32. Wrong (n. 27 above) has identified the same possible foci of Weber's political sociology—voluntaristic legitimation, rationalized ideology and pure domination—that I have outlined here.

Considerable confusion and ambiguity exists in the ways this typology
[of] legitimation has been interpreted and utilized. Do the three types
refer to different *motives* for obeying political authorities? Or do they
represent different *structures* of political power? Or are they different
types of *normative justification* for obeying the commands of a
powerholder?

"The latter view," Wrong argues, "is the correct one: types of legitimacy
are essentially normative principles that are regularly and publicly in-
voked to justify compliance with the commands of an authority rather
than specifications of 'real' motives for obedience." Thus, they are "ideological rather than psychological constructions." ("Introduction," p. 41,
italics added.) However, while Wrong's conclusion regarding Weber's
own understanding of legitimation in the context of his explicitly political sociology is, I believe, correct, he disregards any issues of theoretical
ambiguity involved in that understanding. He makes no reference to the
fact that Weber's earlier definitions of legitimacy did, in fact, refer to
"real" motives—not simply to reflected ideology—or to the even more
significant fact that such a conception could be connected with more
multidimensional empirical treatments of political authority in certain
other sections of Weber's work. Wrong, in other words, shares the same
limiting "consistency bias" I have discussed above.

In the present discussion, I am focusing on the theoretical tendency
toward instrumentalism that dominates Weber's explicitly political sociology. Such instrumental reasoning is evident in the formal conceptual
segments of *Economy and Society*, as well as in the chapters on historical
sociology that will soon be discussed. This is not to say that Weber never
presents any contrary, more multidimensional perspective on "legitimacy." Earlier in this chapter, e.g., we have seen that in the first pages of
his formal conceptual discussion he does so. He also does so, of course, in
the implicit political sociology that informs the works I have discussed in
ch. 2 and ch. 3, sec. 2. In a passage in the speech "Politics as a Vocation,"
Weber also presents a more normatively oriented perspective. "When
and why do men obey," he asks. "Upon what inner justifications and
upon what external means does this domination rest?" He proceeds to
outline the three forms of legitimacy in an anti-instrumental way.

To begin with, in principle, there are three inner justifications, hence
basic *legitimations* of domination. First, the authority of the "eternal
yesterday," i.e., of the mores sanctified through the unimaginably ancient recognition and habitual orientation to conform. This is "traditional" domination. . . . Second, there is the authority of the extraordinary and personal gift of grace (charisma), the absolutely personal devotion and personal confidence in revelation, heroism, or other
qualities of individual leadership. . . . Finally, there is domination by virtue of "legality," by virtue of the belief in the validity of legal statute and

functional "competence" based on rationally created *rules*. (Gerth and Mills, *From Max Weber* [n. 26 above], pp. 78–79, italics in original.)

The point, in other words, is not that Weber did not "know better," but that, theoretically, he set himself on an instrumental track in the main body of his formally political work. On this paradox, see the conclusion to the present chapter.

33. For the connection of prophecy and charisma, see, e.g., Weber, *Ancient Judaism* (New York, 1952), pp. 294, 395, and Weber, *The Sociology of Religion* (Boston, 1963), pp. 46–47, 106–107, 270–271. Parsons made this broader claim for the role of "charisma" in his "Introduction" to *The Sociology of Religion* (pp. xxxiii–xxxiv). The same position is taken by S. N. Eisenstadt in *Max Weber on Charisma and Institution Building* (Chicago, 1968), pp. lx–lxi, passim. In their stretching of the concept of charisma, Parsons' and Eisenstadt's essays must be seen as original theoretical contributions in their own right, not as true interpretations of Weber's work. Karl Deutsch's insertion of "charisma" into Weber's theory of power must be viewed in a similar way. It is interesting that Deutsch clearly tries to find in "charisma" an alternative to Weber's more instrumental conception of order, i.e., to "the idea that there is no other order in the world than [that] introduced by some external power." With charisma, he reasons, Weber found that "the systems of the world, in the absence of sovereignty, are not completely chaotic" (Deutsch's discussion of Raymond Aron's "Max Weber and Power Politics," in Otto Stammer, ed., *Max Weber and Sociology Today* [New York, 1971], pp. 116–122, quoting p. 18.)

In biographical terms, it is interesting to note, the connection between charisma and legitimation seems to make perfect sense. The leading historian of Weber's career, Wolfgang J. Mommsen, believes that Weber first turned to a formal analysis of political legitimation and charisma after he had done substantial reading about the prophets of ancient Israel (Mommsen [n. 21 above], pp. 101–102).

Yet, for all the empirical possibility and biographical connection, the fact remains that in terms of theoretical logic Weber's analysis of charisma primarily followed a very different path.

34. Max Weber, "The Sociology of Charismatic Authority," pp. 245–252 in Gerth and Mills (n. 26 above), p. 246; *ES*, p. 1112.

35. Ibid., pp. 246–247; *ES*, pp. 1112–1113.

36. Ibid.

37. Ibid., p. 1121.

38. Ibid., p. 1122.

39. Ibid., p. 1123.

40. Ibid., p. 1125.

41. Ibid., p. 1124 (*WG*, p. 844).

42. Ibid., p. 1126.

43. Ibid., p. 1127. The digression which follows in *ES* (pp. 1127–1133) on the origins of democratic suffrage in the exceptional case in which the power of selection devolves upon the ruled is, indeed, a multidimensional example of how a political formation can emerge from the search for meaning by masses of people. It is interesting to note, however, that in his lengthy discussion of the same issue of democratic suffrage in the text of his analysis of "legal domination," Weber reverts to an explanation of origins purely in terms of interests. (I discuss this at some length below.)

44. Ibid., p. 1139.

45. Ibid.

46. Ibid., p. 1141 (*WG*, p. 850).

47. Ibid.

48. For an example of this multidimensional analysis, see, e.g., *The Sociology of Religion* (n. 33 above), pp. 186–188.

49. The present interpretation, then, supports Shils' observations about this part of Weber's analysis of charisma: "In Weber's chapter on the transformation of charisma," Shils writes, "the institutionalization of charisma was confined to ecclesiastical, monarchical, and familial institutions, where the sacred and the primordial are massively or tangibly present." Even here, however, Weber "tended to think of such charismatic patterns as lacking the genuinely charismatic element, and as greatly supported by considerations of 'interest' in guaranteeing stable succession and continuing legitimacy" (Edward A. Shils, "Charisma, Order, and Status," *American Sociological Review* 30 [1965]: 199–213, esp. 202). This brilliant interpretive essay by Shils stands alone as a critique of Weber's handling of the charisma concept. Its drawback, from the present perspective, is that Shils, in his emphasis on Weber's views of contemporary society, has conflated the "religious" and "political" treatments of traditional society in Weber's work and thereby implied a more satisfactory utilization of charisma in parts of Weber's political sociology than, I think, can actually be sustained. It has been very difficult for liberal thinkers to accept ideologically—and, indirectly, to comprehend analytically—the seemingly paradoxical Realpolitik of Weber's theory of political charisma. Even Mommsen, who is often so realistic about these tendencies in Weber's work, writes as if the identification of "charismatic leadership and charismatic domination" results only from the terminological problem that *Herrschaft*, the word for domination, implies a personal relationship. Yet the only counter-examples of this conflation Mommsen can find are from Weber's religious writings (*The Age of Bureaucracy* [n. 21 above], pp. 79–80).

50. *ES*, pp. 1140–1141. This is precisely the passage that Shils notes as the instance where Weber "comes closest" to a satisfactory elabora-

tion of charisma ("Charisma, Order, and Status," p. 202, n. 3). However, this passage is not an explanation of "office charisma" as such but an analysis of the variation that can occur within it.

51. *Max Weber on Law in Economy and Society* (n. 22 above), p. 336; *ES*, p. 954.

52. *ES*, p. 1007, italics added.

53. Ibid., p. 1006.

54. Ibid., p. 1011.

55. Ibid., p. 1008.

56. Ibid., p. 1010.

57. Ibid., p. 1015.

58. Ibid., p. 1028.

59. Ibid., p. 1027.

60. Ibid., p. 1040.

61. Ibid.

62. Ibid.

63. Ibid., pp. 1025, 1019.

64. Ibid., pp. 1042–1043.

65. Ibid., pp. 1044–1053.

66. Ibid., p. 1046 (*WG*, p. 774).

67. Ibid., p. 1049.

68. Ibid., pp. 1058–1109.

69. Ibid., p. 1079.

70. Ibid.

71. Ibid., p. 1057.

72. Ibid. The critical role of these external conditions in promoting Western feudalization are further elaborated in the later section, "The Military Origins of Feudalism" (*ES*, pp. 1077–1078).

73. Because of the unfortunate effort to read Weber as a highly consistent theorist, most interpreters have tried to camouflage the striking instrumental tendency in this central portion of Weber's historical sociology, when, indeed, they have recognized it at all. Once again, Shils is an exception in his ability to recognize the inadequacies of Weber's treatment even while he draws upon it for inspiration. In the autobiographical essay that forms the Introduction to the second volume of his collected papers, Shils talks about the theoretical problems he encountered when he began to examine "tradition" and "traditionalism" in Third World nations.

> I had to occupy myself with tradition with even more reason once I had extended my interests to Asian and African societies. . . . Max Weber was of little help here; despite the richness of his treatment of patrimonial authority as the major type of traditional authority, he in fact made little effort to elucidate the nature of tradition, nor did he even specify

wherein lay the traditionality of patrimonial authority. (Edward A. Shils, *Center and Periphery: Essays in Macrosociology* [Chicago, 1975], p. xxxiv.)

It would be more correct to say that Weber did not specify the normative sources of patrimonial traditionalism, for he certainly did expound a systematic and detailed theory of the instrumental sources and effects of its arbitrary and stereotyping forms. Shils' insight into the weaknesses of this part of Weber's theory might be compared with the account by Jere Cohen, Lawrence E. Hazelrigg, and Whitney Pope. These authors rightly note Weber's failure to integrate his formal conceptualization of legitimation and domination with his historical discussion of the impact of religion, and they note also that Weber's explanation of traditional authority was primarily antinormative. The difficulty here is that they accept this internal strain as if it made perfect theoretical sense, and the antinormative theory of tradition is, for them, perfectly adequate. ("De-Parsonizing Weber: A Critique of Parsons' Interpretation of Weber's Sociology," *American Sociological Review* 40, no. 2 [1975]: 229–241, see 231–233.

74. *ES*, p. 1068, italics added.

75. Ibid., p. 1105. It should be noted, however, that this reductionist approach to the *origins* of the feudal ethic did not automatically mean that Weber could not give the ethic independent causal status in terms of its *effects*. There are certain sections in Weber's discussion of feudalism which emphasize the long-term significance of the feudal conception of individual honor for the development of the West. E.g., he describes the ethic as contributing to the notion of "rights," to constitutionalism, and to "the idea of the social contract as the basis of the distribution of political power" (ibid., p. 1082). Unfortunately, these thoughts on the relevance of the feudal ethic remain undeveloped and unconnected to Weber's general political analysis of the transition to modern life.

76. This section occurs in ch. 15, "Political and Hierocratic Domination," which focuses on the organizational aspects of the different religious institutions in traditional society.

77. Ibid., p. 1192.

78. Ibid.

79. Ibid., p. 1193 (*WG*, pp. 906–907).

80. Ibid.

81. Ibid., p. 1192.

82. Ibid.

83. Ibid. (*WG*, p. 905).

84. Ibid., p. 1064.

85. Ibid., p. 1063.

86. Ibid., p. 1062 (*WG*, pp. 788–789). In "Politics as a Vocation," Weber also refers to the unique English case as providing the historical opportunity for an antibureaucratic institutional breakthrough, and here the instrumentalism of his perspective is even more clearly evident. The same decentralized structural position is described as decisive. It is portrayed as the result of an instrumental strategy by the prince to create a group to fight against local lords. This group then used its new-found position, in turn, to wage a self-interested struggle against the prince. Any altruistic elements of the gentry's action are explained on the basis of rational expediency.

> A patrician stratum developed there [in England] which was comprised of the petty nobility and the urban rentiers; technically they are called the "gentry." The English gentry represents a stratum that the prince originally attracted in order to counter the barons. The prince placed the stratum in possession of the offices of "self-government," and later he himself became increasingly dependent upon them. The gentry maintained the possession of all offices of local administration by taking them over without compensation in the interest of their social power. The gentry has saved England from the bureaucratization which has been the fate of all continental states. (Gerth and Mills [n. 26 above], p. 93.)

For Weber to have interconnected his multidimensional analysis of English development and the instrumental analysis of traditional society, he would have had to elaborate the relationship between English patrimonialism and Anglicanism, the relatively traditionalistic Protestant form that preceded the rise of English Puritanism and the English revolution. David Little makes precisely this analysis in his excellent historical analysis, *Religion, Order, and Law* (n. 25 above). Little claims to be following the direct path that Weber himself laid down. Nonetheless, it would be more accurate to say that, inspired by the multidimensional strand of Weber's thought as filtered through the synthetic theoretical framework of Parsons, Little has filled in the empty blanks of Weber's political sociology of English history, blanks that existed because of Weber's own instrumental bent. Another work in historical sociology that carries out the kind of multidimensional analysis of English development for which Weber's own work implies the necessity, and which does so within a generally Weberian framework, is Michael Walzer's *Revolution of the Saints* (Cambridge, Mass., 1965). Instead of treating the gentry simply as a naturally instrumental status group, Walzer demonstrates how the cultural outlook of this class, influenced primarily by Anglicanism, was revolutionized by the impact of Puritanism. Walzer claims that he is opposing Weber's analysis because he is focusing on religion's impact on political, not economic, affairs; yet, as we have seen above, the political and revolutionary impact of Western religion was actually among Weber's major interests. Walzer does not see this interest because in Weber's analysis of political aspects of the English case his instrumentalism eliminated any normative reference.

It should be noted, perhaps, that what I am documenting in the text is the limiting impact of Weber's "sociological epistemology" on his ability to formulate his empirical insights. I am not saying that Weber did not "know," while writing this section of *Economy and Society*, that both ideal and material factors played a role in the creation of modern political and economic liberalism. Rather, I am saying, at the minimum, that because of certain theoretical limitations he was unable to express this intuitive and empirical knowledge, and, at the maximum, that these theoretical blinders prevented him, in this particular moment, even from *seeing* the empirical world in as multidimensional a manner as he did when writing some of his other work. On rare occasions, Weber explicitly indicated precisely this knowledge, combining the political analysis of traditional society with references to the religious factors that inhibited or promoted modern individuation. E.g., in his political essays on Russian development, written in the midst of the essays on Puritanism, he refers at one point to the unique constellation of factors which had encouraged European liberalism and which, he believed, were not present in the Russian case. This constellation brings together both sides of the causal chain.

> The historical development of modern "freedom" [in Europe] presupposed a unique and unrepeatable constellation of factors, of which the following are the most important: first, overseas expansion[;] secondly, the characteristic economic and social structure of the "early capitalist" period in Western Europe; thirdly, the conquest of life through science[;] finally, certain ideal conceptions which grew out of the concrete historical uniqueness of a particular religious viewpoint, and which, working together with numerous unique political circumstances and the material preconditions mentioned above, combined to fashion the "ethical" and "cultural" character of modern man. (Quoted in David Beetham, *Max Weber and the Theory of Modern Politics* [London, 1974], p. 46.)

Yet even in such informal political essays, Weber's thinking about the preconditions of modernity frequently takes an instrumental path. In explaining the lack of freedom in Germany and Russia, he often focuses primarily on the pervasiveness of German feudalism with its local particularistic control, and on the overweening strength of Russia's patrimonial officialdom, which simply on material grounds excluded the Russian bourgeoisie from assuming power (see, e.g., Beetham, p. 157).

I should note, finally, that Weber does refer, in one sentence of his three-page discussion in *ES*, to the influence of Puritanism on the bourgeois class (p. 1063). This occurs, however, in an after-the-fact manner that actually serves to emphasize its residual status vis-à-vis the developments described. For an additional, much briefer reference in *ES* to the origins of the Western bourgeois class purely in terms of the decentralized power of Western traditionalism, see p. 1103.

87. *ES*, pp. 1086–1087.

88. Weber, *The Agrarian Sociology of Ancient Civilization* (London, [1908] 1976), pp. 53–60.

89. Ibid., p. 61.

90. Ibid., pp. 62–63.

91. Ibid., pp. 62–63; cf. p. 364.

92. Ibid., p. 67.

93. Ibid., p. 60.

94. Ibid., p. 64.

95. Ibid., p. 365. For an interesting essay on the usually unacknowledged similarities between this monograph and Marx's theory of ancient capitalism and agrarian relations, see Jonathan M. Wiener, "Max Weber's Marxism," *Theory and Society* 11 (1982): 389–401.

96. Thus, the great importance of Bendix's work of synthesis and analysis (*Max Weber*, n. 21 above) has been that he elaborated the Hobbesian element of "domination" in Weber's political sociology more than any commentator before him. Yet, Bendix's interpretation is weakened because of his insistence that this element is not, in fact, really Hobbesian, but encased in a multidimensional perspective. Bendix's approach to Weber's political sociology emphasizes the role of legitimacy in a manner that obscures the theoretical problems in Weber's treatment. Trying to achieve more an accurate reproduction of Weber's intellectual product than a critical evaluation—and, as I will argue in ch. 6, actually ending up with a revision of it—Bendix reaffirms the continuity between the "religious" and "political" writings, a continuity that, in fact, only sporadically exists. Thus, Bendix argues that Weber's "essay on Judaism is only the starting point of an explanation that occupied him for the rest of his life," and that "his studies of ancient civilization, his sociology of law and of the types of domination, his essay on the city and his lectures on general economic history—all are continuations of the sociology of religion." He insists that Weber's "political sociology . . . supplement[s] the initial essay on the Protestant ethic." (Pp. 279–280.) And in the final pages of his intellectual portrait, after he has drawn clear lines between Weber's commitment to the "meaningful," nonrational aspects of action and his formal conceptualization of political legitimacy (pp. 476–477), Bendix elaborates what he believes to be the central relationship Weber drew between *Ancient Judaism* and modern legal-rational domination (pp. 478–486). Yet in making these connections he is interweaving elements whose theoretical relationship was extraordinarily problematic in the original work. (The same kind of relationship is artificially "postulated" in the recent, insightful work of Schluchter in his essays "The Par-

adox of Rationalization: On the Relation of Ethics and World" and "Value Neutrality and the Ethic of Responsibility," in Guenther Roth and Wolfgang Schluchter, *Max Weber's Vision of History* [Berkeley and Los Angeles, 1979], pp. 11–118.)

Of perhaps even greater importance for the contemporary understanding of Weber's political sociology is the interpretation offered by Talcott Parsons in his brilliant study *The Structure of Social Action* (New York, [1937] 1968), some details of which were elaborated a decade later in his equally penetrating Introduction to Weber's *The Theory of Social and Economic Organization* (n. 1 above, pp. 3–86). Despite Parsons' greater sensitivity to presuppositional problems in general, and his occasional awareness of their manifestation in Weber's own work, his treatment of the political sociology is more responsible than any other for creating the impression that Weber's analysis successfully resolved the issues raised by the conflict between materialist and idealist traditions. Yet Parsons actually refers hardly at all to Weber's political sociology in *The Structure of Social Action*. When he does so, moreover, he completely obscures the disparity between the multidimensional and instrumental strands of Weber's thinking. He asserts that the primary emphasis of the "political" sociology was on legitimacy, and he links the legitimation concept directly to the themes of Weber's sociology of religion.

Parsons first establishes the cultural referent of the legitimacy concept by linking it to an orientation to "ideas" (p. 650). He then draws the logical conclusion that Weber's notion of political authority is parallel with Durkheim's voluntaristic concept of moral obligation.

> To put the matter somewhat differently, for one who holds an order to be legitimate, living up to its rules becomes, to this extent, a matter of moral obligation.... In both cases [Durkheim's and Weber's] a legitimate order is contrasted with a situation of the uncontrolled play of interests. (P. 661.)

Parsons not only connects the political and religious writings in this general way, but he also specifically asserts that Weber has identified legitimacy with the subjectivity of political charisma: "Charisma is directly linked with legitimacy, is indeed the name in Weber's system for the source of legitimacy in general" (p. 663). And although Parsons admits that Weber did not "originally" conceive the relationship, he himself links legitimacy with the authority derived from prophetic charisma. He even utilizes the very terms "obedience" and "orders" —which, I have maintained, were the crucial focus of rational reduction in Weber's formal definition of domination—to analyze prophecy. The prophet, Parsons maintains, is "qualitatively different from other men in that he is in touch with or the instrument of a source of authority higher than any which is established or any to which obedience can be motivated by cal-

culation of advantage." The "essential problem" for Weber, in Parsons'
view, "is that of the relation of prophetic charisma to the legitimacy of
the orders which govern everyday life" (p. 663). Finally, Parsons implies
that Weber actually provided a clear discussion of the relation between
religious prophecy and the emergence of traditional and rational-legal
domination (p. 664), concluding with the observation that, for Weber,
"the legality of [an] order" must always involve a source "which is, in the
last analysis, charismatic" (p. 665).

In the later treatment, his Introduction to *The Theory of Social and
Economic Organization*, Parsons is more cautious about this direct connection, but in the end comes down on the same side of the issue. He criticizes Weber's utilization of charisma in the political context as
exclusively connected "with the claim to authority of an individual personal leader," and questions whether the "important distinction between
the pattern of legitimacy and the modern bearer of authority" is "sufficiently worked out" in Weber's discussion (p. 75). Such doubts appear to
imply an awareness of the instrumental structure of Weber's political sociology—particularly in view of Parsons' criticism in the same essay of
Weber's tendency to dichotomize rational and nonrational action, a criticism I have referred to in ch. 2, sec. 1. In fact, however, Parsons refrains
from making any such critique, characterizing the problematic area of
Weber's political analysis as only an "explicit treatment" (p. 75). On the
implicit level, Parsons maintains, Weber did successfully connect his religious and political sociology. After citing the use of charisma in the religious writings, he asserts once again that for Weber "all authority has a
charismatic basis in some form" (p. 76). In the later discussion of
Weber's political theory, Parsons carries this purported connection still
further by making the claim, albeit in a qualified manner, that ideas have
a significant independent role in Weber's formulations of political action:
"Though Weber does not analyze it in detail here, of course the character
of the system of ideas in terms of which the charismatic claims of the
movement is formulated has an important influence on the way in which
this routinization works out" (p. 66). Whereas Parsons justifies this statement by referring to Weber's understanding of the conception of "charisma of office" as an outgrowth of the particular Christian formulation
of grace (p. 66), I have demonstrated, to the contrary, that the explanation of office charisma in Weber's political sociology actually derives
from an instrumental conceptualization of institutional struggle. In the
end, as I suggested in ch. 2, sec. 1, Parsons attributes the weakness which
he has recognized in Weber's political sociology to meta-methodological
problems in Weber's approach to building scientific theory. Although
such problems may well exist in their own right, they cannot be mentioned without reference to the presuppositional difficulties about action
and order with which they correspond.

An important, more recent interpretation of Weber's political work, S. N. Eisenstadt's introductory essay to his selections ("Charisma and Institution Building: Max Weber and Modern Sociology," pp. ix–lvi in Eisenstadt, ed., *Max Weber on Charisma and Institution Building* [Chicago, 1968]), indicates the profound influence of this Parsonian interpretation and, indeed, carries its thrust one step further. Inspired also by Shils' formulations, but without acknowledging, as Shils does, the critical limitations of Weber's own usage, Eisenstadt attempts to place the concept of charisma at the very center of Weber's work. Because he does not recognize the prevalence of instrumental theorizing in Weber's sociology, Eisenstadt actually uses instrumental theory as a foil against which he contrasts Weber's supposedly satisfactory resolution of the relationship between charismatic values and more conditionally oriented activity.

> Throughout his work [Weber] indicated that the political, economic, legal, religious, and stratification spheres are not only organizational aspects of any relatively stable social relations or institutions; they do not only constitute means for the attainment of goals which are, as it were, outside of them. They constitute also realms of goals, of "ends" of potentially broader, overall "meanings" toward which the activities of the participants are oriented. (P. 37.)

At another point, he contrasts the multidimensionality of Weber's approach to political action with the more traditional sociological approach, criticizing the latter's politicization of "legitimation" and describing its emphasis on the very term— "obedience" —which the present analysis has found to be so characteristic of Weber's own studies in political sociology.

> As is well known, sociological analysis has continuously stressed that it is the religious and the political spheres that are the most natural foci or institutional abodes of such charismatic qualities and symbols. This contention has often been presented in a rather routine way as deriving mainly from the specific organizational needs of these spheres for legitimation or for keeping people quiet and obedient, thus reinforcing the "semi-conspiratorial" theory of charisma or of ideology. (P. 29.)

Finally, Eisenstadt, like Parsons, attributes the discontinuity which he finds in Weber's work to certain qualities of Weber's methodological understanding of scientific theory, to his "reluctance to engage in full, systemic, formal analysis" (p. 13). I would contend, however, that Eisenstadt's essay must be viewed as an original contribution to multidimensional theorizing in its own right rather than as an objective reading of the theory that actually underlies Weber's political sociology.

97. Parsons, *Structure of Social Action*, p. 533.

98. Schluchter, "Paradox of Rationalization" (n. 96 above), p. 59.

CHAPTER FIVE

1. E.g., Reinhard Bendix in "Max Weber's Image of Society," the concluding chapter of his *Max Weber*, which is intended as an overview of Weber's historical sociology, has noted the description of the prophet in *Ancient Judaism* as one of Weber's fundamental contributions to the understanding of the origins of *contemporary* society (Berkeley and Los Angeles, [1960] 1978, pp. 479–481). This idea of the contribution to modern life of the activism of the salvation religions has perhaps been best formulated in Robert N. Bellah's important essay "Religious Evolution" (*Beyond Belief* [New York, 1970], pp. 20–50), which relies heavily on Weber's religious studies but does not explicitly offer any overall interpretation of Weber's work. Wolfgang Schluchter's "The Paradox of Rationalization: On the Relation of Ethics and World" utilizes the historical insights of Bellah's essay in precisely this manner—to offer an interpretation of Weber's work that draws strong connections between the theory of modernity and the theory of religious rationalization (in Guenther Roth and W. Schluchter, eds., *Max Weber's Vision of History: Ethics and Methods* [Berkeley and Los Angeles 1979], pp. 11–64).

2. For the relation of decentralized feudal "right" to the establishment of modern legal-rational law, see Weber's *Economy and Society* (*ES* as cited in ch. 2, n. 5), p. 1082, and Max Rheinstein, ed., *Max Weber on Law in Economy and Society* (New York, 1954), p. 184. For the relation of feudal right to the voluntaristic aspects of medieval church law, see, ibid., p. 168.

3. Karl Deutsch has characterized Weber's theory of Western development by referring almost exclusively to the phenomena that promoted the normative rationalization which, in ch. 2, I discussed as belonging to only one part—the multidimensional segment—of Weber's work. This passage is worth quoting in full.

> In his [Weber's] view the West grew not primarily from power as such, but out of the self-governing town: this self-administering town grew from a feudal community, that community from the sacrament of holy communion, which first made these men capable of law and organization. The rise of the West, the greatest development of power in the history of the world, came about according to Weber from a chain of events which in their nature are far more relevant to human communication and living together than to men's power to command. ("Discussion of Raymond Aron's 'Max Weber and Power Politics,'" in Otto Stammer, ed., *Max Weber and Sociology Today* [New York, 1971], pp. 116–122, see p. 122.)

4. It is rarely appreciated that although these methodological essays do provide a basis for meta-methodological commitments to what I have called (in vol. 1, ch. 1) the positivist persuasion, Weber's overall purpose in writing them was to allow science to be utilized in political and policy

discussions in a more responsible and morally committed way. If social science were objective, then politicians and policy makers who used its conclusions could be held personally responsible for their judgments, which would then appear, more accurately, to be derived from their ideological beliefs rather than from external reality itself.

5. This little-known passage is worth reproducing at greater length:

> Whoever understands by "democracy" . . . a human mass pulverized into atoms is fundamentally mistaken, at least so far as American democracy is concerned. It is not democracy, but bureaucratic rationalism that tends to have this consequence of 'atomization,' a consequence which is not avoided by its preference for imposing compulsory structures from above. Genuine American society . . . was never a sandheap of this kind, nor yet a building where anyone without distinction could just walk in. It was and is permeated with "exclusiveness" of every kind. The individual never finds sure ground under his feet, either at university or in business, until he has succeeded in being voted into an association of some kind—in the past invariably Christian, now secular as well—and has asserted himself within it. The inner character of these associations is governed by the ancient "sect spirit" with far-reaching consequences. (J. Winckelmann, ed., *Max Weber, Soziologie, Weltgeschichtliche Analysen, Politik*, 4th ed. [Stuttgart, 1968], pp. 393–394, quoted in David Beetham, *Max Weber and the Theory of Modern Politics* [London, 1974], p. 206; for some supporting comments, see also Weber's "Sect, Church and Democracy," *ES*, pp. 1204–1211, esp. pp. 1207–1208.)

Weber goes on to contrast this American case with the German, again emphasizing the decisive force of their variable religious histories.

> It is even now still our fate, that, for numerous historical reasons, the religious revolution of that time [i.e., the Reformation] meant for us Germans a development which did not promote the power of the individual, but rather the importance of officialdom. And so, because the religious community after the revolution as before took the form only of a "church," a compulsory association, there arose that situation in which every struggle for the emancipation of the individual from "authority," every manifestation of "liberalism" in the widest sense, was compelled to set itself in opposition to the religious communities. At the same time we were denied the development of that tradition of voluntary associations which the "sectarian life" had helped to encourage in the Anglo-Saxon world, so different in all these respects. (Ibid.)

For a good discussion of this "political" dimension of Weber's comparative religious sociology, see Anthony Giddens, *Politics and Sociology in the Thought of Max Weber* (London, 1972), pp. 30–33.

6. Max Weber, "Politics as a Vocation," in Hans Gerth and C. Wright Mills, eds., *From Max Weber* (New York, 1946), pp. 77–128, see pp. 115–116.

7. Weber, "Science as a Vocation," ibid., pp. 129–156, esp. pp. 134–135.

8. Ibid., pp. 150–151, 147.

9. Ibid., p. 152.

10. There is also an instance in the public speech on politics where Weber conceives of vocation as essential to the integrity of the contemporary bureaucratic ethos ("Politics as a Vocation," ibid., p. 88), although this ethic is more *wertrational* than the *Zweckrationalität* that characterizes the preceding references. I will refer to this and the other institutional analyses noted here at greater length below.

11. Weber, "The Power of the State and the Dignity of the Academic Calling in Imperial Germany," *Minerva* 11, no. 4 (October, 1973): 571–632. Edward Shils translated these pieces from newspaper articles, letters to the editor, and public speeches that Weber gave between 1908 and 1919. These phrases are quoted from pp. 576, 578.

12. *Ibid.*, pp. 578, 592.

13. Weber, "Class, Status, Party," pp. 180–195 in Gerth and Mills (n. 6 above); *ES*, pp. 926–939.

14. Rheinstein, *Max Weber on Law in Economy and Society* (n. 2 above), pp. 294–296, 318–321; *ES*, pp. 871–873, 892–895. In terms of Weber's explicitly scientific research, mention should be made of one other piece of "potentially" multidimensional analysis that is truly striking. This is Weber's "Methodological Introduction" to a survey that the Verein für Sozialpolitik proposed on the effects of large-scale industry on the lives of workers, written in 1908 (pp. 103–155 in J. E. T. Eldridge, ed., *Max Weber* [London, 1971]). In this proposal, Weber elaborates a number of material factors that conditioned the workers' responses to industrial life: variations in technology, the organic composition of capital, the division of labor, and the quality and level of wages. Yet a constant counterpoint to these instrumental references is Weber's systematic insistence on the "other side," the normative order that conditions the workers' response to external conditions, the extent to which "industry on its side, in its capacity for development and in the direction of its development, is governed by given qualities arising out of the ethnic, social and cultural background, the tradition, and the circumstances of the workers" (p. 104). Weber insists that the relation to factory conditions involves a "learning" process (p. 112), and that only if this voluntary element is understood can the "general 'spiritual' qualities of the workers" accurately be seen: "their 'character,' 'temperament,' and their 'intellectual' and 'moral' state—things which, without a shadow of doubt, have often an important, sometimes a decisive, influence on their suitability for the individual types of industrial work" (p. 124; cf. Weber's discussions of worker socialization on p. 129). This multidimensional perspective is

pervasive. "Even where the circumstances are otherwise absolutely identical," Weber writes, adumbrating the "historical experiment" he conducted in the comparative religion essays, "by no means every new system of remuneration achieves the same results with every labour force. Of especial interest to the inquiry of this survey are just such limitations of the effect of the incentive to work lying in the remuneration system, as well as any differences there may be in the reactions of workers of *different* ethnic, geographical, cultural, social or religious background to the *same* systems of remuneration." (P. 138, italics in original; cf. pp. 149, 150.) It is impossible to reconcile the presuppositional perspective that underlies this proposal with the instrumental thinking that—we will see later in this chapter—so permeates Weber's perspective on modern industrial life.

15. The "Weberian" conception of the rational-legal order as providing a new, more voluntaristic standard of activity vis-à-vis "traditional" authority has been most successfully articulated in contemporary sociology by those interpreters who emphasize the continuity of Weber's thought and, accordingly, utilize the resources he provided in the multidimensional aspects of his work for their own analyses of contemporary political action. Some representative authors and works in this tradition are: Robert N. Bellah, *Beyond Belief* (New York, 1970); Talcott Parsons, *The Evolution of Society*, ed. Jackson Toby (Englewood Cliffs, N.J., 1977); S. N. Eisenstadt, *Tradition, Change, and Modernity* (New York, 1973); Wolfgang Schluchter, "Paradox of Rationalization" (n. 1 above); David Little, *Religion, Order, and Law* (New York, 1969); Michael Walzer, *The Revolution of the Saints* (Cambridge, Mass., 1965); Benjamin Nelson, "Conscience and the Making of Early Modern Cultures: *The Protestant Ethic* beyond Max Weber," *Social Research*, 36 (1969): 4–21; Alvin W. Gouldner, *The Dialectic of Ideology and Technology* (New York, 1976), Reinhard Bendix, *Nation-Building and Citizenship*, 2d ed. (Berkeley and Los Angeles, 1976); Guenther Roth, *The Social Democrats in Imperial Germany* (New York, 1963); Wolfgang Schluchter, *The Rise of Western Rationalism: Max Weber's Developmental History* (Berkeley and Los Angeles, 1981). My point here is not that these writers are incorrect empirically or theoretically. To the contrary, they elaborate further what I consider to have been the major synthetic breakthrough of Weber's work. They are incorrect, however, insofar as they, in fact, claim merely to extend Weber's own view of modern life. (Only Gouldner makes no such claim, presenting himself more as a Marxist than a Weberian; I would read his work, however, more as that of a radical Weberian.)

16. Weber, *The Protestant Ethic and the Spirit of Capitalism* (New York, 1958), p. 181. As Beetham (n. 5 above) puts the relevance of these final pages: "It is ironic that *The Protestant Ethic* should have been read

as providing a general justification for the independent power of ideas in social life, when the conclusion Weber himself drew for modern society was precisely the opposite" (p. 221). Wolfgang J. Mommsen makes much the same point:

> *The Protestant Ethic and the Spirit of Capitalism* is commonly held to prove the case for the autonomy of idealist, and specifically religious forces in history. However, it was by no means intended to be a direct refutation of Marxism. Weber, in fact, came very close to Marx's position when he argued that mature capitalism can survive without the specific mentality which was the offspring of puritan asceticism. In an almost Marxist fashion he described the modern capitalist system as an irresistible social force which coerces men to subject themselves quasi-voluntarily to its objective social conditions, regardless of whether they like them or not. Henceforth they have got to be *Berufsmenschen*, for the system of modern industrial capitalism does not permit otherwise. (*The Age of Bureaucracy* [New York, 1974], p. 55.)

17. In view of the similar ambiguities that occur in Tönnies' *Willkür* ("rational will") and Weber's *Zweckrationalität* (see ch. 2, n. 48), it is revealing that Tönnies in his famous work of 1887 concludes that *Willkür* is capable only of sustaining "business," not a calling. *Wesenwill* ("natural will") can sustain a calling, but rational will makes labor into an instrumental means-end process, one in which "the end should be attained in the most perfect possible way with the easiest and simplest possible means." "If this principle is applied to life as such a business," Tönnies warns, the guiding principle becomes perfectly utilitarian: "the greatest amount of pleasure or happiness with the least amount of pain, effort, or trouble, the smallest sacrifice of goods or vital energy (through labor)." (*Community and Society* [New York, 1963], p. 144.) In the final passage in Weber's *Protestant Ethic*, we see the instrumental understanding of *Zweckrationalität* that corresponds to the instrumental understanding of "rational will." Weber's concept can no more sustain a "calling" than could Tönnies' earlier one. As we noted earlier, Tönnies consciously modeled *Willkür* and the *Gesellschaft* order that this action informed after the instrumental capitalist society portrayed by Marx.

18. Weber, "Socialism," in J. E. T. Eldridge, ed., *Max Weber* (London, 1971), pp. 191–219, see p. 202.

19. Weber, *Aufsätze zur Soziologie und Sozialpolitik* (Tübingen, 1924), p. 414, quoted in Steven Seidman and Michael Gruber, "Capitalism and Individuation in the Sociology of Max Weber," *British Journal of Sociology* 28 (1977): 498–508, see 507. The shift which I am documenting here, and which is, in part, the point of this chapter, has been clearly articulated by Seidman and Gruber: "While Weber saw that the modern world provided an ideal milieu within which individual autonomy could and did arise, he equally recognized that the peculiar combination of univer-

sal structures (economy, polity, law, science, bureaucracy) crystallized into a world in which submission and adaptation progressively replaced self-determination as the paradigmatic form of conduct" (p. 498). They conclude, at least for the general thrust of Weber's work and, in my opinion, correctly that the "acquisition and loss of autonomy by the individual constitutes the implicit problematic for Weber's programmatic investigations into civilizational histories as mediated by the sociological problem of modern capitalism" (p. 506).

Siegfried Landshut's was perhaps the first critique to expound the shared assumptions in Marx's and Weber's views of capitalism, insisting that for Weber as for Marx economy is destiny, that capitalist relations are human relations but appear to be natural and beyond human will, that capitalism is marked by class antagonisms where inequality and exploitation occur side by side with libertarian ideology (*Kritik der Soziologie* [Munich and Leipzig, 1927], pp. 61–62). Karl Löwith took up this theme in perhaps the most famous and compelling presentation of the case for this convergence, arguing that Weber's "rationalization" should be seen in the contemporary world as a more complex and empirically accurate equivalent of Marx's alienation ("Max Weber und Karl Marx," *Archiv für Sozialwissenschaft und Sozialpolitik* 67 [1932]: 53–99, 175–214, partly reprinted as "Weber's Interpretation of the Bourgeois-Capitalistic World in Terms of the Guiding Principle of 'Rationalization'" in Dennis Wrong, ed., *Max Weber* [Englewood Cliffs, N.J., 1970], pp. 101–102). "Both provide, Marx directly and Weber indirectly," Löwith writes, "*a critical analysis of modern man within bourgeois society in terms of bourgeois-capitalist economy,* based on the recognition that 'economy' has become 'destiny' " (*Archiv*, p. 61, italics in original). Löwith sees that Marx and Weber disagree about the historical sources that created this alienation-rationalization, and he tries to present the contemporary situation outlined in Weber's work in a particularly "existentialist" way. He emphasizes that for Weber, in contrast to Marx, the possibility for individual dignity and commitment still remains. But Löwith insists that while Marx and Weber may disagree in their prescriptions for action, they do not disagree on what contemporary alienation is. Abramowski sees the same tendency toward a convergence with a Marxian understanding of alienated instrumentalism in the contemporary capitalist world (*Das Geschichtsbild Max Webers* [Stuttgart, 1966], pp. 163 ff.), though he insists on the same qualification as Löwith about the continuing possibility for individual dignity. In a more specifically Marxist tradition, Jean Cohen produces essentially a similar argument, utilizing Weber in a positive manner to extend and amplify Marx's original theory about the alienation and instrumentalism of modern society. "Weber is important," Cohen argues, "precisely because he anticipated the forms domination would take in advanced industrial society, and their negative implications regarding subjectivity" ("Max Weber and the Dynamics of Rationalized Domination," *Telos* 4 [1972]: 63–86, quoting 63).

I do not accept many of the specifics of these analyses, and would insist on a number of model and propositional differences between Marx and Weber. The main convergence I am interested in documenting is, after all, presuppositional. Still, all of these analysts of Weber's theory of contemporary life are partly correct, and they present an important corrective to those who see the convergence as one between Weber and Durkheim, not Weber and Marx.

The most extensive, textually supported argument for the "Marxist" elements in Weber's analysis is Beetham's reconstruction of Weber's theory of modern politics from his occasional political writings (in newspaper articles, pamphlets, speeches, and letters), many of which are serious scholarly investigations in their own right. Beetham (n. 5 above) concludes that this writing "differ[s] in a number of respects from what is frequently regarded as the typically Weberian approach to political analysis. . . . Such supposedly Weberian emphases as the independence of the 'political' from the 'economic' [and] the importance of ideas, the role of legitimacy in explaining political stability and change, etc., are largely absent from these accounts and even at points explicitly denied" (p. 203). Beetham argues that in empirical and theoretical terms Weber and Marx are similar, the only significant difference being Weber's more conservative, "bourgeois" ideological outlook: "In a number of important respects his perception of his own society, at an empirical level, was similar to that of Marx. What differed was the practical standpoint he adopted as an actor in relation to that structure, the values in terms of which he sought to direct the process of interaction between society and politics. . . . What differed here was not the terms of the analysis, but the particular class standpoint from which it was judged." (P. 241.)

Again, although I argue along some of these same lines, I would depart from Beetham's conclusions in a number of ways. First, even in regard to contemporary capitalist society, Weber's empirical understanding differed significantly from Marx's in terms of his more complex model and in terms of his understanding of the role that the state played in any industrialized society. It was partly upon such *empirical* grounds that his preferences in the political realm differed from Marx's—not simply on the basis of the radicalism or conservatism of his ideology. Weber's espousal of the inclusion of the working class in a bourgeois democratic polity, e.g., derived in part from his empirical belief that such inclusion was possible, which Marx did not share. Second, Weber's ideology was not simply "bourgeois" and "conservative." As will be seen more clearly in the concluding chapter, Weber was actually a sharp critic of "bourgeois" society and should be viewed as a pessimistic liberal reformer, not a conservative (see the argument in sec. 5). Finally, Beetham's understanding of the systematic scientific writings—to which he does not refer at length—accepts the portrait of a consistently multidimensional Weber which I have criticized here.

20. Weber, "The Meaning of Discipline," in Gerth and Mills (n. 6 above), pp. 253–264, quoting p. 253; *ES* (see ch. 2, n. 5), p. 1149, italics added (*WG*, pp. 866–867).

21. Ibid.

22. Ibid., pp. 261–262; *ES*, p. 1156 (*WG*, p. 873). It is revealing to compare this with Marx's very similar description of factory organization—which he takes to be prototypical of the order of contemporary capitalist life—in *Capital*, vol. 1:

> So far as the division of labour re-appears in the factory, it is primarily a distribution of the workmen among the specialized machines. . . . To work at a machine, the workman should be taught from childhood, in order that he may learn to adapt his own movements to the uniform and unceasing motion of an automaton. . . . Since the motion of the whole system does not proceed from the workman, but from the machinery, a change of persons can take place at any time without an interruption of the work. . . . The technical subordination of the workman to the uniform motion of the instruments of labour . . . gives rise to a barrack discipline." (Moscow, n.d., pp. 420–423.)

23. Weber, "Class, Status, and Party," in Gerth and Mills, pp. 180–195, quoting p. 180; *ES*, p. 926 (*WG*, p. 678).

24. Ibid., pp. 194–195; *ES*, pp. 938–939 (*WG*, pp. 688–689).

25. Ibid.

26. Weber, "Some Categories of Interpretive Sociology" (1931), *The Sociological Quarterly* 22 (1981): 151–180, quoting p. 177 ("Ueber einige Kategorien der 'verstehenden' Soziologie" [1913], in Winckelmann [n. 5, above], p. 147).

27. Bendix and Wrong both interpret the bureaucracy essay from such a generalized comparative view. Wrong specifically opposes such an interpretation to the kind of criticism of Weber's theory of bureaucracy which I make in sec. 1, below (Wrong [n. 19 above], "Introduction," pp. 33–36; Bendix [n. 1 above], pp. 425–427).

28. Weber, "Bureaucracy," in Gerth and Mills, pp. 196–244 (*ES*, pp. 956–1005), see pp. 196–197; *ES*, pp. 956–957.

29. Ibid., pp. 197–198; *ES*, pp. 957–958 (*WG*, pp. 703–704).

30. There is some evidence that, informally, Weber empirically recognized an alternative to this type of domination-oriented analysis of bureaucracy even though his more general commitments made it impossible for him to incorporate this alternative into his concepts, definitions, and propositions. For example, in the essay "Parliament and Government in a Reconstructed Germany" he describes bureaucratic workers as engaged by voluntaristic commitments which are stimulated by their subjective appreciation of the independence of the legitimacy and, presumably, the fairness of the bureaucracy itself. "Independent

decision-making and imaginative organizational capabilities in matters of detail," Weber writes, "are usually also demanded of the bureaucrat, and very often expected even in larger matters." He argues, in fact, that "the idea that the bureaucrat is absorbed in subaltern routine and that only the 'director' performs the interesting, intellectually demanding tasks is a preconceived notion of the literati and only possible in a country that has no insight into the manner in which its affairs and the work of its officialdom is conducted." (*ES*, p. 1404.) This "preconceived" notion, however, is exactly the one Weber himself has proposed in the main propositions of his scientific theory. An understanding of the bureaucratic ability to react to external pressures in an activistic way that is motivated by commitment to generalized beliefs would, of course, be more consistent with the multidimensional strand of his work.

31. "Bureaucracy," pp. 198–199; *ES*, pp. 958–959 (*WG*, p. 705).

32. Ibid., p. 199; *ES*, p. 959 (*WG*, p. 705).

33. Ibid.

34. Ibid.

35. Robert Merton, in contrast, takes Weber's work as arguing for the centrality in bureaucratic life of the socialization to duty and obedience (*Social Theory and Social Structure* [New York, 1968], pp. 252–253).

The instrumentalism of Weber's theory does not mean that his view of state bureaucracy is the same as Marx's. It is true, as Beetham (n. 5 above) has well demonstrated, that Weber often views bureaucracy's nonbureaucratic, political "top" as controlled by dominant class interests (p. 66 for the Russian bureaucracy, pp. 152–155 for the German; cf. "Capitalism and Rural Society in Germany," in Gerth and Mills, p. 373). Yet this is not at all economic determinism in Marx's sense of state institutions being completely structured by class interests. The bureaucracy in Weber's work is still an independent institutional entity, with its own developmental laws. In Weber's bureaucracy, economic determinism can, indeed, only occur by controlling the extrabureaucratic executive power of an organization. Thus, e.g., the differential class recruitment to bureaucracy must become an independent variable in any "Weberian" explanation, no matter how instrumentalist. I am arguing, in other words, that Weber's "model," within an instrumental presuppositional framework, is very different from Marx's. I exclude here the Marx of *The Eighteenth Brumaire*, for reasons indicated in vol. 2, ch. 10. Yet even if it were included I would say that Weber conceptualizes in precise empirical theories what remained primarily residual, passing observations for Marx.

36. "Bureaucracy," pp. 207–208; *ES*, p. 967.

37. Ibid., p. 208; *ES*, p. 968.

38. Ibid.; *ES*, pp. 967–968.

39. Ibid. (*WG*, p. 712).

40. Ibid., pp. 209–211, 214–216; *ES*, pp. 969–971, 973–975.

41. Ibid., p. 215; *ES*, pp. 974.

42. Ibid., pp. 212–213; *ES*, pp. 971–973.

43. Ibid., p. 221; *ES*, p. 980 (*WG*, p. 722).

44. The remainder of Weber's bureaucracy essay (ibid., pp. 224–239) concerns itself primarily with issues other than internal operation and external determination. Yet in the very last section Weber raises an issue that departs from his otherwise exclusively hierarchic emphasis: the possibility that bureaucratic power is dependent not on force, instrumental calculation, and passive acquiescence but on "expert knowledge" (pp. 235–239). However, although he begins to discuss some of the ramifications of this possibility, he makes no attempt to integrate the issue with the main thrust of the analysis which proceeded it. Some commentators have recognized how this latter argument about the basis of bureaucratic behavior deviates from Weber's purely hierarchic model. (See, e.g., Peter M. Blau's "Critical Remarks on Max Weber's Theory of Authority," pp. 147–165 in Wrong [n. 19 above], p. 156.) Parsons, in fact, explicitly utilizes the reference to expert knowledge to criticize Weber's bureaucracy essay, in an extremely general way, for emphasizing "coercive power" over "voluntary consent" ("Introduction," pp. 3–86 in Weber, *Theory of Social and Economic Organization* [New York, 1946], p. 59). "The fundamental model he had in mind," Parsons writes about Weber's bureaucracy model in general, "was that of legal 'powers,' particularly powers of coercion in case of recalcitrance" (p. 59). But the prototype of voluntaristic authority by virtue of expert knowledge, Parsons rightly insists, is that of the educated professional whose authority derives from cultural internalization (pp. 59–60, n. 4). These observations, however, are given slight play in Parsons' overall evaluation of Weber's political sociology which generally holds, along with others, that Weber's analysis was consistently multidimensional.

45. For the "functional" perspective as the cause of Weber's problems with bureaucracy, see Blau's remarks:

> What is missing from Weber's analysis is a similar systematic attempt to specify the *dysfunctions* of the various elements and to examine the conflicts that arise between the elements comprising the system. Thus, even if it is true that the hierarchy of authority promotes discipline and makes possible the coordination of activities, does it not also discourage subordinates from accepting responsibility? ("Weber's Theory of Bureaucracy," in Stammer [n. 3 above], pp. 141–146, see pp. 143–144, italics in original.)

I have referred earlier (ch. 4, n. 27) to a more purely empirical criticism of Weber's theory of authority that Blau makes at another point. For a similarly empirical argument—in this case, that the overemphasis in

Weber's theory occurs because he slights importance of informal relations in organization—see Philip Selznick, "Foundations of the Theory of Organizations," *American Sociological Review* 13 (1948): 25–35. (Selznick's masterful analysis of organizational processes in *Leadership in Administration* [New York, 1957] still makes an apparently empirical critique of the hierarchical model, arguing that Weberian organizational theory ignores the phenomenon of leadership; but, in fact, its major polemic is firmly launched at the presuppositional level itself, e.g., Selznick's argument that the organizational analyst must see the possibility for relating administrative strategy to broader considerations of value.) For the ideological and political approach to Weber's overemphasis on hierarchy, see Mommsen (n. 16 above), passim.

46. Thus, e.g., motivation is the central focus of Selznick's analysis in *Leadership in Administration*, which focuses on the problem of making organizational participation voluntary and consensual.

Weber's instrumental analysis would have difficulty, e.g., explaining the kind of revolutionary, ultravoluntaristic bureaucracy represented by the Bolshevik type of party that Lenin established in Russia before 1917— just as Marx's instrumental analysis did not allow a systematic explanation for this ideologically-inspired political phenomenon. (Weber's student, Robert Michels, did utilize Weber's more instrumental theory to explain the Marxist political party of German Social Democracy, but his explanation—leavened by certain psychological assumptions—predicted passivity, resignation, and reformism. It, too, had no theoretical resources for voluntarism.) Just as Lenin had to implicitly revise Marx to justify theoretically the basis for his vanguard party in *What Is to Be Done?* (see vol. 2, ch. 10), Selznick produces a much more culturally- and motivationally-directed organizational theory than Weber's to explain the extraordinary effectiveness of the Leninist party in his *The Organizational Weapon* (New York, 1952).

A similarly revisionist theory is offered by Gaston Rimlinger in "The Legitimation of Protest: A Comparative Study in Labor History," *Comparative Studies in Society and History* 2 (1965): 329–343, in order to explain the passivity of the German proletariat in the face of industrialization, a passivity that made them more vulnerable to the eventual bureaucratization represented by the German Social Democratic party. The English proletariat, in Rimlinger's view, responded to industrialization in an active and rebellious way, a response which made the English workers' movement less open to bureaucratization. Rimlinger works within the Weberian framework, but his analysis is mediated by Bendix's more consistently multidimensional interpretation. The crucial variable, for him, is the more activist Puritanism of British Christianity as compared with the more authoritarian heritage of German Lutheranism, a normative contrast that Weber's bureaucracy theory rarely embraces.

47. Weber, "Parliament and Government in a Reconstructed Germany," *ES*, pp. 1381–1469, see p. 1392.

48. Ibid., p. 1403.

49. Ibid., p. 1414; Weber, *Gesammelte Politische Schriften*, ed. Johannes Winklelmann, 3d ed. (Tübingen, 1971), p. 349, hereafter cited as *GPS*.

50. Ibid.

51. Ibid., p. 1450.

52. Ibid.

53. It is quite possible to make this confusion of Weber's treatment of democratic responsibility in the present context with his analysis of responsibility in ancient Israel because Weber in the parliamentary essay continually invokes many of the concepts first developed in his discussion of prophecy—e.g., the significance of public demagoguery. However, the crucial fact is that in the discussion of contemporary democracy this type of behavior is not connected to motivation generated by transcendent belief; it is treated, rather, as a manifestation of instrumental interest.

54. Ibid., p. 1404.

55. Ibid., pp. 1416–1424. After this section, most of the rest of the essay is taken up with specific suggestions for the postwar German situation in terms of the institutional arrangements which Weber has recommended (*ES*, pp. 1428–1442, 1449–1451, 1459–1462). Weber also discusses how these conditional arrangements can at times impinge on the creation of effective leadership—e.g., by bureaucratizing the mass party and by creating "caesarist" features in mass democracy (pp. 1454–1459).

56. Again, my point here is not that Weber never mentions a more multidimensional approach to charisma. In the beginning of "Politics as a Vocation," e.g., he explicitly connects the modern demagogue of parliamentary democracy with the religious prophet: "Devotion to the charisma of the prophet, or the leader in war, or to the great demagogue in the *ecclesia* or in parliament, means that the leader is personally recognized as the innerly 'called' leader of men. Men do not obey him by virtue of tradition or statute, but because they believe in him. If he is more than a narrow and vain upstart of the moment, the leader [then] lives for his cause and 'strives for his work,' " (Gerth and Mills [n. 6 above], p. 79; *GPS*, p. 508). For the rest of this speech, however, charisma in this normative sense, and with these normative results, becomes a residual category, and the ramifications of this kind of relationship in terms of the variability of normative order are never pursued. The fact of a charismatic relationship is taken as a parameter: it creates an external condition that rational actors and material institutions must take into account.

57. *ES*, p. 1438.

58. Ibid., p. 1427. I noted the same instrumental treatment of "vocation" in the bureaucracy essay. The failure on Weber's part to explain political "responsibility" with reference to political "conviction" in his

essays on democracy and bureaucracy is a major failure. It demonstrates once again, the power of theoretical presuppositions in directing and limiting propositional analysis.

59. E.g., *ES*, p. 922.

60. See the writings discussed by Beetham (n. 5 above, pp. 121–131).

61. "Politics as a Vocation" (Gerth and Mills, n. 6 above), pp. 84–86.

62. Ibid., pp. 88–90.

63. Ibid., pp. 100–101.

64. Ibid., p. 105.

65. Ibid., p. 102.

66. Ibid., p. 110.

67. Ibid., p. 103, italics in original.

68. Ibid. See n. 56 above.

69. Ibid., p. 108; cf. pp. 105–110.

70. *ES*, p. 268, italics in original.

71. The letter, written in 1908, is quoted in Mommsen (n. 16 above), p. 87.

72. The statement can be found in Friedrich Meinecke, *Politische Schriften und Reden*, ed. George Kotowski (Darmstadt, 1958), pp. 49–50; it is quoted in Fritz Ringer, *The Decline of the German Mandarins* (Cambridge, Mass., 1969), p. 131.

73. For an often insightful testimony about the democratic misgivings that Weber felt about the political tendencies he scientifically described, see Karl Loewenstein, *Max Weber's Political Ideas in the Perspective of Our Time* (n.p., 1965), passim; see also the balanced discussion by Anthony Giddens, *Politics and Sociology in the Thought of Max Weber* (n. 5 above), 1972, passim.

It is the miscalculation about Weber's ideology—the notion that he actually approved or wished for the Machiavellianism he described—that mars the otherwise very accurate criticisms which Mommsen and Aron have made against the Realpolitik instrumentalism of Weber's perspective on modern politics. Both commentators have noted the ruthlessness of Weber's vision of international conflict and the way in which this vision of Realpolitik affected his analysis of intranational political life. Mommsen has related this problem mainly to Weber's acceptance of German imperialism, Aron more generally to the historical period within which Weber lived. (Raymond Aron, "Max Weber and Power Politics," in Stammer [n. 3 above], pp. 83–100; Wolfgang J. Mommsen, "Discussion on Raymond Aron's 'Max Weber and Power Politics,' " ibid., pp. 109–116, and also his "Max Weber's Political Sociology and his Philosophy of World History," in Wrong [n. 19 above], pp. 183–194.) Surely, however, the problem relates equally to the failure to postulate the normative mediation of external force which characterizes the entire range of Weber's political sociology. As for Weber's ideology, it is as democratic as it is authoritarian in its evaluative bent.

Aron actually does define Weber's politics as following the Hobbesian tradition, linking this theoretical perspective first to Weber's description of external politics, then to the sociology of domination that controls his vision of internal politics.

> When Hobbes, in his *Leviathan*, looks for an illustration of the state of nature and describes relations between Sovereigns, he gives a radical expression to a classical idea. Weber, who defines the state as having the monopoly of legitimate violence, should logically recognize the heterogeneity between the violent rivalry of states and the rivalry, which is subject to law, between individuals and classes within a state. Now the fact is that Weber who obviously admitted this heterogeneity has rather blurred this distinction. It seems to me he was impressed and to some extent influenced by Darwin's vision of social reality. (P. 90.)

> Theoretically all politics, home and foreign, is above all a struggle between nations, classes or individuals.... Weber never indicated explicitly any difference of character between the internal and external struggle. (P. 85.)

(The only article in English in which Weber relates his visions of internal and external power politics is "Structures of Power," in Gerth and Mills [n. 6 above], pp. 159–179.)

It could be argued, of course, that the vagaries of Weber's discussion of democracy should be interpreted only in historical and empirical terms, not on presuppositional ones. (See Guenther Roth, "Political Critiques of Max Weber: Some Implications for Political Sociology," pp. 195–210 in Wrong [n. 19 above], for such a historical explanation of, and rationale for, Weber's views on politics.) According to this view, Weber is arguing in the specific situation of postwar Germany for specific changes in political conditions; he does not mention cultural conditions because they were not amenable to change at that particular historical juncture. In opposition, I would argue, first and most importantly, that Weber himself makes no historical qualification but speaks about parliamentary democracy in the general sense. Second, this treatment of democracy dovetails too easily with other aspects of his political sociology to be considered a historically specific anomaly. Finally, Weber did not hesitate, in other, more multidimensional segments of his work, to criticize the cultural aspects of German life, and he does so even in articles that appeared in nonacademic media.

74. "What is distinctive about this [Weber's] account of democracy," Beetham writes, "is that it makes no reference to democratic values" (n. 5 above, 112). Niklas Luhmann has shown clearly how Weber's instrumental conception of action allows the relation between authority and the rules that regulate it to be a purely hierarchical and coercive one, and he relates this to Weber's acceptance of an overly narrow conception of

instrumental rationality as the basis of organized action. "Weber sees the contribution of members as essentially a matter of obedient behavior," and "as a result, questions of motivation are neglected" (Luhmann, "Ends, Domination, and System: Fundamental Concepts and Premises in the Work of Max Weber," in his *The Differentiation of Society* [New York, 1982], pp. 20–46, quoting p. 44). While Luhmann suggests that this problem of action occurs because Weber did not conceptualize societies as "systems," I believe that such model commitments are not necessarily connected to presuppositions about action.

75. The monograph is progressively time-ordered in its overall chapter organization, and many of the chapters are themselves chronological.

76. Rheinstein, *Max Weber on Law in Economy and Society* (n. 2 above), pp. 99–100; *ES*, pp. 667–668.

77. Ibid., p. 167; *ES*, p. 713.

78. Ibid., p. 76; *ES*, p. 761.

79. Ibid., pp. 76–77 (see also pp. 73, 86–88); *ES*, p. 761.

80. In terms of classifying Weber's work as a whole, then, the early analyses of law in traditional society would be included in the strand of his writings discussed in ch. 2, while only the following discussion of law in capitalist society should properly be considered part of the more instrumental political sociology analyzed in the present chapter.

Throughout the following analysis, I am careful to speak about Weber's conceptualization of the *functions* of modern law rather than his *explanation* for the development of these functions in historical terms. I do so for the reason that although Weber clearly attributes a formidable determining role to the emergence of strong economic interest-groups, he also cites developments in the normative sphere—in addition to those cited above, the drive for abstraction on the part of legal scholars and "honoratiores" (*Max Weber on Law in Economy and Society*, ch. 7). Such a normative explanation of origins, of course, is no more inconsistent with an instrumental interpretation of modern life than the role of Puritanism in creating capitalism is with the latter's contemporary deterministic form. Considered as a whole, however, Weber's historical explanation of legal development would have to be considered as presenting a theoretically "dichotomized" picture rather than a completely one-dimensional one. E.g., although he clearly related the origins of legal rights to religious influences and specifically linked them to processes in legal thought in contrast to purely economic needs (ibid., p. 131), in the same chapter he develops a general explanation of rights solely in terms of the growth of economic exchange (p. 158; see also the striking "either/or" manner of his references to rational and nonrational determinants, pp. 224–226).

81. Ibid., p. 189; *ES*, p. 730.

82. Ibid.

83. Ibid., p. 191; *ES*, p. 731 (*WG*, p. 563).

84. "Bureaucracy," in Gerth and Mills (n. 6 above), p. 219; *ES*, p. 979 (*WG*, p. 720). It is significant for the relation of this conceptualization to Weber's perception of the dominant role of capitalist economic interest in modern society to understand that he introduces it, in the bureaucracy essay, in the course of his long discussion of the materialist origins of modern bureaucracy. Though the passage cited is an ambiguous one, it seems clear that Weber intends to minimize the individualizing aspects of the modern judge's role.

85. Philip Selznick has criticized the emphasis on coercion in Weber's conception of law, in *Law, Society and Industrial Justice* (New York, 1969), pp. 6–7. I would limit this criticism to Weber's treatment of the special case of law in modern society.

86. Rheinstein, *Max Weber on Law in Economy and Society*, ch. 11. The status of law as pure "means" refers to the distinction between the normative ontological status of law and its instrumental position in epistemological terms made in the preceding paragraph, and it demonstrates the empirical significance of theoretical distinctions that, in themselves, might seem obscure. In my discussion of abstract "theoretical logic" in vol. 1 (ch. 3, sec. 1), I suggested that "sociological materialism" cannot be defined by the actual ontological status of the external and coercive element itself, i.e., whether the ordering elements a theory posits are corporeal entities or not. What determines sociological materialism is the "externality" of an ordering element vis-à-vis the actor, and what decides this externality is the nature of the action which presupposes the collective order described. Whether or not an element of collective order is "ideal" or "normative" in its actual composition, it will be external and coercive vis-à-vis the actor if he is conceptualized, theoretically, as acting toward this rule only in a self-interested and completely rational manner and, therefore, as not internalizing the rule at all. In this case, the ideal element, in itself, can be viewed only as an external element which must be rationally calculated along with external material elements. In the last instance, such purely external norms will be theoretically conceptualized as "backed up" by some kind of physical sanction, but before this "last instance" their coercive status is not attached to material things. These presuppositional issues, it is clear, are extremely important if Weber's theory of contemporary rational-legal society is to be understood, for "norms" per se certainly continue to exist in Weber's theory of modern society.

87. Ibid., p. 298; *ES*, pp. 874–875.

88. Ibid.; *ES*, p. 875 (*WG*, p. 642). The contention that this radical distinction—between a substantively rational law connected to cultural values and a formally rational law unattached to such values—functioned

to support Weber's theory of the absence of voluntarism in modern society is further substantiated by a passage in the essay on parliamentary democracy. Weber speculates here on the absence of freedom in modern life due to excessive bureaucratization:

> How can one possibly save *any remnants* of "individualist" freedom in any sense? After all, it is a gross self-deception to believe that without the achievements of the age of the Rights of Man [e.g., the age of substantively-rational natural law] any one of us, including the most conservative, can go on living his life. (*ES*, p. 1403, italics in original.)

89. *Max Weber on Law in Economy and Society*, pp. 294–296, 318–321; *ES*, pp. 871–873, 892–895.

90. In terms of the multidimensional argument, Parsons argues that formal law indicated for Weber simply a shift from "particularism" to "universalism" *within* the continuing normative reference of the legal system ("Evaluation and Objectivity in Social Science: An Interpretation of Max Weber's Contribution," pp. 79–101 in his *Sociological Theory and Modern Society* [New York, 1967], pp. 79–101, esp. pp. 93–94). It is true that Weber is right to argue that a *completely* substantively rational system would, as Parsons believes, imply "a simple application of ethical orientations" (p. 93) that would be too particularistic for modern life. My criticism is not, however, that Weber's rejection of a purely substantively rational legal system is incorrect but rather that he does not—and cannot, given his presuppositional commitments—conceptualize the alternative of formal rationality as "a level of differentiation of the normative order," as Parsons claims that he does (p. 93). Weber does not do so because he does not actually develop a conception of the role of normative elements in modern life. Parsons, of course, claims that he does, and in this interpretation of Weber's sociology of law presents it as demonstrating the crucial link between religious systems of meaning and political organization (pp. 93–94). But this claim must be viewed as one more manifestation of Parsons' perspective on Weber's work as possessing a unified theoretical framework.

On a more empirical level, Bendix has advanced much the same claim for the multidimensionality of Weber's legal theory. It stipulates, in Bendix's view, that there is a "balance between these principles" of formal and substantive rationality, a balance Bendix roots in the empirical character of modernity itself (*Max Weber* [n. 45 above], p. 484).

An argument for the instrumentality of the legal theory that is pursued on as generalized a level as Parsons' contrary contention can be found in Leo Strauss, *Natural Right and History* (Chicago, 1953). Strauss has forcefully described Weber's inability to connect modern social action to conceptions of "natural right" as an inability to connect action to the influence of broader systems of cultural and ethical values. An effectively similar argument made on methodological, empirical and ideological grounds is presented by Max Rheinstein's evaluative essay introducing the monograph on law. Although Rheinstein, like Bendix, also emphasizes the instances of Weber's recognition of substantive rationality in modern legal life, his detailed analysis of Weber's treatment makes it clear that he understands Weber as regarding formal rationality to be the immanent tendency in modern law. He also emphasizes that Weber directly connects this form of legal thought to the utilitarian kind of *zweckrational* motivation that is associated with economic life under capitalism.

> Modern capitalism constitutes for Weber the very prototype of purposively rational conduct, *viz.* of conduct oriented toward profit and rational choice of the means conducive to that purpose. The categories of legal thought are obviously conceived along lines parallel to the categories of economic conduct. The logically formal rationality of legal thought is the counterpart to the purposive rationality of economic conduct. Indeed, there are many indications that Weber at some stage of his work regarded it as possible that a peculiar relationship existed between the logically formal rationality of legal thought and the purposively rational kind of economic conduct and thus with modern capitalism. But Weber's own work shows that this connection is not one of absolute correlation. ("Introduction," pp. xxvii–lxiii in *Max Weber on Law in Economy and Society*, p. l.)

Despite the latter disclaimer, it can be argued that the implicit point of Rheinstein's essay is to criticize Weber's emphasis on the dominant role of formal rationality in modern legal life. He attempts to dislodge any inherent connection between modern life and formally rational law by relating Weber's radical distinction between formal and substantive rationality to his methodology of ideal types rather than to a judgment of empirical fact (pp. xlviii–xlix), thus following Parsons' emphasis on methodological as opposed to presuppositional criticism of Weber's work. In addition, he offers a sociology-of-knowledge explanation for the postulated disjuncture, citing the manner in which formalistically minded legal scholars were forced to play a central modernizing role in the industrialization of continental Europe as opposed to their less central role in the modernization of England and America (p. li).

Mommsen takes a similar sociology-of-knowledge approach to the legal sociology, though viewing it less equivocally as of a purely instrumental type: "Weber gloomily depicted the kind of society which would come closest to a full implementation of all the elements listed under the type of pure legal rule. It would be administered by an almighty bureaucracy in accordance with a closely knit network of laws and regulations of a purely formalistic nature, which would leave little or no space for individually-oriented creative action. In such a system moral values would be of little avail, for the organizational structure would only take into account technical considerations. . . . Eventually all individual initiative would be suffocated by the iron force of a network of purely instrumentally-legal stipulations." (*Age of Bureaucracy* [n. 16 above], pp. 81–82.)

The instrumentality of Weber's views of modern law can perhaps most effectively be indicated by the fact that the Frankfurt-school Marxist Jürgen Habermas has used the Weberian conception of law to document what he views as the purely technical, instrumental rationality of the capitalist social system. Taking his cue from Weber's treatment, Habermas links the historical development of law only to the external forces of bureaucracy and industrialization.

> Formal law corresponded to objective conditions insofar as the two great processes which fundamentally changed the interconnections of *dominium* and *societas* asserted themselves within the territorial states of the sixteenth century: that is, the centralization and at the same time the bureaucratization of power within the modern state apparatus . . . as well as the expansion of capitalist trade. (*Theory and Practice* [Boston, 1973], p. 62.)

Assuming such a history of purely external reference, Habermas can find grounds for arguing that modern law eliminates cultural experience and, with it, the possibility for voluntarism.

> Formal law frees the conduct of citizens within a morally neutral domain, releasing them from the motivations of internalized duties and liberating them to look after their own interests; therefore the limitations which result can now only be imposed externally. . . . The universe of private autonomy, to which the law secures the right, is the psychological motivation of coercion, of obedience. When actually in force, formal law is sanctioned solely by physically effective force, and legality is fundamentally divorced from morality. (Ibid., pp. 84–85.)

Perhaps the most nuanced discussion of Weber's approach to modern law—a discussion which tries to resolve but actually revises Weber's original ambiguity—is Schluchter's in *The Rise of Western Rationalism* (n. 15 above), pp. 82–121. For a discussion of this work, see ch. 6, n. 21.

91. For Weber's discussion of these issues, see, e.g., "Socialism" (n. 18 above), esp. pp. 208–211; also "Status Groups and Classes," in *ES*, pp. 302–307.

92. "Class, Status, Party" (n. 13 above), p. 181; *ES*, p. 927.

93. Ibid., p. 187; *ES*, p. 932.

94. Ibid., pp. 194–195; *ES*, pp. 938–939.

95. Ibid., p. 187; *ES*, p. 932 (*WG*, p. 683).

96. Weber, "Ethnic Groups" in *ES*, pp. 385–398, quoting p. 385, italics in original.

97. "Class, Status, Party," p. 181; *ES*, p. 927.

98. Ibid., p. 180; *ES*, p. 926.

99. Ibid., p. 181; *ES*, p. 926.

100. Ibid., pp. 183–184; *ES*, p. 929; cf. *ES*, p. 305.

101. Ibid., p. 186.

102. Ibid., p. 193; *ES*, p. 937; cf. "Socialism" (n. 18 above), p. 193.

103. "Class, Status, Party," p. 187; *ES*, p. 932.

104. Ibid., p. 188; *ES*, p. 933.

105. Ibid., p. 191; *ES*, pp. 935–936.

106. Ibid., p. 192; *ES*, p. 936.

107. Ibid., p. 188; *ES*, p. 933.

108. Ibid., p. 194; *ES*, p. 938.

109. Ibid., p. 195; *ES*, p. 939.

110. Ibid., p. 194; *ES*, p. 938. For a fuller discussion of this phenomenon, see, e.g., Weber's analysis as presented in Beetham (n. 5 above), p. 80.

111. The quasi-Marxist, purely instrumental approach to stratification that lies at the heart of "conflict theory" is, therefore, thoroughly rooted in Weber's own work. In one of the books that laid the foundations for this approach, John Rex insists that status should be viewed simply as an attempt at the legitimation of class interest. The very conflict over status demonstrates, in his view, that there is no overarching normative order beyond the ideology promoted by political and economic interest groups. (*Key Problems in Sociological Theory* [London, 1961], pp. 148–150.) Status, Rex writes, is simply the "means" by which a class "legitimates its position" (p. 153). In the non-Marxist tradition, of course, the reductionist tendency of Weber's position can also promote the instrumentalization of status. The massive quantitative comparative study conducted by Donald Treiman, *Occupational Prestige in Comparative Perspective* (New York, 1977), takes what Treiman calls a "structural" approach to prestige. The work achieves this appearance of materialism, however, simply by converting important elements of subjective status— e.g., the cultural knowledge that gives prestige—into a form of "power." This reduction too can be read as "orthodox" Weberianism.

It was precisely against this reductionistic tendency in the original theory that Edward A. Shils tried to reconnect Weber's "status" concept to "charisma" as a carrier of cultural meanings in his seminal essay, "Charisma, Order, and Status" (pp. 256–275 in Shils, *Center and Periphery: Essays in Macrosociology* [Chicago, (1965) 1975]). Influenced by Shils, S. N. Eisenstadt emphasizes the vital multidimensional understanding that there are two fundamentally different ways of conceptualizing the "status" concept. He criticizes the positivist discussion of prestige for not connecting the concept more closely to culture, although he reads Weber in a polemical way as himself asserting that this connection must always be maintained.

The central concept in later sociological analysis of stratification, largely derived from Weber, is that of prestige. As is well known, prestige has been presented in most analyses of stratification as one of three major dimensions of stratification, power and wealth being the other two. But at the same time prestige was the least analytically specified dimension. Both the bases (or criteria) of prestige and the structural implications of its differential distribution have been abundantly described but not fully explored in their basic analytical implications. They were to some extent taken for granted, often subsumed under, or related to, the concept of "style of life," which often served, like the concept of prestige itself, as a sort of general residual category in the studies of stratification.

... However, important implications for these problems can be derived from Weber's own work.... Among the most important of these implications is that the sources of prestige, of the deference which people render to others, are rooted not only in their organizational (power, economic, etc.) positions, but also in their differential proximity to those areas which constitute the institutional foci of charisma. ("Max Weber and Modern Sociology," pp. ix–lvi in Eisenstadt, ed., *Max Weber on Charisma and Institution Building* [Chicago, 1968], p. xxxiii.)

An important work that bridges the conflict, exchange, and cultural approaches to status is William J. Goode, *The Celebration of Heroes* (Berkeley and Los Angeles, 1979), though Goode's cultural references are not as strong as they should be.

Dick Atkinson is the interpreter of Weber's work who has most forcefully recognized the strains and instrumental tendency in his analysis of class (but cf. the insightful discussion by Schluchter, *The Rise of Western Rationalism* [n. 15], pp. 78–81). Weber's "explicit intention," Atkinson writes, "is to combine objective and subjective factors in conceptualizing class situation." Yet Weber "seems unaware of these problems when he suggests that only 'persons who are completely unskilled, without property and dependent on employment without regular occupation, are in a strictly identical class "situation." ' " Atkinson asks, "Do itinerant, unskilled and unemployed labourers share an identical class situation? Are there really no other class divisions based partly on subjective criteria within this 'objective' situation?" (*Orthodox Consensus and Radical Alternative* [New York, 1972], p. 72.) Atkinson recognizes that by connecting class consciousness to "communalization" Weber implicitly contradicts the instrumental reasoning upon which the class-status distinction is based.

This [emphasis on communalization] completely contradicts his [Weber's] main and formal distinction between 'class situation', which he sees as being objectively determined prior to any interest which may be rationally deduced from it, and 'status situations', which *are* the subjective estimations and actions of these actors who, thereby, form their status situation. If both class and status situations are formed only by virtue of the action of men in relations with other men, then there can be no prior, objectively independent analysis of class situation. (P. 75, italics in original.)

On close examination the distinction between class and status breaks down. The analysis of false-consciousness, of subjectivity, is the analysis of status. So the analysis of complex divisions within one class, let alone the incorporation of the subjectivity of one class by another, must of necessity proceed in terms of analysis similar to that adopted by Weber's consideration of status. (P. 115.)

112. See, e.g., Richard Ashcraft, "Marx and Weber on Liberalism as Bourgeois Ideology," *Comparative Studies in Society and History* 14 (1972): 130–168, esp. 152.

113. Thus, Roth contends that "Weber insisted on realism in politics because the politically dominant Right adhered to idealist and romanticist notions to provide motive and cover for irresponsible power politics" and that "Weber insisted on realistic politics also because for decades the sterile left-wing liberal opposition of Imperial Germany stuck to 'principles' regardless of political feasibility" ("Political Critiques," pp. 55–69 in Reinhard Bendix and Guenther Roth, *Scholarship and Partisanship: Essays on Max Weber* [Berkeley and Los Angeles, (1971) 1980], p. 68). Earlier in the same essay, Roth dismisses critical arguments about the lack of normative reference in Weber's understanding of modernity by stressing its realism and objectivity in a different way:

Since sociological analysis properly endeavors to look at the world dispassionately or, more correctly, from a "theoretical" perspective in the strict contemplative sense of the word, it must appear relativist and Machiavellian to all those who, for ideological reasons, cannot recognize any dividing line between political sociology and political ideology (p. 55).

Much of this liberal position hinges on a pragmatic, normatively oriented interpretation of "Politics as a Vocation." Shils ("Introduction," in his *The Intellectuals and the Powers and Other Essays* [Chicago, 1972], p. vii) and Wrong ("Introduction" [n. 19 above], pp. 58–59) both cite Weber's notion of the "ethic of responsibility" as an example of his commitment to forms of political liberalism and moderation, as manifesting what another liberal interpreter, Benjamin Nelson, has described as the Weberian "social reality" principle ("Discussion of Herbert Marcuse's Industrialization and Capitalism,'" in Stammer [n. 45 above], pp. 161–171). See also Loewenstein (n. 73 above).

114. Ringer describes Weber as a "heroic pessimist" (n. 72 above, p. 158), one who sought to "uphold a heroic ideal of rational clarification in the face of tragedy" (p. 163). Ferdinand Kolegan discusses Weber's "cul-

tural pessimism" that even a socialist like Tönnies shared, though he argues that Weber never shared Tönnies' radically anti-urban, anti-industrial sentiments ("The Concept of 'Rationalization' and Cultural Pessimism in Max Weber's Sociology," *Sociological Quarterly* 5 [1964]: 355–373). "A Liberal in Despair" is the title of the last chapter in Mommsen's *The Age of Bureaucracy.*

115. Quoted in Mommsen, "Max Weber's Political Sociology and His Philosophy of World History," *International Social Science Journal* 17 (1965): 32 (reprinted in part in Wrong [n. 19 above]). Cf. Abramowski's statement that "important features of Weber's own ideal of personality are interwoven into the portrayal of the ethical emissary prophets of Israel and of the rational method of conduct of the Puritans" (*Das Geschichtsbild Max Webers* [n. 19 above], p. 162).

In a letter written two years after the letter of 1906 quoted in the text, Weber allows us more insight into the relationship between the high value he placed upon Puritanism and his vision of decline: "It is an inwardly difficult and typical situation: *none* of us could *by himself* be a sectarian—Quaker, Baptist, and so on. Historically speaking the time for sects or anything of the sort is past. On the other hand, the fact that our nation has never gone through the school of hard asceticisms *in any form* is the source of everything that I find so hateful in it *as well as in myself*!" (Quoted in Mommsen, p. 32, n. 4, italics in original.)

Puritanism, we must remember, was the first historical subject to which Weber gave serious and continuous attention after he recovered from his long nervous breakdown. As Arthur Mitzman has shown at great length in *The Iron Cage* (New York, 1970), this breakdown was at least partly stimulated by the anxiety and guilt that Weber experienced in his rebellion against his father. Although Weber eventually recovered his capacity to work, he never fully resolved the emotional issues that burdened him. Can it be purely coincidental that Weber concluded that the Puritans, too, presented forefathers to whom contemporary men could not live up?

116. "Science as a Vocation," in Gerth and Mills (see n. 6 above), p. 139.

117. Ibid., p. 147. For an insightful discussion of this strand of Weber's theory of modernity, see Steven Seidman, *Liberalism and the Origins of European Social Theory* (Berkeley and Los Angeles, 1983), ch. 11.

118. "Science as a Vocation," p. 152, italics in original.

119. The ambivalence in Weber's attitude toward the science he so championed is perhaps difficult for readers in the Anglo-American liberal tradition to comprehend, but it is an accurate reflection of the social and cultural attitudes of the "accomodationist" group of German intellectuals that initiated German sociology. This group, of which Weber was such an important member, did not accept the extreme antimodernist re-

actions of the conservative "mandarin" intelligentsia; at the same time, however, they did not completely dissociate themselves from some of the attitudes that underlay it. The mandarins regarded Anglo-Saxon and French intellectuals, from as early as the seventeenth century onward, as embarked on a dangerous path that would undermine *Kultur*, the very integration that supplied "meaning" for intellectual life. They associated these intellectuals, in short, with "science," and science almost exclusively with practical manipulation, rational technique, and environmental control. (For a good background discussion of this attitude see Ringer [n. 72 above], pp. 85 ff.) Although the extreme conservatism of these mandarin sentiments has largely dissipated today, there are strong echoes of this sensed antipathy between a culture in which science has a prominent place and a culture that can provide normative order in the writings of contemporary "Frankfurt school" Marxism—by Horkheimer, Adorno, Marcuse, and Habermas. This shared ideological reaction helps explain the ease with which these theorists, particularly Habermas, have been able to assimilate an important strand of Weber's work, a strand that is tied to the kind of instrumental thinking that Marx employed.

120. "Science as a Vocation," p. 154.

121. Ibid.

122. Weber, "Religious Rejections of the World and Their Directions," in Gerth and Mills (n. 6 above), pp. 323–359, see pp. 350 ff.; cf. "Science as a Vocation," pp. 141–142.

123. Ibid., p. 155.

124. Mitzman documents this development in an extraordinarily interesting, if sharply one-sided, way: "Weber, in his postbreakdown *Weltanschauung*, shared with Marx the perception of an ever-increasing rationalization and efficiency of social systems, but, for many reasons, he saw this as a dead-end progress, heading only to the 'cage of bondage.' . . . Unable to accept this bondage in his inner life, he tended to divide his thought into a public, historical *Weltanschauung* (comparable to Marx, but without the utopian dialectic) and a private a-historical ethic (comparable to Nietzsche . . .). He was, however, too much the sociologist to view his private code as totally without historical and social foundations. Instead, alongside the series of ideal types which he used to typify the various aspects of the process of rationalization, Weber established a parallel series which exemplify a world of doomed and rejected historical alternatives." (*The Iron Cage* [n. 115 above], p. 188.) These alternatives—the antonyms to modern existence which he privately longed for but believed to be publicly inaccessible—emerged in Weber's later work as ambivalent paeans to Eros, aesthetic sensation, and mystical release. Weber had surprisingly close social ties with the romantic poet and literary figure Stefan George and his circle, who espoused an adamant form of antimodernist cultural

reaction. (Ibid., pp. 260–270.) Although Weber's continuing commitment to equality and individual liberty made him reject the elitist implications of George's circle as an impossible basis for a modern industrial society (a criticism which Mitzman does not sufficiently emphasize), Weber was attracted to their spiritual commitments and yearning nonetheless. This complex relationship is reflected in a public defense Weber made of George and his circle in 1910: "George and his pupils in the final analysis serve, 'other Gods' than I, no matter how highly I may esteem their art and their intentions. This is not altered by the fact that I do feel an inner necessity to give my most unconditional purely *human endorsement* to the unvarnished genuine seriousness with which George personally faces his mission." (Quoted in Marianne Weber, *Max Weber* [New York, (1926) 1975], pp. 459–460; on Weber's relation to Nietzsche, see n. 132 below.) While Mitzman's insight into Weber's ambivalence about modernity is salutary, his general perspective on Weber's sociological theory underplays his continuing commitment to rationality, and for this reason cannot be accepted as such.

125. "Science as a Vocation," p. 142 (*Gesammelte Aufsätze zur Wissenschaftslehre*, 3d ed. [Tübingen, 1968], p. 598).

126. Ibid., p. 153.

127. "Religious Rejections" (n. 122 above), p. 342.

128. Ibid., p. 347 (*Gesammelte Aufsätze zur Religionssoziologie*, 3 vols. [Tübingen, 1920–1921], 1:560), cf. pp. 344–345.

129. Ibid., p. 342; cf. p. 350.

130. Leo Strauss articulates the purely individualistic, noncollective status of the options Weber presents to the free individual as follows:

> He was forced to dignify what he called "purely 'vitalistic' values" to the same height as the moral commands and the cultural values. The "purely 'vitalistic' values" may be said to belong entirely to the "sphere of one's own individuality," being, that is, purely personal and in no way principles of a cause. Hence they are not, strictly speaking, values. (*Natural Right and History* [n. 90 above], p. 46.)

Strauss clearly perceives, moreover, the historical rupture that Weber postulated in order to rationalize the theoretical break from the influence of normative order. "What seems at first to be an invisible church," Strauss writes about Weber's attitude toward the Protestant ethic and its relation to modernity, "proves to be a war of everybody against everybody or, rather, pandemonium" (p. 45).

I cannot go along, however, with the contemptuous dismissal by Strauss of Weber's commitment to such individual values as representing an ideological withdrawal from political responsibility. Although Weber did not offer to the individual any normative resources upon which to draw, he insisted, nonetheless, on the need to maintain individual integrity and responsibility for one's own actions. Nobody has brought out more clearly this Weberian insistence on an "existential" commitment than Löwith. It is worth quoting his insistence at some length:

> The positive fact, however, of this lack of belief in something that would transcend the "fate of our time" and the "demand of the day"—in objective, existing values, meanings, validities—is the subjectivity of a rational responsibility in the form of a pure self-responsibility which the individual assumes for and toward himself. . . . Placed into this world of bondage, the individual as "man" belongs to himself and relies totally upon himself alone. . . . With this final affirmation of the productivity of opposition, Weber stands in the most extreme contrast to Marx, who on this score remained a Hegelian, because he wanted to abolish the "contradictions" of bourgeois society. . . . Weber affirms this self-alienated humanity (as Marx puts it) because . . . to act in the midst of this specialized and indoctrinated world . . . with the passionate force of negativity . . . was the meaning of "freedom of movement." . . . What Weber created for himself with his method was a "platform of negativity" on which the human hero "in a very plain sense of the word" should now bestir himself. ("Weber's Interpretation of the Bourgeois-Capitalistic World in Terms of the Guiding Principle of 'Rationalization,' " in Wrong [n. 19 above], pp. 101–122, quoting pp. 119–122; this translation is a selection from Löwith's "Max Weber und Karl Marx.")

131. This concluding section should put into perspective the major liberal interpretation of Weber as providing the theoretical undergirding for contemporary society as a secular community of rational faith. This perspective is primarily the work of Talcott Parsons, who, as we will see in ch. 6, not only gained insight from Weber's sociology but used it to legitimate a multidimensional perspective that was primarily his own. As I have indicated in the text, the pivotal empirical point in this liberal, multidimensional reading is Weber's theory of secularization. It is interesting, then, to quote the reading of the last pages of *The Protestant Ethic* offered by one of Parson's major students, Neil J. Smelser: "By virtue of its conquest of much of Western society capitalism had solidly established an institutional base and a secular value system of its own—economic rationality. Its secular economic values had no further need for the 'ultimate' justification they had required during the newer, unsteadier days of economic revolution." (*Essays in Sociological Explanation* [Englewood Cliffs, N.J., 1968], p. 135.) Smelser reads the secularization theory in a "weak" way: the final pages of *The Protestant Ethic* are speaking only about economic values, and Weber is arguing that these become specialized and functionally differentiated from value commitments, like religion, which are of a more general and ultimate kind. This is certainly a plausible reading of empirical secularization, but

it denies the theoretical and ideological tensions that permeate Weber's work.

The most ambitious recent reading along these lines of Weber's modernity theory is Wolfgang Schluchter's. Schluchter is right to point to the humanitarian ideological commitment that underlies Weber's contemporary theory, but he is wrong, I believe, to contend that Weber's work contains a full-fledged "institutional analysis" of the conditions which could sustain an ethic of vocation and critique ("Value Neutrality and the Ethic of Responsibility," in Guenther Roth and Schluchter, *Max Weber's Vision of History* [Berkeley and Los Angeles, 1979], p. 74). Indeed, more than any other contemporary interpretation Schluchter's demonstrates that the reading of Weber as a multidimensional theorist of modernity depends on a "weak" theory of secularization. Schluchter's presentation of Weber's historical sociology as describing the emergence of a "dualistic anthropocentrism," where normative order and instrumental pressures are locked in permanent conflict, presents a history that is filtered through the much more consistently multidimensional history of religious rationalization produced in the work of Talcott Parsons and Robert N. Bellah (Schluchter, "The Paradox of Rationalization" [n. 1 above], passim, esp. p. 15, n. 13, and p. 21, n. 29). That this reading is as much an implicit revision of the weaknesses of Weber's theory as an objective reading of its actual content is explicitly acknowledged when Schluchter writes that "we are ready to argue in his [Weber's] own terms against him," and when he rejects a more instrumentalist reading on the grounds that "this interpretation does not provide any solution" to the problems outlined in Weber's description of modern life (ibid., p. 53 and ibid., n. 150). (The same kind of strategic rereading occurs, in an even more ambitious way, in Schluchter's *The Rise of Western Rationalism* [n. 15], passim; cf. ch. 6, n. 21.)

The liberal interpretation that insists on the continuity between the world of faith and the secular order—the continued possibility for ethical commitment and institutionalized values—fails to come to grips with the Nietzschean dimension of Weber's thought. Weber's affirmation of Puritan culture and his simultaneous affirmation of secular rationality and the end of religion involve him in the same dilemma that Nietzsche first articulated, that of simultaneously denying and affirming God. Walter Kaufmann puts the dilemma this way: "To escape nihilism—which seems involved both in asserting the existence of God and thus robbing *this* world of ultimate significance, and also in denying God and thus robbing *everything* of meaning and value—that is Nietzsche's greatest and most persistent problem" (*Nietzsche* [New York, 1956], p. 86). Like Nietzsche, Weber is at once a traditionalist and an antitraditionalist. It is this paradox, indeed, that makes both thinkers so difficult to interpret in terms of their ideological leanings and lends to their thought the peculiar sense of tragedy.

There are strong and direct echoes of Nietzsche in Weber's formulation of the problem of secularization. It was Nietzsche who defined the problem of "de-deification" as the fundamental crisis of modern life (see *The Gay Science*, ed. Walter Kaufmann [New York, 1974], secs. 108–109). In the famous parable "The Madman," e.g., Nietzsche writes: "The madman jumped into their midst and pierced them with his eyes. 'Whither is God?' he cried; 'I will tell you. *We have killed him*—you and I. All of us are his murderers.' But how did we do this?" To explain, he cites the effects of mechanical laws which Weber will later call the inexorable rationalization of nature: "What were we doing when we unchained this earth from its sun? Whither is it moving now? Whither are we moving? . . . Is there still any up or down?" This metaphysical atomization evokes in Nietzsche the same feelings that Weber later expressed: "Do we not feel the breath of empty space? Has it not become colder? Is not night continually closing in on us?" (Ibid., sec. 125, italics in original.)

Nietzsche is aware that the death of God presents the only true hope for real individualism (sec. 23), a liberation which depends on the polytheism of many gods that will allow many norms (sec. 143). It was, indeed, to support this kind of individuation that Nietzsche wrote *The Gay Science*: "Among Europeans today there is no lack of those who are entitled to call themselves homeless in a distinctive and honorable sense: it is to them that I especially commend my secret wisdom and *gaya scienza*" (sec. 377). Yet in his prophetic way, Nietzsche feels that such individuation is unlikely. He foresees the shadows of irrationality, and he predicts doom and apocalypse rather than freedom. European society is "corrupted" and "exhausted"; the passions are suppressed and weakened (sec. 23, 47). "The ancient national energy and national passion that became gloriously visible in war and warlike games" Nietzsche rues in a passage that also finds echoes in Weber's later writing, "have now been transmuted into countless private passions" (sec. 23). It is this disappointment and pessimism about the possibility for individual integrity in the age of disbelief that leads Nietzsche to his speculations about the superman, new Caesars, and new tyrants—even though the acceptance of these would involve the illusory reestablishment of faith. Weber, of course, does not follow Nietzsche in this latter speculation, but his ideological problematic is not so distant from Nietzsche's own.

CHAPTER SIX

1. I have referred to the interpretive works of most of the authors cited here at some length in the discussions and notes in earlier chapters (see Author-Citation Index). As for C. Wright Mills, his fundamental interpretive work was the essay written with Hans H. Gerth, "Introduction: The Man and His Work," in Gerth and Mills, eds., *From Max Weber:*

Essays in Sociology (New York, [1946] 1958), pp. 3–74. Mills elaborated this instrumentalized version of "Weberian sociology" in his subsequent, extremely influential research and theory, e.g., *The Power Elite* (New York, 1959). (Mills' work is discussed later in the present chapter.) For the case made by Irving M. Zeitlin, see his *Ideology and the Development of Sociological Theory* (Englewood Cliffs, N.J., 1968), pp. 111–158.

2. The clearest early statement of this synthetic strategy is Talcott Parsons and Edward Shils, "Values, Motives, and Systems of Action," in Parsons and Shils, eds., *Towards a General Theory of Action* (New York, 1951), pp. 47–278. Cf. the not unsympathetic comment by Donald G. Macrae to the effect that when Parsons discovered Weber's work in the 1920s "it was at once an invention and a discovery" (*Max Weber* [New York, 1974], p. 99).

3. Parsons, "An Outline of the Social System," in Talcott Parsons, Edward A. Shils, Kasper Naegele, and Jesse R. Pitts, eds., *Theories of Society* (New York, 1961), pp. 30–79; Parsons, *The Evolution of Societies*, ed. Jackson Toby (Englewood Cliffs, N.J., 1977).

4. Robert N. Bellah, *Beyond Belief* (New York, 1970); Clifford Geertz, *The Interpretation of Cultures* (New York, 1973); David Little, *Religion, Order and Law* (New York, 1969). There is no single work or group of works in which Parsons' strain toward normative overemphasis occurs; it is, rather, an analytical dimension of most of his oeuvre. See vol. 4, *The Modern Reconstruction of Classical Thought: Talcott Parsons*, chs. 8–9.

5. Neil J. Smelser, *Social Change in the Industrial Revolution* (Chicago, 1959); S. N. Eisenstadt, *The Political System of Empires* (New York, 1963). For a discussion of these strains within the Parsonian tradition and their links to the interpretation of classical theory, see the concluding chapter of vol. 4 and also my "Paradigm Revision and 'Parsonianism,' " *Canadian Journal of Sociology* 4 (1979): 343–358.

6. Reinhard Bendix, *Nation Building and Citizenship* (Berkeley and Los Angeles, [1964] 1977) and *Kings or People* (Berkeley and Los Angeles, 1978).

7. Seymour Martin Lipset, *Political Man* (New York, 1960), esp. pt. 1. There are sections in Lipset's later writings where this perspective is further elaborated: *The First New Nation* (New York, 1967), ch. 9; *Revolution and Counter-Revolution* (New York, 1968), ch. 2, 6, 9.

8. *The First New Nation*, esp. chs. 1 and 4–8; *Revolution and Counter-Revolution*, pt. 3.

9. Guenther Roth, *The Social Democrats in Imperial Germany* (New York, 1963).

10. Ralf Dahrendorf, *Class and Class Conflict in Industrial Society* (Stanford, Calif., 1959).

11. Randall Collins, *Conflict Sociology* (New York, 1976). (The kind of aggressively antinormative position that Weber's political history legiti-

mates is starkly revealed by a more recent statement in Collins' work on individual interaction: "I believe that the terminology of norms ought to be dropped from sociological theory" ["On the Microfoundations of Macrosociology," *American Journal of Sociology* 86 (1981): 984–1014, quoting 991, n. 3]. Yet if one considers Weber's multidimensional history of Western development, could a more "anti-Weberian" statement be found?) For the more multidimensional elements in Dahrendorf's later work, see, e.g., *Society and Democracy in Germany* (New York, [1965] 1979), pp. 52–53, where reference is made to the contributions of Parsons, particularly the way Parsons interwove religious and political factors in his explanation for the unevenness of German development.

12. Irving Louis Horowitz, *Three Worlds of Development* (New York, 1968); Samuel P. Huntington, *Political Order in Changing Societies* (New Haven, Conn., 1968). For an argument that criticizes such modernization theory precisely for its reliance on the instrumental elements of Weber's work, see Jeffrey Prager, "Moral Integration and Political Inclusion: A Comparison of Durkheim's and Weber's Theories of Democracies," *Social Forces* 59 (1981): 918–950, esp. 938–946.

13. Mills, *The Power Elite* (n. 1 above).

14. John Rex, *Key Problems in Sociological Theory* (London, 1961).

15. David Lockwood, "Some Remarks on 'The Social System,'" *British Journal of Sociology* 5 (1956): 134–145, and "Social Integration and System Integration," in George K. Zollschan and Walter Hirsch, eds., *Explorations in Social Change* (Boston, 1964), pp. 244–257, esp. pp. 253–255.

16. Georg Lukács, *History and Class Consciousness* (Cambridge, Mass., [1923] 1971).

17. Jürgen Habermas, "Technology and Science as Ideologies," in his *Toward a Rational Society* (Boston, 1970), pp. 81–122, and idem, *Legitimation Crisis* (Boston, 1975).

18. Weber's work seems, e.g., to have strongly affected Ralph Miliband's *The State in Capitalist Society* (New York, 1969) and also Nicos Poulantzas' *Political Power and Social Classes* (New York, 1978).

19. In Bendix's case this is particularly interesting. Bendix seems to have arrived at the notion of "citizenship"—the empirical focal point of his middle and later work—after an encounter with the thought of T. H. Marshall. Though not a Marxist in any strict sense, Marshall was a key intellectual figure in the British socialist tradition, and he mediated this socialist focus on class exploitation through Weber's work. It is quite possible, in fact, that it was through an encounter with the writings of this Weberian socialist thinker that Bendix first became alerted to the possibilities of Weber's notion of "citizenship" and to the key role of *The City*. Only when Bendix's writing moved into the realm of "citizenship" analysis did it become fully multidimensional in scope. Ironically, Parsons' encounter with T. H. Marshall had the opposite effect: it allowed him more

firmly to integrate a non-normative political dimension into his analysis of modern society—an integration that he made, like Bendix, by viewing Marshall's work through the prism of *The City*.

20. I have pointed to these claims for similarity in earlier chapters. See Parsons' two principal works of Weber interpretation: *The Structure of Social Action* (New York [1937] 1968) and his "Introduction" to Weber, *The Theory of Social and Economic Organization* (New York, 1947).

21. This is very much the central polemic of Parsons' *The Evolution of Societies* (n. 3 above). It is also the accomplishment, and a very important one, of the work by one of Parsons' most distinguished students, Robert Bellah, in *Beyond Belief* (n. 4 above). Both works achieve a multidimensional Weber by formulating an independent conceptual schema to integrate his work with the more normative emphases of Durkheim. Another essay by a student of Parsons that reveals a striking and explicit attempt to integrate the traditions of Parsons, Weber, and Durkheim is Edward A. Tiryakian's "A Model of Societal Change and Its Lead Indicators," in Samuel Z. Klausner, ed., *The Study of Total Societies* (New York, 1967), pp. 69–97. Donald N. Levine's searching essay, "Rationality and Freedom: Max Weber and Beyond," *Sociological Inquiry* 51 (1981): 5–21, presents another example. Influenced by Parsons, though not a student or direct follower, Levine conducts a scholarly analysis of the philosophical roots of Weber's conception of rationality, as well as a systematic analytical discussion of the conception itself and its relevance for the fate of rationality in contemporary society. Yet despite its greater textual fidelity, Levine's work follows Parsons by "reading into" Weber's work a fully multidimensional perspective which is as much about what Weber "would have said" about modernity if his work had been more truly synthetic as it is about the actual corpus.

Schluchter's essays in Guenther Roth and Wolfgang Schluchter, *Max Weber's Vision of History: Ethics and Methods* (Berkeley and Los Angeles, 1979), also articulate this extrapolation of Weber's work: though not a "Parsonian," Schluchter mediates Weber's latent instrumentalism primarily through Parsons' own theory rather than through Durkheim's. Schluchter's subsequent monograph, *The Rise of Western Rationalism: Max Weber's Developmental History* (Berkeley and Los Angeles, 1981), gives a reading of Weber which draws upon the normative tradition of sociological theory to maintain the "true multidimensionality" of Weber's work. On the one hand, Schluchter is explicit about his use of contemporary multidimensional theories to "read" Weber's work in a more satisfactory way. He seeks a "reinterpretation that follows his [Weber's] way of posing the problem without fully accepting his solution" (p. 5), realizes that such a reinterpretation must "extract" (ibid.) from Weber's writings, and systematically draws upon the concepts of Parsons, Luhmann, and Habermas to make such an extraction possible.

On the other hand, however, Schluchter maintains that the essentials of his reinterpretation are perfectly consistent with—in fact, represent merely an elaboration of—Weber's writings.

This ambiguity about the status of Schluchter's analysis is perhaps most clearly presented in his discussion of Weber's account of rational domination. Schluchter begins with what he insists is Weber's central theoretical contribution in this regard—a "developmental" theory about the movement from personal and traditionalist to impersonal, rational domination, a movement, he believes, that especially involved ethical and normative change. Schluchter's own contribution, within this context, is to demonstrate that Weber, within his abstract theory of evolutionary stages, distinguishes a range of fundamentally different historical paths. Through a "strategy of exposition," he will analyze Weber's discussion of the "historical variants of basic configurations of legality and of the manner in which they may favor the formal or the substantive rationalization of law and administration" (p. 108). At this point, however, Schluchter's "exposition" is interrupted by his acknowledgement that Weber's own theorizing often seems to ignore the normative, ethical dimension of rationalization. Thus, he writes that "in order to do this [i.e., carry out the search for historical variants], we must interpose another consideration." This consideration involves the following:

> Weber *tends* to identify legality with formal rationalization . . . so that substantive rationalization appears not as a component of the guiding principle of legality but as its counter principle [i.e., as] the intrusion of ethical imperatives, utilitarian pragmatism or political maxims into the autonomy of the legal and administrative apparatus, which functions as a "rational machine." . . . This is the *impression* conveyed by Weber's description of the dialectic of formal and substantive rationalization under the conditions of legal domination. And this *impression* is reinforced by the fact that [e.g.,] he *tends* to use the conceptions rational, legal and bureaucratic synonymously. (Pp. 108–109, italics added.)

Schluchter clearly hesitates about whether such weaknesses really exist in Weber's work or whether they have been mistakenly read into it. He suggests (ibid.) that if Weber had lived to write his chapter on the development of the modern state this confusion might have been cleared up. Yet he acknowledges, at the same time, that there are "also systematic reasons" for the impressions Weber's work leaves. When Schluchter goes on to present a detailed, and extremely interesting, discussion of normative aspects of political development, drawn from sources outside Weber's work, he clearly implies that these systematic reasons have to do with Weber's own theoretical failures. One aspect of the detailed discussion which follows is, indeed, explicitly revisionist: "If we want to remedy Weber's shortcoming, we must extend our analysis of the relation between ethic of responsibility and enacted law" (p. 109). Yet there are various points where Schluchter continues to refer to the discussion merely as an "elaboration" (p. 110). It is only after six pages of detailed, "extra-Weberian" discussion that Schluchter suggests "now we can move on to the historical variants of domination" (p. 115), the very discussion of which he originally indicated would involve simply an exposition of Weber's thought.

It seems to me that Schluchter has not merely teased out the "developmental" strand of Weber's empirical historical analysis; rather, while trying to maintain the gist of Weber's empirical analysis he has challenged Weber's theory on crucial, more generalized levels—in terms of its social-system model, its ideology, and its presuppositions.

22. Bendix, "Two Sociological Traditions," in Bendix and Roth, *Scholarship and Partisanship: Essays on Max Weber* (Berkeley and Los Angeles, 1971), pp. 282–298, asserts an inseparable gulf between Durkheim's and Weber's sociologies. This essay is the explicit response by Bendix to Parsons' argument for the convergence of these two classical thinkers, made more than thirty years before. In the context of this debate, Bendix's position has much to recommend it—but *only* in this context. Bendix's essay is limited because it refers primarily to the more specific levels of the scientific continuum, particularly to models and to propositions; it is also informed by a misreading of Durkheim as an anti-voluntaristic theorist. If Weber's work is read in a way that gives more play to generalized concerns, and if Durkheim's thrust is viewed more accurately, it becomes clear that there are, indeed, important areas of overlap between Weber's writing and Durkheim's. Parsons was more sensitive to this overlap precisely because he saw more clearly these generalized elements. Even in terms of more generalized issues, however, Parsons greatly exaggerated the convergence.

It is the double failure of orthodox Weberians to incorporate the insights of Durkheim and of "functionalist Durkheimians" to incorporate the instrumental sensitivity of Weber that has created two very distinct traditions of contemporary non-Marxist political sociology. For an illuminating discussion of this division, see Prager, "Moral Integration and Political Inclusion" [n. 12 above].

23. The preceding chapters have presented descriptions of Weber's understanding of the modern state and democracy, contemporary law, and modern rationality. I have not discussed at any length Weber's views of contemporary education. Although for Durkheim this subject was crucial, Weber hardly touched upon it, and he neglected it precisely for the reason that he saw little prospect for normative order in the modern world. "The field of education," he observed, is "that area which everywhere provides the most important opening for the impact of domination [*Herrschaftsstruktur*] upon culture" (*Economy and Society* [Berkeley and Los Angeles, 1978], p. 1090). In the period of legal-rational domina-

tion, a purely technical and efficient version of education prevails. Whereas charismatic education attempts to produce a "new soul," and traditional education concerns itself with cultivating certain "ways of thought," modern education, Weber insists, seeks "simply to *train* the pupil for practical usefulness for administrative purposes [*Zweck*]" (*The Religion of China* [New York, 1951], pp. 119–121, italics in original). No single instance could better show the enormous distance that separates Weber's understanding of modern order from Durkheim's than this exemplary disagreement over education.

Works of Weber

Following are the works cited in the text and notes, listed chronologically according to date of original publication or, if unpublished, date of composition. I have included the original language edition only when it was a primary reference.

Die römische Agrargeschichte in ihrer Bedeutung für das Staats-und Privatrecht, [1891], 1962.
"Die Verhältnisse der Landarbeiter im ostelbischen Deutschland," *Schriften des Vereins für Sozialpolitik* 55 (1892).
"Privatenqueten über die Lage der Landarbeiter," *Mitteilungen des ev.-soz. Kongresses* 3 (April–July 1892).
"Die ländliche Arbeitsverfassung," *Schriften des Vereins für Sozialpolitik* 58 (1893).
"Developmental Tendencies in the Situation of East Elbian Labourers," [1894], *Economy and Society* 8 (1979):177–205.
"Economic Policy and the National Interest in Imperial Germany," [1895], in W. G. Runciman, ed., *Max Weber: Selections in Translation*, 1978.
"The Stock Exchange," [1896], in Runciman, ed., *Max Weber: Selections in Translation*, 1978.
"The Social Causes of the Decline of Ancient Civilization," [1896], in Weber, *The Agrarian Sociology of Ancient Civilizations*, 1976.
Roscher and Knies: The Logical Problems of Historical Economics, [1903–1906], 1975.
" 'Objectivity' in Social Science and Social Policy," [1904], in Weber, *The Methodology of the Social Sciences*, 1949.
The Protestant Ethic and the Spirit of Capitalism, [1904–1905], 1958.
"Church and Sect in North America," *Die Christliche Welt* 20 (1906).

"The Protestant Sects and the Spirit of Capitalism," [1906], in Weber, *Gesammelte Aufsätze zur Religionssoziologie*, 1920–1921.

"Capitalism and Rural Society in Germany," [1906], in H. H. Gerth and C. Wright Mills, eds., *From Max Weber: Essays in Sociology*, 1946.

"Methodological Introduction," [1908], in J. E. T. Eldridge, ed. *Max Weber*, 1971.

"The Power of the State and the Dignity of the Academic Calling in Imperial Germany," [1908–1919], *Minerva* 11, no. 4 (1973):571–632.

The Agrarian Sociology of Ancient Civilizations, [1909], 1976.

Gesammelte Politische Schriften, 1911.

"Some Categories of Interpretive Sociology," [1913], *The Sociological Quarterly* 22 (1981):151–180.

"Religious Rejections of the World and Their Directions," [1916], in Gerth and Mills, eds., *From Max Weber: Essays in Sociology*, 1946.

"The Social Psychology of World Religions," [1916], in Gerth and Mills, eds., *From Max Weber: Essays in Sociology*, 1946.

The Religion of China: Confucianism and Taoism, [1916], 1951.

The Religion of India, [1916], 1958.

"The Meaning of 'Ethical Neutrality' in Sociology and Economics," [1917], in Weber, *The Methodology of the Social Sciences*, 1949.

"Parliament and Government in a Reconstructed Germany," [1917], in Weber, *Economy and Society*, 1968.

Ancient Judaism, [1917–1918], 1952.

"Socialism," [1918], in Eldridge, *Max Weber*, 1971.

"Science as a Vocation," [1919], in Gerth and Mills, eds., *From Max Weber: Essays in Sociology*, 1946.

"Politics as a Vocation," [1919], in Gerth and Mills, eds., *From Max Weber: Essays in Sociology*, 1946.

Gesammelte Aufsätze zur Religionssoziologie, 1920–1921.

"Structures of Power," [1922], in Gerth and Mills, eds., *From Max Weber: Essays in Sociology*, 1946.

Gesammelte Aufsätze zur Soziologie und Sozialpolitik, 1924.

"Methodological Introduction," [1924], in Eldridge, ed., *Max Weber*, 1971.

General Economic History, [1927], 1950.

From Max Weber: Essays in Sociology, 1946.

The Theory of Social and Economic Organization, 1947.

The Methodology of the Social Sciences, 1949.

Law in Economy and Society, 1954.

The City, 1962.

The Sociology of Religion, 1963.

Gesammelte Aufsätze zur Wissenschaftslehre, 3d ed., 1968.

Soziologie Weltgeschichtliche Analysen, Politik, 4th ed., 1968.

Economy and Society, 1968.

Max Weber: Selections in Translation, 1978.

Author-Citation Index

This index is intended as a combination bibliography/name index. Every article and book referred to in the text and notes is included here (with the exception of works by Weber), but authors are included only if their work is specifically cited. If the work of an author mentioned in the text is cited only in the notes, the page of both text and note references is indexed.

Subject Index

Action: *affektuell*, 25–26, 152; ends of, 16, 24, 26–27, 29, 31, 36, 40, 79, 92, 113; empirical, 29; external conditions of, 11–12, 24–26, 31–33, 37, 40–41, 55, 60, 77, 79, 92, 94, 106, 115; idealist approach to, xv–xvi; insane, 30; internal subjective reference of, 28–31, 78, 114; and interpenetration of internal and external elements, 40, 44–45, 53, 55; instrumental-rational, 27, 33, 55, 60, 79, 87; materialist approach to, xv–xvi, 27; means of, 16, 24, 27, 29, 31, 36, 79, 86, 92, 106, 113; modern economic, 36–37, 39–40, 55, 79; moral ends of, 17; multidimensional understanding of, xv, 27, 33, 53, 55–56; nature of social, 24; problem of, xv–xvii, 2, 22–27, 29, 33, 55, 69, 184, 200; as product of different analytic orders, 33, 41; prophetic, 44; relation between means and ends of, 24–29 passim, 31, 37, 92, 100; religious, 40; *traditionell*, 25–26, 152; utilitarian aspects, 15, 37, 40, 79, 106; voluntaristic, 14, 23–24, 32, 96;

wertrational, 25–27, 33, 80, 152–153, 156; *zweckrational*, 25–29 passim, 31–36 passim, 48, 69, 83, 90, 100, 102, 116, 122, 135, 153–156, 203
————, instrumental, xv, xviii, 1–3, 11–12, 24–25, 27–28, 33, 64, 70, 94, 96, 101, 103, 153–154, 199; collectivistic form of, xvii; individualistic form of, xvii
————, nonrational, xv, 3, 38–39, 69, 78, 184; collectivistic form of, xvii; individualistic form of, xvii, 3
Ad hoc explanation, 67, 122
Alienation, xviii, 101, 153, 191
Ambivalent theorizing, 58–59, 68, 73, 80–81, 118
America, 99, 112. *See also* Democracy
Analytic referent, 26
Analytic understanding of the individual, xviii. *See also* Concrete understanding of the individual
Analytic v. concrete frames of reference. *See* Concrete v. analytic frames of reference
Ancient Egypt, 91, 95
Ancient Israel, 44–45, 70–75, 84, 98,